Learning Science
Teaching

Learning Science Teaching

Keith Bishop and Paul Denley

 Open University Press

Open University Press
McGraw-Hill Education
McGraw-Hill House
Shoppenhangers Road
Maidenhead
Berkshire
England
SL6 2QL

email: enquiries@openup.co.uk
world wide web: www.openup.co.uk

and Two Penn Plaza, New York, NY 10121-2289, USA

First published 2007

A catalogue record of this book is available from the British Library

ISBN-13: 978 0335 22235 3 (pb)   978 0335 22234 6 (hb)
ISBN-10: 0335 22235 8 (pb)   0335 22234 X (hb)

Library of Congress Cataloging-in-Publication Data
CIP data applied for

Typeset by RefineCatch Limited, Bungay, Suffolk
Printed in the UK by Bell and Bain Ltd, Glasgow

The *McGraw·Hill* Companies

Contents

Preface

If you are early on in your learning journey as a science teacher or are involved in helping beginning- and early-career teachers on their way, then this book is written for you.

Its twofold message is that whatever your learning journey, 1) learning science teaching is an intellectual pursuit, and 2) the path to accomplishment is found by those science teachers whose mission is to be continuously-learning teachers. And, of course, that is why we have called this book *Learning science teaching*.

So what will you find in this book? Above all, you will hear the voices of 14 highly accomplished teachers of secondary science talking about their professional knowledge and their professional learning journeys. Why these science teachers? They were recommended to us by their peers and colleagues, not just because of their ability to enthuse and inspire their students into learning science, but because they are the kinds of teachers we could all learn from. Documented in this book, then, are the life experiences of science teachers who, by consensus, demonstrate very high levels of accomplishment.

What do we mean by 'highly accomplished? We hope that will be revealed as you read this book. How did we capture their voices? We used a very simple technique called video stimulated recall (VSR) to get these teachers to talk to us in depth about their practice. A camcorder is set up in the corner of the class and left to run for a whole lesson. After the lesson, we asked the teacher to view the recording, stopping and starting it to talk us through what happened and tell us about their decision-making. We also conducted a pre-VSR interview to get them to talk particularly about how their practice has changed over time – how did they teach at the beginning of their learning journey, and what is different now?

This book is organized around Chapters 3–5 which describe and interpret the practice of the highly accomplished science teachers. By chance we managed to observe roughly equal numbers of physics, biology and chemistry lessons. Every now and then we write a short commentary on what appears to us to be a particularly significant aspect of practice (see the Appendix for a summary). One idea of using these commentaries is to alert you to literature sources that will help you to explore the aspect further.

Chapter 1 explores the knowledge base of science teaching. In it, we reject the idea that the science teacher's learning journey is just the acquisition of a static body of knowledge, and invent a spinning top as a metaphor to highlight its dynamic nature. Without doubt, these highly accomplished science teachers have acquired a huge amount of knowledge about science teaching through their careers. What matters and makes the difference, though, is what they do with it, and that is the substance of Chapter 2. In Chapter 2 we concentrate on the thinking that underlies the way these teachers manipulate (or transform, as we prefer to call it) their subject knowledge and all the other kinds of knowledge we discuss in Chapter 1; a process we refer to as *pedagogical reasoning*.

If every student is to become scientifically literate then understanding how science works is fundamental. Chapter 6 takes as its stance that your own understanding, as a science teacher, of how science works, wittingly or unwittingly, will inevitably affect the way you teach. We have tried to look at how the knowledge these highly accomplished science teachers have, about the nature of science, influences their thinking and practice. In effect, we are inviting you to do the same.

As part of our research we also held conversations with small groups of students taught by these highly accomplished science teachers. Therefore, we have called Chapter 7 'The student voice'. You will see there's plenty of evidence to suggest that listening to your students is vital if you are to know about the impact you are having. What sort of job do you do in helping your students see how school science and the real world of science connect?

We then turn our attention in Chapter 8 to how professional learning occurs. The chapter's main theme comes from the highly accomplished science teachers – if you are not proactive in your reflection and analysis, your learning will be restricted. Professional learning is complex. We see how these teachers create opportunities to develop their professional learning capacities and how learning from others is a key part of their practice. In fact, the health and vitality of professional learning communities depends on teachers like these.

Our journey through this book concludes in Chapter 9 through an examination of the relationships between professional *knowledge*, professional *learning* and professional *development* in the light of what we have learned from this group of highly accomplished science teachers. We explore what we have called the *professional learning capacities* a little further and offer you a model of professional learning to consider.

How should you use this book? We suggest you dip into it as you like. The easiest material to read is in Chapters 3, 4 and 5 which contain only a few references to academic literature. Whether you are a beginning teacher or a more experienced teacher looking to support beginning- and early-career teachers, we hope you can hold up the content as a mirror to your own practice. By the way, we are absolutely *not* offering you any kind of definitive model of teaching science, only a rich set of experiences, insights and interpretations that might stimulate your own thinking about what you know and can do. If, as a result, you find you can engage more deeply in the discourse of the pedagogy of science learning and teaching, then we have been successful in our task.

In the other chapters you will find much more reference material. We have done this deliberately so that if, for example, you are on a teacher training programme that requires you to submit work at M level, you will find lots of sources to direct your study. Knowing that many readers will be experienced qualified teachers looking to develop their skills as mentors or looking for new directions for their departments, we have purposely included a large number of books. Books are often easier to get hold of and they quite often contain really good synopses of academic literature. If, perhaps, you are doing a Master's degree, and as you have access to library resources, it is up to you if you want to go further and hunt down the original sources.

In this book we show how highly accomplished teachers learn both through their own endeavours and from the various communities of pupils and practitioners with whom they work. We show how they work within their communities and make meaning from their experiences. As they grow, their sense of identity develops, helping them to establish their role both as learners and teachers.

Finally, by getting teachers to talk in depth, we aim to give you a deeper understanding of practice by making the professional knowledge of highly accomplished science teachers explicit. There is a huge body of research literature developed over the last 20–30 years that tries to pin down the knowledge base for teaching. Through reading this book we hope you can begin to plan or map out the beginnings of your professional learning journey. As aspiring science teachers in the early part of your career, we hope you enjoy making meaning from what you've read as you pursue the goal of becoming highly accomplished teachers of science yourselves.

Acknowledgements

We would like to thank all the highly accomplished science teachers whose wealth of knowledge and experience made this book possible. In particular, 'Aaron', 'Alison', 'Derek', 'Emma', 'Eric', 'Iain', 'Isabel', 'Jodie', 'Orla' and 'Ursula' gave us their time to talk through their thinking as science teachers and how they continue to learn. They, together with the other five highly accomplished science teachers we observed also provided us with their numerous ideas and approaches to science teaching which we believe make this book stimulating to read. We are grateful to the headteachers of their schools who gave access to classes and allowed us to use video as the means to capture the events and episodes which form the foundations of the research.

But it was not only the teachers that provided us with insights into how they learn and continue to learn. We should also acknowledge the contribution of the students who were refreshing in their clarity and honesty about what engages them in learning science. It is the authenticity that stems from their voices that enables us to make sense of those insights and helps us to see just how these highly accomplished science teachers develop their practice.

We particularly wish to thank Kevin Dawes for the many conversations that helped us to shape the programme of research that provides the foundation of this book. As a head of science, and a passionate physicist, Kevin provided the basis of many of the lines of inquiry which we followed through with all the other highly accomplished science teachers.

Finally, we are also very grateful to all our colleagues within the science education community in local authorities and in higher education institutions for their recommendations. They were able to identify their colleagues in schools who not only fitted the bill, as highly accomplished science teachers, but also had the skill and capability to articulate their practice in language accessible to beginning-teachers.

This book represents the bringing together of our own experience of working with teachers and others in the science education community over the last 20 years. Although we cannot name them all, we would acknowledge our debt to them for shaping our own ideas and influencing the development of the themes explored within.

1 Professional knowledge of the science teacher: a worldwide perspective

The focus of this chapter is on these two questions:

- What do you need to know to be an accomplished science teacher?
- How do you develop or acquire that knowledge?

But before addressing those questions directly, we should perhaps explore the status of teaching. Teaching is notoriously hard to define. Is it an art or a science? Is it a craft? All these words can be used to describe different ways of looking at teaching. Most teachers would agree that it is more than a job and many would describe it as a profession. There is some debate about whether or not teaching is a 'true' profession like medicine or the law, which are often cited as such. It has been suggested that to classify it as such, limits our conception to a technical role operating from a given set of rules and knowledge. Teaching is beyond that, particularly in a subject like science where we are constantly being encouraged to consider new knowledge and new ideas about teaching.

If teaching is a profession, then teachers should be considered as professional but what do we mean by that word? Here again we have a debate about possible meanings. The word can be used simply to mean someone who gets paid for what they do (in contrast to amateur) or it can refer to expectations about the sort of conduct which might be expected from individuals. This leads to the characteristic of professions being, at least to some extent, self-regulating. Here teaching as a profession runs into problems. Although there have been recent attempts to set up General Teaching Councils, these bodies do not have the same constitutions, operational procedures or relationships with their members that apply to bodies like the General Medical Council or the Law Society. Some time back, Etzioni (1969: v) considered teaching as a 'semi-profession'. In comparison with more established professions like medicine or law, he considered that the newer professions like teaching were different:

Their training is shorter, their status is less legitimised, their right to privileged communication less established, there is less of a specialised body of knowledge, and they have less autonomy from supervision or societal control.

Another influential writer in this area is Donald Schön. His book *The reflective practitioner* (1983) is subtitled *How professionals think in action* and was one of the first attempts to make sense of professional learning and the character of professional knowledge in a time of widespread technological and societal change. Schön suggests a move from what he terms 'technical rationality' to 'reflection in action' in the way that professionals operate. Technical rationality may have served us well in the past, but in more uncertain times we need to be able to respond to situations which are not amenable to rational analysis, which is where reflection in action comes in. More recently, Guy Claxton (1997) contrasted 'knowing what to do' with 'knowing what to do when you don't know what to do'. 'Knowing what to do' is like technical rationality – a knowledge base within the profession which can be drawn upon to guide practice. 'Knowing what to do when you don't know what to do' is about having a repertoire of tools to construct solutions to as yet undefined problems – a different sort of intelligence for these changing times.

Before we drift too far away from the classroom, this sort of debate does have some meaning for teaching. Teachers in general, but perhaps science teachers in particular, have to face new challenges all the time in both what they teach (because that is constantly developing and changing) and how they teach it. This idea of reflection-in-action which Schön identifies as being a more appropriate characteristic model for professionalism in times of change requires teachers to take control of their professional learning, and particularly to value the tacit knowledge that they hold and which guides their classroom practice. It is this tacit knowledge that we try to draw out in later chapters of this book. Becoming a professional science teacher is not a case of learning a predefined set of procedures and a static body of knowledge, it is about engaging with a dynamic and exciting subject and facing the challenges of presenting to students in an accessible way.

Eric Hoyle (see discussion in Stenhouse 1975: 142–4) suggested that a distinction could be made between 'restricted' and 'extended' professionals. Restricted professionals are not 'bad' teachers – indeed they plan and prepare their teaching conscientiously and care for their students. But they do not look beyond their classrooms and do not have the same desire to learn for themselves, and from themselves and others, that the extended professionals do. Our desire is to support teachers in this transition from the restricted to the extended and is behind our notion of the learning science teacher.

Because of all this uncertainty about status, and particularly this question of autonomy, it may be hard for teachers to argue for what ought to be a right for professionals to take responsibility for their professional learning and to define for themselves the mechanisms by which it is achieved. For many teachers, professional learning is seen to be limited to whatever 'in-service training' is made available to them. The important difference between in-service training which is 'done to you' and professional learning which you control yourself, may be totally obscured by the culture in which schools are embedded. Our intention through this book is to encourage science teachers to take charge of their professional learning for themselves and to provide some ideas about how to do that.

There is another thread running through our approach. One of the really positive aspects of a science teacher's daily life comes from working with others. Science teachers tend to work in departments. Indeed, there may be more contact and interaction between science teachers than other subject specialisms. There is a lot of interest currently in professional learning communities and encouraging their establishment in schools. Those advocating this could do well to look at many successful science departments. The importance of this is not just in recognizing that science teachers do not usually work in isolation but that they recognize the value of the community of practice in which they work. Lave and Wenger (1991) have developed the idea of 'situated learning', claiming that much of the most valuable learning associated with professions and other jobs more generally, comes through the practice situation. Knowledge is acquired in the context of social relationships in what they refer to as a 'community of practice' – a concept not dissimilar to the professional learning community which just emphasizes the learning dimension more overtly. William Hanks (in Lave and Wenger 1991) suggests that 'learning is a way of being in the social world, not a way of coming to know about it'.

We will return to the notion of professional learning within communities of practice in later chapters, but now we wish to turn to the question of whether it is possible to define the knowledge that underpins accomplished teaching.

Knowledge bases for teaching

It is an attractive idea that if we could define the knowledge needed for teaching, it might assist new teachers to be able to structure their professional learning to acquire it. Many attempts have been made to do this. One of the best known is that proposed by Lee Shulman and his associates at Stanford University in the 1980s (see Wilson 2004 for a collection of Shulman's key writings) which suggests the following category headings:

- content knowledge;
- general pedagogical knowledge;

- curriculum knowledge;
- pedagogical content knowledge;
- knowledge of learners;
- knowledge of educational contexts;
- knowledge of educational ends, purposes and values.

Newton was determined to find seven colours in white light because of the religious and mystical symbolism associated with the number seven – Shulman has come up with the same number here (although he does suggest these categories as a minimum number). Of these, the greatest interest has been shown in the fourth – pedagogical content knowledge (PCK), perhaps because it is the hardest to define, perhaps because it may be more associated with the best quality teaching. Whatever the reason, it has received much attention, particularly in science education. We explore PCK and our interpretation of it a little more below.

This and other attempts to define knowledge categories need to be seen in the context of their time. In the mid-1980s it was possible to think of teachers as professionals with some degree of autonomy (at least at a collective if not individual level) about their practice and therefore some control over their professional development. In the 1990s there was the emergence of a climate of accountability associated with what is often referred to as the 'standards movement' – standards both for the classroom (like our own National Curriculum in England and Wales) and for teachers.

Shulman himself was involved in the development of professional standards for accomplished teachers for the National Board for Professional Teaching Standards (NBPTS 2005) which was set up as an independent body in the USA. Codifying professional knowledge for the purposes of certificating teachers requires the adoption of a rather brutal and mechanistic approach which allows little blurring of boundaries or recognition of complexity – it can be atomistic and even simplistic. Nevertheless, this is necessary if the resulting framework is to be fit for purpose.

The NBPTS standards have been developed recognizing the need for definitions to take into account both subjects and the age of students. These are the standards for science for teachers of early adolescents (11–15). There are 13 separate standards divided into four groups:

Preparing the way for productive student learning
1 Understanding early adolescents
2 Knowledge of science
3 Instructional resources

Establishing a favourable context for student learning
4   Diversity, equity and fairness
5   Engagement
6   Learning environment

Advancing student learning
7   Understanding pedagogy
8   Science inquiry
9   Contexts of science
10 Assessment

Supporting teaching and student learning
11 Family and community outreach
12 Professional collaboration and leadership
13 Reflective practice

Across the Pacific, the Australian Science Teachers Association (ASTA 2007) developed its own set of professional standards based on the NBPTS approach. The resulting document recognizes the difficulties of the atomistic approach and is more descriptive in defining its standards. There are 11 elements divided into three broad areas:

Professional knowledge
1   Of science and science curricula
2   Of teaching, learning and assessment
3   Of students and factors affecting their learning

Professional practice
4   In designing appropriate and coherent learning programmes
5   In creating and maintaining challenging but safe learning environments
6   In engaging students in developing scientific knowledge through inquiry
7   In looking for ways of extending students' understanding of major scientific ideas
8   In developing students' capacity for informed decision-making
9   In using a variety of strategies to monitor and assess students' learning

Professional attributes
10 To analyse, evaluate and refine teaching practice to improve student learning
11 To work collegially within and beyond the school to improve science education

We introduce these frameworks now because we will return to them later in this book, but, for now, the questions which we would ask are:

- Are these lists of elements or standards a 'knowledge base' for science teaching?
- Are they sufficiently comprehensive to describe fully the knowledge that you need to be a good science teacher?

The major difficulty here is recognition that while some aspects of teaching are amenable to definition in this way, some clearly are not. This was recognized as early as the 1960s by writers like Michael Oakeshott (see the discussion in Eraut 1994: 65) in making the distinction between technical knowledge (amenable to written codification) and practical knowledge (expressed only in practice and learned through practice). These ideas go back to Aristotle and the distinction the Greeks made between *techne* and *praxis* – different forms of knowledge. More recently, Kessells and Korthagen (see discussion in Loughran 2006a) have used two more Greek ideas about the nature of theory – the twin constructs of *phronesis* and *episteme*. Phronesis is the way theory develops out of and can guide experience and practice; episteme is the sort of theory generated through more traditional research and which is often treated with some concern, particularly by teachers. A more constructive parallel might be the distinction between conceptual and procedural understanding in science (Duggan and Gott 2002). Korthagen's perspective (2004) is supported by others like Fenstermacher (1994) who distinguishes between the sort of knowledge created by educational researchers (formal knowledge) and the more practical knowledge generated by teachers through experience. The tension is that although the knowledge of episteme is easier to define and codify, the knowledge of phronesis may be more attractive to and highly valued by teachers.

A notion which appears frequently in the literature is that of 'tacit knowledge'. This construct is usually credited to the philosopher Michael Polyani and was first expressed in the 1960s. The attraction of the idea in many fields, not just teaching, may be associated with a desire not to have all of our actions reduced to tick-box competencies but to retain some sense of something we hold to be holistic and personal about what we do. This does create a problem for novices in whichever field. If an important component of practice is tacit (and by definition difficult to codify or articulate) then how can it be passed on from generation to generation? A chapter in John Loughran's book *Developing a pedagogy of teacher education* is entitled 'Making the tacit explicit' (2006a: 43–62). Putting aside the logical inconsistency of the statement, we subscribe to the sentiment and it could serve to some extent as a subtitle for this book. We have tried in our accounts of the practice of highly accomplished teachers, in later chapters, to both present the knowledge which can be identified or at least inferred from practice using the commonly held categories as well as trying to give at least some feel for the tacit knowledge using some of the strategies that Loughran advocates. For example, as we will discuss later, we have found value in using video stimulated recall (VSR) to provide a way for teachers to pick out key decision-making points in their lessons and explain their thinking. In this way, we hope that science teachers, early on in their careers, can learn through the accounts and reflections of others and can aspire to the sort of high quality science teaching we have seen.

Before leaving the knowledge base of science teaching, we would like to come back to Shulman's category of pedagogical content knowledge, because of its perceived importance in identifying high quality teaching and also to present our own perspective on how it might be conceptualized.

Pedagogical content knowledge (PCK)

Since Lee Shulman first proposed the idea of PCK in the mid-1980s, many writers and researchers have been trying to capture the essence of what it actually is. Others have questioned how helpful the idea is and there has been criticism of the construct (see Turner-Bisset 1999). In one of his two seminal articles at the time all Shulman says about PCK is that it is, 'that special amalgam of content and pedagogy that is uniquely the province of teachers, their own special form of professional knowledge' (Wilson 2004: 22). Shulman then picks out PCK as being of special interest:

> It represents the blending of content and pedagogy into an understanding of how particular topics, problems, or issues are organised, represented, and adapted to the diverse interests and abilities of learners, and presented for instruction.
>
> (Wilson 2004: 228)

Having given a glimpse in his own article of what PCK might be about, Shulman moves on to consider other matters and leaves others to develop ideas about its characterization. In the other (and slightly earlier) seminal paper, Shulman does give some indication of what might be included in relation to teaching in a particular subject area (he was clear about the context-specific nature of PCK – PCK in science would be different from PCK in geography):

> . . . the most useful forms of representation of those ideas, the most powerful analogies, illustrations, examples, explanations, and demonstrations – in a word, the ways of representing and formulating the subject that make it comprehensible to others.
>
> (Wilson 2004: 203)

In science, this illustration of PCK has led to the association with the models, metaphors and analogies that are used to teach the subject and some of the stories of science which science teachers use to develop understanding of concepts. Undoubtedly there is knowledge here – one has to know these stories or analogies before one can use them – but Shulman goes a little further in suggesting that possession of this knowledge on its own is not enough:

> Since there are no single most powerful forms of representation, the teacher must have at hand a veritable armamentarium of alternative forms of representation some of which derive from research whereas others originate in the wisdom of practice.
>
> (Wilson 2004: 203)

This means that decisions need to be made in planning lessons or even during lessons themselves about which alternatives from the 'armamentarium' to choose. This is an additional knowledge dimension – not only knowledge of the forms of knowledge, but also knowledge of where and when to use them. Thus, perhaps it would be better to see PCK as being a 'meta-knowledge' – a knowledge about knowledge – rather than just another component of the basic knowledge elements of teaching.

The overall concept embodied in PCK seems to have particularly inspired researchers in the field of science education where perhaps the nature of the subject stresses the importance of the organization and representation of knowledge when that knowledge is often concerned with concepts of an abstract and intellectually challenging nature. For further reading on this we can recommend Loughran (2006b), Gess-Newsome and Lederman (1999) and, for some very practical ideas, Loughran *et al.* (2006).

We would like to propose our own metaphor for how we see the relationship between PCK and the other knowledge base elements that Shulman proposes. We would like to think of professional knowledge being similar to a spinning top (see Figure 1.1) with coloured segments (the knowledge categories) that are to some extent discrete and readily distinguished from one another when the top is still, but which merge to form a different colour when spun. If you use the right colours, when you spin the top it appears to be white and the component colours are no longer visible in themselves. The new colour is generated from the components but is different from them. Maybe this is what Shulman was thinking of when he referred to 'an amalgam' and a 'blending' of knowledges and maybe this is why there has been so much difficulty in 'freezing' PCK to define it – it has been described as an 'elusive butterfly'. Perhaps one reason for the problems is that PCK can only be 'seen' in action – it is a dynamic construct which is not amenable to static representation.

Thus, we do not see pedagogical content knowledge as being a separate static colour but rather being the dynamic colour generated in practice through

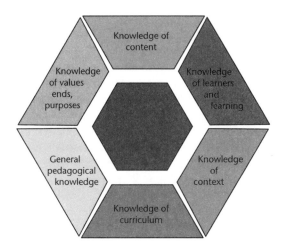

Figure 1.1   The 'spinning top' – a metaphor for professional knowledge.

the capability of the teacher to be able to combine or blend the individual knowledge bases together – to 'spin the top'. In our accounts of the practice of highly accomplished teachers in Chapters 3–5, we have used this spinning top device at the end of each one to identify elements of professional knowledge which the teacher has drawn on in the lessons discussed. We hope that the account itself gives a feel for the dynamic and interactive way in which professional knowledge is used by these teachers.

We have tried to identify their professional knowledge by using the six categories Shulman originally proposed with one minor modification. Shulman included 'knowledge of learners' as one category but we have extended this slightly to 'knowledge of learners and learning'. Knowledge about teaching is found in 'general pedagogical knowledge' and arguably knowledge about learning could be considered to be there as well but, particularly in science, knowing about individual learners would seem to go together with an understanding of the processes involved in their science learning.

As far as PCK is concerned, we will discuss the metaphors, stories and alternative representations that our teachers used in the lessons we observed, but they are discussed in the context of those lessons – not separated out and isolated. We feel that such separation of instances where PCK is evident, from the context, can tend to devalue or almost trivialize the key message. Our hope is that your understanding of PCK will emerge through the discussion and analysis of the practice of these teachers as being more about the thinking behind the selection and application of knowledge than the individual 'bits' of knowledge themselves. Our position on this is closer to Kathryn Cochran and colleagues in her notion of 'pedagogical content knowing' – PCKg (Cochran *et al.* 1993).

Experts, expertise and accomplishment

In this penultimate section we will divert slightly from considering what it means to be professional to other ways of looking at high achievement more generally. What do we mean by an expert and what does an expert teacher look like? A rather unhelpful answer to that question is to say that he or she demonstrates expertise, but what do we mean by that? David Berliner (2004) discusses a number of generally accepted characteristics of experts (not just teachers) to define what we might mean by expertise. It is seen in terms of the following:

- automaticity and routinization of everyday operations in the field;
- sensitivity to the demands of the task and social situation;
- the way problems are represented;
- fast pattern recognition capabilities;
- perception of meaning in patterns;
- domain specificity.

He makes a telling point about the distinction between expertise and experience, 'experience alone will not make a teacher an expert, but it is likely that almost every expert pedagogue has had extensive classroom experience' (Berliner 2004: 200–1). Or, to put it a bit more cruelly, a comment was made about a fellow teacher, 'Has he got ten years' experience, or one year's experience ten times?!'

Berliner investigated expert teachers and revealed some more linked characteristics which underpinned their teaching:

- knowledge of the cognitive abilities of their students;
- personal knowledge of their students;
- a history with their students;
- student expectations of good teaching even if it was challenging.

A further finding was the recognition of a distinction between 'crystallized' and 'fluid' expertise. In the former, individual experts are able to respond in familiar situations through learning from past experience. Fluid expertise is the response to unfamiliar situations and was characteristic of the top experts. We referred to Guy Claxton's work earlier and his 'knowing what to do when you don't know what to do' comes in here too, suggesting a sort of metacognitive capability characteristic of expert practice.

Berliner suggests a five stage model for teacher development which takes the teacher from novice, through advanced beginner, competent and proficient to expert status. Along the way, the whole *modus operandi* changes:

novices are deliberate, advanced beginners are insightful, competent teachers are rational, proficient teachers are intuitive but expert teachers are 'arational'. Berliner (2004: 202) says that, 'They are acting effortlessly, fluidly, and in a sense this is arational because it is not easily described as deductive or analytic behaviour.'

He further suggests that expert teachers operate in a qualitatively different way to novices – but what is this qualitative difference and is it something that everyone can acquire? It seems that expertise seen in this way is not a question of accumulating knowledge, even less one of accumulating experience; it is about developing that fluidity associated with the 'adaptive expert'.

Sternberg and Horvath (1995) recognize the difficulty of listing characteristics of expert teachers and suggest that, rather than being identical, experts bear more of a 'family resemblance' to one another than they do to non-experts and that this resemblance can help to define a 'prototype' for the expert teacher. This is built up from psychological research and its features are divided into three broad areas – knowledge, efficiency and insight. The last of these alludes back to the earlier discussion about the difficulty of defining something as ephemeral as 'insight'.

These characterizations of 'experts' are useful up to a point and, indeed, the teachers we have worked with demonstrated many of them, but we have not chosen to use the word 'expert' either as a noun or an adjective to describe them. We have chosen the phrase 'highly accomplished teacher'. We have taken the notion of accomplishment as having certain other connotations which 'expert' does not have. The word is used by the NBPTS in the USA to define a level of performance which can be recognized by a national system of certification. The term 'highly accomplished teacher' is used in the National Professional Standards framework developed specifically for science teachers in Australia. In neither case is there an explanation as to why they chose the idea of accomplishment. It is a term often associated with the arts – with music particularly. 'Expert' has a somewhat harder edge. We would suggest that, by choosing to see our teachers as highly accomplished rather than expert, we are recognizing both the definable characteristics and the more elusive qualities which contribute to their success. This quotation is attributed to Leonardo da Vinci, 'It had long since come to my attention that people of accomplishment rarely sat back and let things happen to them. They went out and happened to things'.

The 'process-content' debate

The purpose of this chapter is to provide some sort of foundation in identifying the professional knowledge which might characterize the highly accomplished science teacher. We have considered professionalism, what we mean by expertise and accomplishment, and different approaches to defining professional knowledge. As you will see in later chapters, we have witnessed accomplishment in the practice of the teachers with whom we have been working not just in terms of them possessing particular sorts of knowledge, but in terms of their ability to deploy that knowledge effectively. It does not matter how good a teacher's knowledge is, if he or she cannot use it to design and execute effective teaching. Thus, we are as much concerned in this book with teacher *thinking* as we are with teacher *knowledge*. Of course, the knowledge base is important but, no matter how strong it is, it is insufficient in itself to result in accomplished teaching. We have noted how Shulman's knowledge categories have been widely used and accepted, particularly his notion of PCK but there is another side to Shulman's coin which does not always get as much attention. Shulman recognized that as well as having knowledge, teachers need to be able to do something with it. He developed the idea of 'pedagogical reasoning' (Wilson 2004: 233) and identified stages in the process of planning and teaching where this type of thinking is employed. Others have used terms like 'didactic transposition' (Ogborn *et al.* 1996: 61) to describe a process of translating knowledge into a form which is appropriate in the classroom setting. In some ways, this parallels the 'process-content' debate in science teaching – should we be teaching the 'facts' of science or the 'methods' or science? As in that debate, the issue is not to choose between one or the other but to maintain an appropriate balance between the two. In this book, the balance (in considering how accomplished teachers come to be so) could be seen to be on the side of 'process', on teacher thinking, and particularly the way teachers' thinking is evidenced through their decision-making before, during and after teaching episodes. This is not to deny the importance of knowledge but rather to suggest that it is the way different professional knowledge bases are knitted together which gets to the heart of high quality science teaching. The next chapter picks up on this theme by examining the transformation of knowledge and pedagogical reasoning in more detail.

2 Transforming science knowledge

As a beginning- or early-career teacher you may wonder how highly accomplished science teachers often make the job look so straightforward. Even when things appear to be going wrong, nothing seems to fluster them. Strangely, they seem to know exactly what to do and when to do it in order to put things back on track. You will know that it is not as easy it looks because on occasions your experiences with similar classes resulted in your plan going awry and you found it difficult to rescue the situation.

You probably also have that feeling that highly accomplished science teachers are good at engaging the students in the subject matter, but you are not quite sure how they do it despite your best efforts at trying to copy what they do. If students do appear to go off-task, highly accomplished teachers seem to be able to read the class situation and make on-the-spot decisions to adjust their plans. Such flexibility is something you really admire, but when you try changing your plans you find that you lose the students' interest or you end up failing to meet the objectives you set out with.

Clearly these teachers are manipulating their knowledge in ways that most other teachers are not. If all the highly accomplished science teachers knew the same things, it would of course be ideal if we could simply write down what it is that they know. But we do not believe that would capture the essence of what their practice is about. In fact, it is our view that it is what highly accomplished science teachers *do* with their knowledge that makes the difference. In other words, it's not just what they know, it is what they do with it that matters!

This chapter is about how highly accomplished science teachers use their professional knowledge to engage their students in learning science and about how they utilize that engagement to result in learning. This is the process that Shulman (1987) calls 'transformation' and why we have called this chapter 'Transforming science knowledge'. We will talk about transformation in more detail later, but first we need to say something about how we get at the professional knowledge of the highly accomplished science teacher, and find out more about what they do with it. The idea is that if we can expose their thinking to more open scrutiny, others may be able to learn from their example. In other words, if you can get highly accomplished science teachers to articulate what they know, beginning- and early-career teachers may begin to see the journey they have taken and perhaps be able to use those insights to enhance the rate at which they develop their professional knowledge bases.

Making professional knowledge explicit

Research into teacher thinking tells us that teacher decision-making is complex, contextual, and involves issues of values and beliefs. This chapter enables us, therefore, to explore what kinds of knowledge teachers draw on in their thought and action, how those knowledge bases interact, and how context and situation influence their thinking. It also enables us to recognize that teachers of different science disciplines have their own specialized forms of knowledge (Calderhead and Miller 1997) and allows us to begin to explore how the science teacher's knowledge may be specialized and distinctive.

The question that matters then, is whether it is possible for highly accomplished science teachers to make more explicit to the rest of us what it is that they are doing. We think one way to do this is to get them to talk about their decision-making as a way of 'getting inside their heads' to explore their thought and action. Throughout our research we asked them to talk in terms of their pre-active, interactive and post-active decision-making, an approach taken from the enormous body of research into teacher thinking that began in the 1980s (see particularly Clark and Petersen 1986). Mostly, our highly accomplished science teachers had not heard of these terms before. However, they found the idea of describing their practice in terms of their decision-making quite easy to understand as they acknowledged that this is exactly what they are doing all the time. Normally, of course, they just do not need to talk about it!

Pre-, inter- and post-active decision-making

To find out about their *pre-active decision-making*, we spent a lot of time asking the highly accomplished science teachers about their planning and preparation decisions. We wanted to know what kinds of things they consider when deciding on how to choose the content and the activities for a series of lessons on any particular topic. One highly accomplished science teacher talked a little about how he goes about the process. He was referring to the new GCSE science specification:

'Most lessons have learning outcomes which are in lots of ways unachievable let's say. So let's use the reflex action for example. How do kids learn all that in one lesson? I don't think they can. So what bits am I going to get them to try and learn and what bits aren't I? I suppose that's my starting point. That comes from a knowledge of syllabus, assessment and where it falls in the bigger picture and experience of teaching the course. So then I think "OK, I want them to learn this, this and this. How am I going to get them to do that and engage them in the first instance? When they walk through the door how am I going to get them to get on-task or listen to me or sit down and get their bags away?" A lot of those decisions probably come from my knowledge of the class, the kids sitting there.'

By *interactive decision-making* we wanted the highly accomplished science teachers to tell us about the decisions they were making during the lesson. What were they looking for as the lesson proceeded? What factors caused them to reassess the development or progress of a lesson? What would make them change tack? Interactive decisions could relate to any of these, for example:

- organizing equipment and apparatus;
- monitoring students actions/behaviour/reading students' behaviour;
- monitoring students' understanding;
- changing sequences;
- monitoring activity time;
- managing transitions;
- monitoring and assessing learning;
- modifying a plenary.

In this extract this teacher is carefully assessing where the students have got to in the practical activity and is weighing up the educational benefits of different courses of action to decide what would be the best option given the time available:

'. . . it's having high expectations. If they don't finish all the practical, does it really matter? Have they got enough evidence that they can still make a conclusion from it? I was aware that there were four students here who'd finished and I didn't want them sitting around doing nothing while the rest of the kids were working. They would have got on with the work actually if they'd done the questions. I'd also made the decision halfway through the practical when I saw what time we had left that none of them had time to do the questions on their own individually.'

To learn about the highly accomplished science teachers' *post-active decision-making*, we asked the them to consider how they use their reflections on their experiences and how they build what they learn from those analyses into their professional knowledge. In this instance the reflections of this highly accomplished science teacher resulted in a general change in practice:

> 'What I've done in recent years is, rather than spend a lot of time in whole class discussion about presenting hypotheses or tabulating results I've tried to get them started doing something [on their own] and work with individuals as much as I can. When you get down to the individual level you very quickly get to ask a lot of questions which give you a fair idea of what they know, what they understand and where the misconceptions are. And I've found that really gives you a much better insight into their understanding.'

The three extracts above are intended to give you a flavour of the thinking that highly accomplished science teachers engage in. Interestingly, what they think is expressed in plain language and is easy to relate to. None of it could be regarded as particularly sophisticated, but it does represent practice that is supported by a clear rationale. Whatever they do, it can always be seen to be purposeful.

In Chapters 3–5 we explore the thinking of the highly accomplished science teachers in much more depth. However, in the meantime, we will look more closely at this concept of transformation.

Transformation

Lee Shulman (1987: 15) argued that 'the knowledge base of teaching lies at the intersection of pedagogy and content'. He coined the term 'transformation' as part of a larger process that he called *pedagogical reasoning*, which he uses to describe how teachers draw on their professional knowledge to make decisions about what to teach and how to teach it (see Figure 2.1).

Shulman argued that:

> To teach is first to understand. We ask that the teacher comprehends critically a set of ideas to be taught. We expect teachers to understand what they teach and, when possible, to understand it in several ways. They should understand how a given idea relates to other ideas within the same subject area and to ideas in other subjects as well.
>
> (1987: 14)

Above all else, Shulman makes understanding the subject matter the most

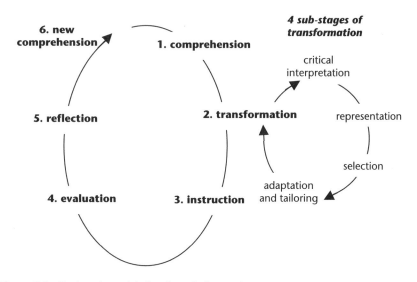

Figure 2.1   Shulman's model of pedagogical reasoning.

important thing a teacher has to do. This is the first stage of pedagogical reasoning: 'comprehension'. After that the teacher can begin the process of transforming that content into material designed for the students. Shulman sees this as a highly complex process involving four sub-stages representing the intersection of pedagogy and content.

Although Shulman coined the term 'transformation' as the process that leads to the development of PCK, it is also worth noting that Ogborn *et al.* (1996), through research into explaining science in the classroom funded by the Economic and Social Research Council (ESRC), offer another perspective on the process. They discuss the idea of 'reworking [subject] knowledge' within the European concept of *'didactic transposition'*. More importantly, they provide a range of examples to illustrate precisely what they mean by reworking subject knowledge and what didactic transposition means in practice. They are well worth exploring as a way to help you understand better your own capacity to blend subject matter and pedagogy (see Ogborn *et al.* 1996: 58–76).

To try to flesh out further what is implied by the terminology associated with transformation, we will illustrate the ideas with a range of examples drawn from our observations and discussions with the highly accomplished science teachers. But before we do that we will just say a little about the implications of the term 'comprehension' as used by Shulman.

Comprehension

To a science teacher, the idea of it being necessary to understand the content is self-evident. How could it be otherwise! Shulman, however, is implying that just to understand it in one way is not sufficient; you should be able to understand it in multiple ways so that you have alternative explanations, should students find one approach difficult. In addition to that, *comprehension* also means you should be able to show the students how the content relates much more broadly to other concept areas so that you can help them see how the different areas of science content are linked, and even more importantly, how the science is relevant to their lives outside the classroom.

This is not arguing that a science teacher should be the fount of all knowledge and cannot possibly admit to not knowing something. In fact, the belief that students often have that science teachers should be able to answer all questions of science is one of the myths of science teaching that we would wish to dispel.

One of the highly accomplished science teachers vented his frustration with less experienced colleagues who were frightened of admitting ignorance:

> 'There's still this stigma [about not knowing the answer], which I can't really believe still exists, where if a child asks a question that the teacher doesn't understand, they'll skirt round the issue and give them the wrong answer, or say "Be quiet" because they don't actually want to show the kids that they don't know everything.'

He went on to explain how this really should not be an issue, as a science teacher who really understands science will be someone who has the higher-order skills to know how to find out if there is something he or she does not know or understand and, just as importantly, who will be able to interpret what he or she finds out and explain it to the students at an appropriate level.

Within Shulman's concept of pedagogical reasoning a key attribute for any teacher is that of self-awareness with regard to knowing precisely the limitations and boundaries of your subject knowledge. This attribute was evident in all the highly accomplished science teachers. We liken it to the concept of 'conscious incompetence', a concept borrowed and adapted from research into group dynamics originally thought to stem from Luft and Ingham (1955) and more often represented as Dubin's dichotomy, shown in Figure 2.2 (Dennison and Kirk 1990). Concern arises, however, where a teacher has not only failed to develop a deep knowledge of the subject matter but is also not fully aware of his or her limitations – i.e., a state of 'unconscious incompetence'. In these circumstances, the danger is that the teacher is unable to recognize the conceptual problems that could be created for the students.

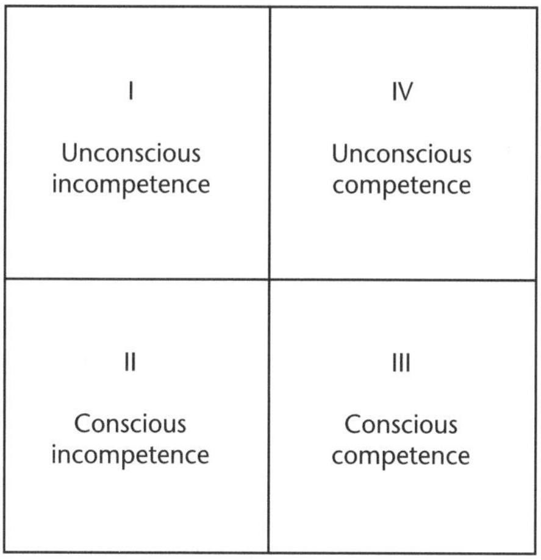

I Unconscious incompetence	IV Unconscious competence
II Conscious incompetence	III Conscious competence

Figure 2.2   Dubin's dichotomy.
Source: Dennison and Kirk (1990)

Another of the highly accomplished science teachers warned against the dangers of inadequate subject knowledge but added a slightly different dimension to the discussion. Here she identifies the contribution to effectiveness that extended knowledge of the background, 'the little stories and anecdotes', can make:

> 'I feel subject knowledge is very, very critical. You have to have a good subject knowledge and then you can start talking about it. If you're trying to teach something you're not sure of you nearly always get found out by pupils because sometimes they want to pursue the topic and you just don't have the background, the little stories and anecdotes, the uses of the subject knowledge and all this sort of thing to just quickly put in and if you can put those in like that it makes you a much more effective teacher.'

This view begins to tie in with Shulman's process of transformation and the construction of the highly specialized knowledge base of PCK, referred to in Chapter 1.

The sub-stages of transformation

The nature of PCK, the nature of its existence and its description, is addressed and documented in many books and articles (see *Examining pedagogical content knowledge*, by Gess-Newsome and Lederman 1999). It is not our intention to try to identify PCK in the highly accomplished science teachers involved in this research, but rather to focus on the processes that would be involved in its production. Key among these is what Shulman refers to as 'transformation' and which he subdivides into four sub-stages. Here we look at these sub-stages in more detail through the words and actions of the highly accomplished science teachers themselves. The four sub-stages are *critical interpretation, representation, selection* and *adaptation and tailoring.*

Critical interpretation

In these days when so many choices about what to teach in science are already made through National Curricula, GCSE/A level specifications, government sponsored schemes of work, school-based schemes of work and national testing, beginning- and early-career teachers can be forgiven for not stepping or thinking 'outside the box' and designing activities that they might feel better fit the learners they are to teach. However, it became very clear from our research that the highly accomplished science teachers, we were working with, all take a very critical approach to deciding what to teach. These extracts give a flavour of the thinking some of them used in relation to the way they thought about the content, its sequencing and representation:

> 'In my case, definitely I try and plan the lesson around how they'll learn. It's not necessarily based around what the National Curriculum or scheme of work says, or even what pieces of equipment I have.'

> 'And I kind of allocate that in my mind per lesson and then start thinking how I'm going to teach them that. And having decided what you want to teach them, some suggestions will be in the scheme of work. But you'll have to think, "Is that suitable for that group? I think they might struggle with that so I'll have to put in extra bits and pieces." '

In each case the highly accomplished science teachers are engaging critically with the material and making decisions about how to teach it. It is through this process that they draw on their past experiences and their stored professional knowledge to bring a range of contextual factors into their decision-making. Recent research by Berliner (2004) reinforces this message about how the professional knowledge of the expert teacher is highly contextualized. It is precisely what we found as all of our highly accomplished science teachers conceived and planned their lessons based on a very deep knowledge of the students, the extent to which they had developed good relationships with them and the physical environment in which they were working.

Representation

It is within this process of representation that most of the evidence for teachers possessing PCK seems to be found. Shulman described PCK as:

> Within the category of PCK I include, for the most regularly taught topics in one's subject area, the most useful forms of those representations of those ideas, the most powerful analogies, illustrations, examples, explanations and demonstrations – in a word, the ways of representing and formulating the subject that makes it comprehensible to others . . . PCK also includes an understanding of what makes the learning of specific topics easy or difficult: the conceptions and preconceptions that students of different ages and backgrounds bring with them to the learning of those most frequently taught topics and lessons. If those preconceptions are misconceptions, as they so often are, teachers need knowledge of the strategies most likely to be fruitful in reorganising the understanding of learners, because those learners are unlikely to appear before them as blank slates.
>
> (Shulman 1986: 9–10)

This definition includes the kind of background knowledge, anecdotes, and so on that one of the highly accomplished science teachers was referring to above. In fact all of our teachers were at pains to demonstrate how they spend a good deal of their time trying to find ways of representing the material in ways appropriate for their learners.

In the research we had dozens of examples of representations designed by the teachers intended to make the abstract concepts of science more concrete. All the time they located their thinking in terms of the students. Of course, they could only do this because they all made huge efforts to find out as much as possible about their students' capabilities.

One highly accomplished science teacher recalled how he had been influenced by another teacher's approach to representing a scientific concept:

> 'He came into the room carrying a huge polystyrene block that he said he'd rescued from the river. It was a bit of packaging, but enormous, almost the same size as him. He came into the room and said, "This is how I'm going to teach density." And he had a small lead block and this massive polystyrene block, and then that led on to how you would talk about mass per unit volume.'

For this teacher, the comical images evoked by this approach had been an inspiration and showed him that with some imagination and a sense of humour you can capture the students' interest and engage their attention.

Once you have got that, you have got a chance. Without it, you are lost, was his view.

In another example this teacher had also been strongly influenced by another teacher's quirky effort to grab the students' attention:

> 'He had a huge pendulum which he hung from the ceiling with a 5kg weight on the end and he asked one of the students there to hold it under his chin and then let go and not to move.'

The students were invited to advise the student whether he should or should not move and to explain their reasons. So would the student have confidence in the principle of the conservation of energy?! See Gibbs (1999) for lots more ideas like these.

Many of the representations talked about as being indicative of PCK are metaphors, analogies and models. Interestingly, all the highly accomplished science teachers went to great lengths to research and examine how their subject knowledge and understanding could support the incorporation of these representations in their teaching. In other words, they themselves needed a deep enough knowledge to be clear in their own minds about the limits of such representations so that they could be confident in dealing with the students' questions and enquiries. For example, one teacher recognized both how models can break down and how the point, or points, of breakdown make for extremely useful teaching points. Moreover, she said she could monitor the students' learning by the extent to which they could identify not only how a model shows analogical similarity to the target concept, but also by how and where it failed to represent the target concept:

> 'They've done a thick piece of wire being like a motorway and a thin piece like a single track road. And why more electrons can be pushed down a thick wire and therefore there's less resistance. That kind of idea. But when they try to explain different materials, some were trying to say that this road was like a rougher one, it had more traffic lights and things. And I said, "No, think about what you're saying. Is the model starting to break down there?" '

Modelling in science education is a remarkably fertile area for classroom research. See Halloun (2006) for a superb introduction to its subtleties and complexities.

Selection

The choice of activity, model, analogy, and so on may be determined by all sorts of reasons. Principal among them, though, stems from highly accomplished science teachers' knowledge of the pupils, their cognitive abilities, their attitudes, their predispositions towards the subject matter and their predicted behavioural responses given the nature of the task. Reasons associated with teachers' in-depth knowledge of their students again demonstrate the contextually determined nature of decision-making.

We encountered many examples of highly accomplished science teachers selecting specific activities because of their potential to engage the students. In many cases, they were drawing on the knowledge and experience of previous episodes where students had been motivated by the approach. Often these activities were called triggers, hooks or starters, all with the intention of providing a way into the lesson that would have the students on-side from the outset.

These ideas were drawn from all kinds of sources. Much of the time they were just simple exercises (e.g., matching ideas, true/false exercises), but all reinvented with a contextual twist that made them relevant to the students. One of the teachers liked to use the historical accounts of scientific events from the *Faber book of science* (Carey 2005), while another would use simple ideas from *The little giant book of science experiments* (Press 1998), from the 'Science notes' in the Association for Science Education's (ASE) journal *School Science Review*, or from *Science UPD8* (see www.ase.org.uk).

Adaptation and tailoring

This fourth sub-stage of transformation represents the part of the process where the teacher adds his or her distinctive twist, tweak or modification to the sequence of concepts, or to an activity or some other facet of the content of the lesson. This is part of the pre-active and interactive decision-making process that results in materials and activities designed specifically for the students in the class, or that take into account particular conceptual or procedural difficulties, pitfalls or misconceptions.

Our research found that all the highly accomplished science teachers could be regarded as innovative in this respect. Essentially, they are all inveterate risk-takers, keen to try out new ideas, strategies or approaches on the basis that they are much more likely to learn about teaching science if they are prepared to take some risks. Put simply – nothing ventured, nothing gained!

> 'I take risks and I'm probably better equipped to deal with the failures but I still will fail sometimes and have to put it down to experience that I'll lock away in my mind as "I'm not doing that again" or "if I do it again I'll do it in a slightly different way".'

> 'When I first started teaching "half-life" it was simply done by taking raw data out of a book and drawing a graph and possibly using a

protactinium decay source to collect some data and draw a graph. But I actually came up with the idea of getting my students involved by them being an atom and decaying in a random process. And the first time I tried it I can remember shaking with fear that this was just going to be a disaster.'

For all our highly accomplished science teachers, learning to teach science is a journey. The journey takes many twists and turns, but always at the centre is the notion of pedagogical thought utilizing the concepts of reflection and analysis.

Learning to transform the content

While it is possible to identify disparate extracts of other teachers' practice to illustrate the sub-stages Shulman describes, it is obvious from talking to highly accomplished science teachers that the process is an integrated one. The four sub-stages are not discrete, they influence and affect one another. The adaptation and tailoring of ideas and materials involves processes of selection and critical appraisal.

So what does the overall process of transformation look like? We asked some of our highly accomplished science teachers to write about their learning journeys in particular topics. Where did they start from in their thinking and where are they now? This approach drew inspiration from some previous work we had undertaken in a European project where we asked teachers to explain the thinking behind the activities and approaches they had designed to achieve specific teaching goals (Bishop *et al.* 2000). In other words, we wanted to see if teachers could highlight points in their own practice where pedagogy and content intersect.

Transformation in practice: teaching about the heart

In this example, Jodie begins by discussing her starting points for teaching the topic of the heart to a group of Year 10 (14–15 age group) students:

'The heart was a topic which I found difficult to teach at first. Part of the reason for this is that I had not encountered the detailed workings of the heart since I studied A level myself, and also because I was still at the stage where I felt I ought to "know everything", and was rather nervous that I might be asked a question that would reveal that I was not, in fact, all-knowing!'

Like many beginning- and early-career teachers the starting point is what you were taught yourself. Jodie adopted a traditional approach without making any real changes which could be shown to have her stamp on them:

> 'I think when I started teaching the topic, it seemed logical to begin with the heart itself, as it is at the centre of the circulatory system. I delivered a fairly didactic lesson on the structure and function of the heart. The pupils would draw a diagram of the heart and the features of the heart in their books, and learn the heart and the labels for homework. By doing this, I felt that the pupils would be familiar with the heart and the features of the heart for the next lesson which was the heart dissection. We would carry out the dissection, and afterwards have a discussion about what we had seen.'

On reflection, Jodie was disappointed with the outcome of the heart dissection despite the students being engaged in the activity. Where she had thought she had prepared them to relate the diagram to the real thing, little of this occurred in practice:

> 'This method did not work as well as I had hoped. For a start, the pupils were so interested in the heart that they tended to "rush in" and cut it into pieces without examining each part and noticing the structures. Also, because the vocabulary of the heart was new to them, they were not using the correct words to describe what they were seeing, and thus were not internalizing the structures and function of each structure, and relating it back to their theoretical work was more difficult.'

By talking to the students and examining their drawings it was clear to Jodie that this approach, although simple in construction, was not resulting in learning:

> 'Although [the] pupils enjoyed the activity, it was not as good a learning experience as I wanted it to be. Assessment of the learning indicated that pupils had learnt some of the vocabulary of the heart, but not how it related to the actual position on the heart. For example, pupils labelled the atria and ventricles wrongly, and were confused about which was the "right" side and which the "left" side of the heart. Many could not indicate the correct direction of blood flow through the heart, or explain why the muscular wall on the "left" ventricle needs to be thicker that that on the "right". This indicated a lack of understanding of the important functions of the heart, as well as superficial learning based more on factual recall than understanding. I felt that pupils would not make such mistakes if they had a real understanding of how the heart functioned.'

This of course was a learning experience for Jodie. Her initial assumptions about the learning sequence and conceptual development needed to be reconsidered. She decided she needed a 'big idea' to provide a clear theme within the teaching sequence. In this case, Jodie's critical engagement with the content led her to identify 'form and function' as the big idea. Her thinking was that if you could get the students to understand why things are the way they are, then they should have a basis for being able to generate explanations for themselves:

> 'The next time I taught the topic, I changed the order of study. I could now see that a good understanding of the vessels and function of the heart was essential before the pupils undertook the dissection. The heart pumping cycle is the key way in to understanding why the heart is structured as it is and we did this once the structure of arteries, capillaries and veins was mastered (using a combination of microscope work and Plasticine modelling).'

Now Jodie had to decide on how to represent the heart and the circulatory system. She had already rejected her original ideas and now needed to develop her rationale for another approach. Jodie decided the way forward was to get the students involved in a memorable activity. She decided that they themselves would 'model' the functions of the heart and the reasoning was that she could create opportunities to explore their thinking as the modelling process took place:

> 'I devised a model for the pumping cycle of the heart, and, with the help of the pupils, arranged the classroom so the tables formed four "chambers" of the heart. Pupils played the part of blood, picking up oxygen in the lungs and delivering it to the respiring cells, while travelling through the classroom and the "heart" in the same way the blood would. Absolutely key to this model was including the whole class, and regularly "freezing" the action so I could ask an individual pupil where they were in the circulatory system, what they were carrying, where they were going next etc.'

In recognition of the varying cognitive abilities of the students, Jodie adapted and tailored the model to suit their learning and attitudinal needs:

> 'This meant that there was repetition of ideas, and it also gave me the opportunity to assess the learning of each pupil in the class, and modify my teaching where necessary. Later, pupils were also able to evaluate this model for accuracy, for example pointing out that one of the drawbacks of the model was that valves were not present.'

Very cleverly, Jodie had built assessment opportunities into the modelling process so that she could make judgements about the extent of the learning and whether the students had sufficient knowledge to progress to the dissection activity. Not only was Jodie trying to model the heart with a dynamic representation and highlight the similarities, she was also encouraging the students to identify the failings of the model. Clearly, the students could only point out the failings of the model if they understood how the heart and circulatory system functioned:

'Only when I was absolutely confident that the pupils had a clear understanding of exactly how the heart worked did I ask pupils to carry out the dissection. With so many "hooks" about the circulatory system to "hang" their learning on, pupils were much more able to notice and retain the pertinent features of the heart, and have a much more valuable discussion about how the structures in the heart enable it to carry out its vital role.'

Since her initial learning experiences gained from teaching the heart, Jodie now summarizes below how she currently conceives the approach as a whole. Having developed her subject knowledge through research and reappraised completely her thinking about how the students learn, she has transformed the subject matter into a set of activities which she believes is now fit for purpose.

Activity	Teacher thinking
At the start of topic, a group of pupils take part in a role play that has a pupil being 'dissected' by a 'doctor'.	This emphasizes two important learning points – that much of our knowledge of physiology originally came from the dissection of cadavers, and also the reasoning behind the labelling of the sides of the heart counter-intuitively (on a diagram of the heart, the right-hand side appears on the left, just as a mirror image would).
Heart dissection comes towards the end of the heart and circulation topic.	At the end of the topic, pupils are more easily able to make links between the structures and functions of the heart, and how these relate to the rest of the circulatory system.

Activity	Teacher thinking
Comparison of heart diagram from textbook with actual heart that has been dissected; differences identified and diagram evaluated.	Encourages pupils to really analyse how the features of the heart fit together.
Differences identified and diagram evaluated.	Identifying any differences between the diagram and the actual heart helps the pupils to appreciate when scientific diagrams are useful and why they are generally used instead of photographs.
Heart dissection is carried out by me as a demo using the digital visualizer with images projected onto the whiteboard, simultaneously with the pupils dissecting their hearts.	Pupils (even those who do not wish to carry out the dissection themselves) have the experience of the heart dissection and clearly see all the features, even if they cannot find them all on the heart they are dissecting. Class discussion can follow about each part of the heart as all pupils are looking at the same part at the same time. Also eliminates the need to deal with the same problem (e.g., one of the atria is missing) 20 times, as all pupils would discover the problem at the same time.
Modelling used to show the heart pumping cycle.	Moving around the room helps learners (especially kinaesthetic learners) engage with what is going on. Allows a complex system to be simplified. Provides opportunity for pupils to evaluate and improve a model.
Pupils encouraged to make gestures that match the vocabulary of the heart, for example a V with their two hands when the word 'ventricle' is used.	These gestures help pupils to link the key vocabulary to the correct place in the heart. They help kinaesthetic learners to internalize the vocabulary.

The sequence of activities is conceived as a whole, with how students learn at its centre. There is a clearly established learning framework designed to promote conceptual development, and where at any point students' learning can be monitored. Running through the sequence is a theme Jodie can use to keep the students on track. At all stages, she has the opportunity to encourage the students to relate form and function. The whole approach is personalized, interactive, and allows Jodie the opportunity to improvise and respond as necessary to the students' learning needs.

3   Physics

In this chapter we look closely at three teachers, Eric, Alison and Aaron, teaching mainstream topics that involve concepts in physics. The topics featuring in these lessons are radioactivity, relative density/buoyancy and kinematics, topics that happened to be the ones being taught by our highly accomplished science teachers at the time we negotiated to visit; there was no deliberate choice made to choose one topic or class above another.

Like all the other lessons we explore in this book, we are not trying to suggest that this is how to teach any particular topic. Our focus is solely the professional knowledge of these highly accomplished teachers, how they acquire it, how they develop it and, of course, how they use it.

Section 1: Radioactivity

The context

The lesson is an 'able' Year 10 group of 25 14–15-year-old students, for one hour. It is set in a large urban Catholic mixed comprehensive school that caters for a broad spectrum of student ability.

The lesson

This is just one a of a series of lessons introducing the topic of radioactivity. In this lesson the 'big idea' is about the concept of radioactive half-life. It is one of a series of lessons that Eric has planned in order to introduce the topic of radioactivity.

The key ideas that Eric wants the students to engage with in this particular lesson are:

- radioactive decay is random;
- the target does not become radioactive;

- the rate of decay is most rapid at the start;
- it is possible that some particles will never decay.

Eric makes no assumptions about what the students might or might not remember, so at the start he refers to the work on alpha and beta decay introduced the previous week. Displayed already as the students enter and settle down is a preparatory question that requires them to write the 'nuclear equation' for the radioactive decay of bismuth 211.

Activity 1	Teacher thinking
Linking activity – exploring a nuclear equation for the radioactive decay of bismuth 211.	'What I was doing there in a way was showing students the power of the scientific equation. Look what we can do! We can summarize this whole thing with just a few symbols on the board. That's amazing isn't it?'
	'So I wanted to go through the process of them writing down that a particular atom was going to turn into something else somehow, and it did that by getting rid of part of its nucleus. Once we got that idea then we could move on to do the simulation which would then lead on to half-life.'
	'So we did a couple examples of decay equations and they'd had some practice the week before of an alpha decay and I wanted to lead that on to beta decay. In fact one of the reasons for doing beta decay was that I knew I was going to touch on carbon 14 and that that would have led me on to talking about isotopes.'

Conceiving the lesson: conceptual progression
Highly accomplished science teachers tend to conceive their teaching holistically. By this we mean that no lesson is an island, it fits into a more complex structure where different concepts are carefully developed either side by side, or in preparation for one another. The teacher thinking, shown above, indicates how Eric is putting ideas in place to prepare the way for conceptual progression.

Immediately afterwards, Eric explores common 'myths' or ideas that he knows from experience the students often hold. The week before he had given the students some true/false statements to answer to find out what they thought.

As well as concentrating on the science itself, Eric aims to develop a context to help the students appreciate its potential relevance to them by asking them

Activity 2	Teacher thinking
Linking activity to recap previous week's work and to set the context to introduce the concept of half-life.	'This lesson on radioactivity was to consolidate some work we'd done previously which had touched upon radioactive decay but to lead into the idea of half-life. The week before I'd given them a number of statements which were things that the "everyday man in the street" might say about radioactivity.'

to judge the statements – for example, 'foods preserved by being irradiated with gamma rays become radioactive' – as true or false.

This is Eric's main start to the lesson where he introduces the concept of isotopes and decay:

'Now bismuth is number 83 in the Periodic Table and that means that it has 83 protons. But the number of neutrons that it has in the nucleus can vary. It's definitely got 83 protons because if it had any other number of protons it wouldn't be bismuth. If it had 82 it would be lead. If it had 84 it would be polonium. But it's got 83. What's different about the different versions of the atom is the number of neutrons that it's got. And the one that's got a total mass of 211 happens to be unstable. So it starts "spitting" out bits of its nucleus in the form of an alpha particle.'

Metaphor
During the stimulated recall Eric explained his use of the word 'spitting'. From experience he knew the metaphor of 'spitting' would capture the students' imagination. He used it deliberately, although he was well aware of the risk if the students were to think this was an opportunity to test their own prowess at spitting. Nevertheless, he believed its pedagogical value was worth exploiting:

'. . . spitting is an occurrence which is well within their realms of understanding! . . . and obviously if you spit you're getting rid of part of yourself and I wanted to get over to them that the unstable atom would be getting rid of part of itself . . .'

Modelling
What follows now is the main activity designed by Eric to try to engage the students and take them on a short journey of discovery about the nature of radioactive decay and the concept of half-life.

To start with Eric says to the students:

> 'Right – what I'm going to do is to model radioactive decay so you can get understanding of what half-life is. There was a statement that you wrote down a week or so ago which said something like, "If a radioactive substance has a half-life of three days then it's all gone in six days." Quite a logical statement . . . what we are going to do is find out whether the statement is true or not.'

Eric goes on to explain that they are going to be involved 'by being an atom and decaying in a random process'. Each student will have a small piece of paper and a coin. The coin decides whether an atom decays or not and the paper represents the decay particle which the students will throw at him if they are to decay! He says:

> 'We're going to do it by representing radioactive decay among ourselves. You are all going to represent a radioactive atom. You have a piece of paper which I want you to screw up into a little ball. This is your little radioactive particle. Now listen carefully! There are rules about this – now if you are radioactive then you have the potential to spit out a particle.'

During the stimulated recall Eric talked about his early concerns. Putting himself in front of the class and telling them to throw bits of paper at him was inevitably a risk.

Activity 3	Teacher thinking
Simulation of radioactive decay.	'When I first started teaching half-life it was simply done by taking raw data out of a book and drawing a graph and possibly using a protactinium decay source to collect some data and draw a graph. But I actually came up with the idea of getting my students involved by them being an atom and decaying in a random process, and the first time I tried it I can remember shaking with fear that this was just going to be a disaster.'
	'Having done it probably 20 times now, I know that I can get away with it and it's never failed. I think for trainee teachers, they possibly couldn't believe you could do it and get away with it, but you can.'

COMMENTARY

Modelling

There is huge amount of confusion relating to the use of models in teaching science. For example, what is the role of models in the creation of scientific knowledge? This is an epistemological question concerned with the theory of knowledge. A pedagogical question involving models, however, would be quite different. Such a question would be asking how representational models might be used to make abstract concepts appear more concrete to students rather than helping them to establish theory.

Throughout the lesson and the various associated discussions, Eric used the terms 'model' and 'simulation' synonymously. A legitimate question to ask is whether and how a simulation differs from a model. It could be argued, for instance, that a simulation is a dynamic model involving time and that it differs in that respect from a representational model, such a scaled-down version of a bridge.

See Chapter 6 for more discussion of models and modelling, or Gilbert and Boulter's (2003) chapter in the *International handbook of science education*. For an easily accessible discussion about the issue consult the Stanford University website (http://plato.stanford.edu/entries/models-science/). These sources help the reader to make distinctions between teaching models and models as theory, as well as providing vital insights into the advantages and drawbacks of models as pedagogical tools.

Eric informs the class he will be protecting himself and makes sure they understand the rules. At this point all the students are fully engaged. The prospect of being able to 'attack' their teacher legitimately is clearly an enticing one!

> 'Now can I just point out one or two things. First of all, you flick your coin and it's either head or tail and you decay or not. You need to throw the paper not the coin! Right? I will be standing here as a target. I'll be protecting the vulnerable parts of my anatomy. Do we all understand the rules?'

Developing relationships

Eric believes in doing things out of the ordinary, setting up humorous situations or even being prepared to make a fool of himself. He saw it all as part of the relationship-building process. However, the students who took part in the focus group later thought that Eric's approach was 'quirky!'. A brief extract from their discussion about learning science gives a flavour of what they thought:

'He's a bit eccentric though.'

'Like he climbs on the table.'

'And remember he rode along the desks.'

'Oh yes, with the bike. That was brilliant. It was like, "What are you doing?" '

'And that train thing, he took ages to get it working but he got it working eventually.'

'He's so passionate about what he does and you really want to learn.'

Next, Eric wants to introduce the concept of chance or randomness. The device to provide the element of chance is the flip of a coin:

> 'Now what I don't want you to do is put it [the paper] in your mouth and start spitting it, but you will be allowed to throw it in a minute. Listen. Whether you throw your radioactive particle out is dependent upon chance. Hence the coin.'

Eric uses his general pedagogical knowledge to put in place a few management organizers, just as any science teacher would. But here it works because the students appreciate that Eric has made the effort to create relationships. They trust him and they reciprocate:

> 'So in a minute what will happen is everybody will flick their coin, or you can just have it in your hand because it's going to be either a head or a tail. I will say either head or tail and then I will tell those people that they are decayed or not. So it's a completely random process. If you decay you then throw your radioactive particle. You obviously need a target. I will be the target and I'll stand up here. This is the one and only opportunity you get to throw a piece of paper at me. You can throw it as hard as you like.'

Risk-taking

Over the years Eric has learned to predict how each new group will respond. He has tried out a number of other 'quirky' ideas already, so this would not be a leap into the unknown, or a recipe for chaos. But now he has got their attention with the opportunity to throw something at him he can try to get across the concept of randomness in radioactive decay:

> 'If you don't decay, if you got the head and I said tails, don't think, "Oh that's not fair" and chuck the piece of paper anyway, because what will happen is we'll then do it again and then we'll do it again and again and again. However long it takes until we've got everybody to decay. Now it's really important that you follow the rules, because if you don't then the simulation won't work.'

A student not wishing to forego some additional opportunities to test his arm asks, 'Please can we practise?'

Eric is working to get over the idea that you cannot predict which particles will decay, only that a similar proportion will, over a given interval of time. He now wants to get across the next point about the nature of radioactivity:

> 'Can I just point out one or two things? First of all I got hit by a few particles but I've not become radioactive as a result. It just hurt a bit and that's what happens with radioactive decay. And if you're hit by it, you just get hurt by it. You don't become radioactive.'

Here Eric is making sure he revisits the 'myths' about radioactivity that he had got the students talking about in the previous lesson. Step by step, he is steadily using the simulation to address the four key ideas:

> 'Next point about radioactive decay. First of all, at the beginning, two times ago, that was when I was potentially going to get hurt the most. So radioactive substances actually become less harmful as time goes on because once the radioactive particle has decayed that's it. It's now stable. So it's not going to do any harm any more . . . So at the beginning that was when it was most harmful to me. Now as time has gone on it's becoming less harmful. There's only potentially a few particles left to decay.'

While it is impossible for us to convey any sense of atmosphere in the class, 25 'engaged' students are now wondering where this is all leading. Eric remains firmly on track with his intentions to achieve student learning and moves on towards the concept of half-life:

> 'So some radioactive substances never get rid of all their radioactivity, even after an "infinite" amount of time. There will still be some radioactive particles in there. It's a completely random process whether the individual atoms decay or not. They might do. They might not. It might take a second, it might take a million years. But what we are able to do is to say roughly what fraction of the particles will decay each time.'

COMMENTARY

Developing relationships and 'risk-taking'

A common theme across our highly accomplished science teachers is the stress they place on the need to develop really effective working relationships with the students. Eric made the point that you cannot undertake any form of risk in terms of your teaching unless you have the students' trust and co-operation. Eric likened risk-taking to:

> 'Standing on the edge of a cliff. If you want to see what's over the cliff you have to stand right on the edge. Obviously you don't want to go over the edge but if you stand back you never find out what's over the edge.'

Like other highly accomplished science teachers, risk-taking was an essential part of learning to be a science teacher (see Berliner 2004). However, Eric emphasized that gaining trust and co-operation is not painless, although over the years, and with experience, it got easier.

How to go about forming effective relationships is part of the science teacher's professional knowledge that comes from knowledge of students, past experiences, general pedagogical knowledge and knowledge of how to make the subject matter sufficiently engaging for the students. For example, knowledge of students' relative abilities is a crucial factor in the planning of lessons and deciding what the students *do* need to know in contrast to what they *do not* need to know. Loughran (2006b: 112) makes this point very clearly.

However, this is not about taking foolish risks, it is about taking *calculated* risks. Interestingly, most of the highly accomplished science teachers also wanted to create an atmosphere where events were not always entirely predictable. Why? Because they said this kept the students guessing and increased their chances of getting student engagement.

Active processing – sketching graphs

In Eric's view it is one thing to get the students engaged in the concepts, but that does not necessarily result in understanding. He, therefore, incorporates further activities designed to revisit the ideas and require the students to translate the information into another form. In this way, Eric can deal with the problems that may have resulted from students misinterpreting the simulation. For this process, he uses a computer program that begins with a large number of particles that then decay over time. Using gradually increasing time periods, for example 10s, then 20s then 50s, the simulation provides the class with the data necessary to plot a simple graph that, in turn, provides Eric with the chance to explore the concept of half-life mathematically.

Activity 4	Teacher thinking
Simple computer simulation of radioactive decay. Eric describes the computer simulation that he created to deal with some of the deficiencies of the student simulation.	'It's an entirely random process so you can't tell which atoms are going to decay, but you can tell what fraction are going to, which is the idea of half-life really, and certainly how it's used in industry. That's where its use is. Not knowing which particles but what fraction is going to decay and so that's the idea of that particular simulation and it allows the students to plot a graph that shows the exponential decay of the sample and it will never fail.'

But before they start drawing Eric asks the students to predict the shape by drawing a simple sketch that brings together time and decay before continuing with an interrogation of the shape of the graph, its properties and how to use it to express half-life. He then goes on to point out that although he thinks this check on learning is appropriate for this particular class, it is conceptually quite difficult and he may not do it for all classes.

Activity 5	Teacher thinking
Predicting the shape of the graph before actually plotting it.	'Twofold really. It's feedback for yourself. Have they understood this concept? And it also gets the students to think as opposed to just taking some numbers and drawing a graph. They've got to think about what the shape is going to be. So there are two purposes: one for the student and one for yourself as the teacher.'
	'With other classes that part of the exercise wouldn't be worth it. This particular class could have coped with that, I think; and that's a judgement you'd have to make.'

The graph-sketching activity is worth noting in terms of what Eric is c with it. Most importantly he is asking the students to 'actively process' the ideas developed through the modelling activity. He then uses it (1) as a check to get a sense of the extent to which the students understand the concepts, and (2) as vital feedback for him to decide how to proceed – assessment for learning in practice!

COMMENTARY

Teaching for understanding

Striving to 'teach for understanding' is a commonly expressed aim for most science teachers. Why would it be otherwise unless, for instance, you believe the time it takes to get students to understand interferes with preparing them for examination success. In fact, teaching for understanding is one of those values that appears to transcend all the highly accomplished science teachers' practice.

We would maintain that all initial teacher education (ITE) programmes of science education promote 'teaching for understanding' as a goal. However, is it necessarily clear what the concept of 'teaching for understanding' actually means? A good starting point is Douglas Newton's book *Teaching for understanding* (2000). You might also explore *Improving subject teaching* (Millar *et al.* 2006) where specific teaching interventions have been designed to allow teachers to promote and monitor students' understanding of scientific concepts.

Having established he can move on, Eric identifies the need to emphasize the context again so that the students do not forget how the school science they are learning connects with the world outside. He, therefore, returns to the statements that earlier the students had to decide were true or false. In the light of these activities could the students evaluate their original ideas? The discussion provides him with another opportunity to monitor the students' learning.

Reinforcing conceptual understanding

As a plenary activity to generate some discussion, Eric plays a short, but carefully chosen, video.

We asked Eric how he had changed his teaching over the years. He told us that at the beginning of his career, he would use data from a book and get the students to draw graphs. But he was not satisfied with this as it failed to engage the students' interest, probably because they were not involved in any active or meaningful way. Evidence from student focus groups within this study

Activity 6	Teacher thinking
Video playback.	'I don't use videos very often. They've got to be worth more than just giving a 20-minute break for the teacher. I think the students have really got to engage with the video and this is a good one. It shows the particles decaying; so they have that reinforced again. Graphics on the video show little particles whizzing around and "spitting" out bits and pieces. Then it looks at a decay curve and just uses some of the ideas we'd been talking about for the previous few lessons.'

suggests very strongly that when students are engaged in activity they are more likely to be involved in the learning process.

COMMENTARY

Student engagement

It cannot have gone unnoticed in recent times how striving for 'student engagement' is almost like the search for the Holy Grail. If you find it, then all else follows. Maybe! But student engagement does not come without effort, and it is like trying to hit a moving target. It would not be the same for every student, group or class.

Some students, of course, might be oriented towards science, but many (or most!) are not. Eric's somewhat 'quirky' approach, as the students put it, is therefore all part of a repertoire constructed to capture their interest. Engagement comes through unpredictability, surprise, fun, humour, stories and being prepared to do odd things. Eric reads widely and considers that a lot of the knowledge he exploits stems from his professional reading. For example, he would draw on resource material, such as John Carey's *The Faber book of science* (2005), a book containing all sorts of strange science stories, historical tales and poetry offering fascinating starting points or contexts for the imaginative science teacher. Another book of this kind, recommended also by the *New Scientist*, is *The velocity of honey* by Jay Ingram (2004).

Such professional reading, including the history and philosophy of science, is a key part of Eric's own education as a science teacher, which he uses to vary the approach to suit the age, ability and aptitudes of the classes he teaches. Alongside his assimilation of the usual curricular material, this is the raw material he manipulates to dream up alternative approaches to presenting the subject matter. Significantly, the students themselves acknowledged this depth of knowledge and were keen to express their appreciation through sentiments such as, 'He treats us like adults,' 'He teaches more than we need to know, but it's interesting' and 'It's his enthusiasm.' They liked what they called his 'random facts' that often grabbed their attention.

Reflections on a teaching and learning model

Towards the end of the VSR process we asked Eric to sum up his construction of this particular lesson. In response Eric said:

> 'Yes, I think that's what you aim to do all the time. You have to try and decide what you want the pupils to have learned by the end and that needs to be clear in your mind, but of course things happen during lessons that you can't legislate for and I think there are lots of decisions that have to be made during the lesson that you're going to leave bits out/put things in depending on what's happening. For this particular lesson I knew what resources I had; I knew roughly how long various parts of it were going to take, and because I've got the experience I guess I was able to fit it all in almost seamlessly. It would have looked like the kids were doing exactly what I wanted all the time, which isn't the case. So you cut short some things. I knew that, for example, if I hadn't started the video by 10.00 a.m. then I wouldn't have had time to show it, so that means there's an eye on the clock; I need to speed this little bit up a bit, maybe get them to finish their graph while the video is going on. These are decisions you make all the time. Actually you're manipulating the lesson as it goes along to try and get it to fit the overall aim, which is, "What do I want the students to have learned by the end of this?" and you've got a number of activities up your sleeve, and you use them or not as the case may be.'

This summary was consistent with Eric's analysis of how the lesson proceeded. As with all the other highly accomplished science teachers, Eric carefully managed the duration of the activities and frequently reassessed what had been achieved and what needed to be changed in order to maintain progress and achieve the learning intentions. Significantly, it was the learning intentions that determined the activities and how they related to one another rather than the activities being an end in themselves, an approach consistent with the kind of objective-driven practice advocated by Gott and Duggan (1996). The idea of 'manipulating the lesson as it goes along' also resonates with the idea that to meet the needs of different learners the teacher has to be sensitive to the development of the lesson. Here Eric constantly made references to previous experiences, but what was so striking was his ability to analyse the material he prepared and differentiate it in terms of intellectual outcomes structured to match the capabilities of the students in the class.

Eric's background

Eric's story for coming into science teaching from a degree background in engineering nearly 20 years ago was not straightforward, but early opportunities to do voluntary work with children made him think that perhaps there was something in teaching that was worth more exploration than he first thought. Throughout his career, Eric has seen himself as being on a continuing learning journey. Having reached the position of leading a science department, his move into initial teacher education as a part-time tutor now provides another source of inspiration and a range of new sources for learning.

Eric's beliefs and theories (personal philosophies) about science teaching

The driving force behind Eric's approach to science teaching is an intuitive belief in the importance of engaging the students in the content in such a way that they develop an intrinsic interest in science. In parallel, Eric also believes that it is vital to develop the kind of relationships with the students that will allow him that possibility. Eric was unequivocal about the need to make the science relevant through the use of everyday, recognizable contexts.

Engaging the students' interest in the subject is one thing, getting them to engage intellectually is another. For this reason, Eric felt it was absolutely vital that he should be able to explain the science well and bridge the gap between what the students already know and what he wants them to know (see Ogborn *et al.* 1996 for an analysis of what we mean by 'explaining'). However, not only does Eric want to be seen by his students as a science teacher who is good at explaining, it is also his belief that they too should be able to use their science knowledge and understanding to start on the journey of trying to explain scientific phenomena for themselves:

> 'It's an explanation of phenomena which you observe around you all the time. Why is the sky blue? Why is a bridge able to span a river without falling down? It's trying to explain things that you can observe and you can take that to origins of the universe in that direction or the size of atoms in another.'

Eric's beliefs are arguably what Argyris and Schön (1974) would call 'theories in use'. It seems to us that Eric's belief system with regard to building relationships with the students, getting them engaged in the work through contexts they can relate to, are actually the theories that govern his approach.

Eric's professional knowledge
Significantly, Eric's experience as head of science in a large Catholic comprehensive school also provided him with some interesting opportunities to rethink his understanding about the nature of science:

> 'The fact that it's [science] probably a "best guess" at explaining phenomena around us as opposed to "this is what somebody has said, so I'm going to go along with that because it makes sense to me".'

At the beginning of his career Eric said he had little time for reading other than to develop his subject knowledge, but through the years he has read extensively about the history of science, exploring how scientific ideas have developed over time, and he now readily incorporates such material into his lessons.

Developing subject knowledge inevitably comes with time, but knowing 'how' you understand it is crucial. Despite having had a successful school and university career in physics, Eric made a fundamental reassessment of his understanding of the subject matter. He described the feelings he encountered:

> 'I'd done well at physics in school myself because I'd learned it but I didn't really understand it, so when it came to teaching it I was almost learning it again properly . . . you've almost got to unlearn or try not to take for granted knowledge you've had for a number of years but try to get down to the level of the pupil.'

As a starting point, Eric uses his own weaknesses in understanding the physics to appreciate the difficulties students have. He talked of 'wrestling with the ideas before you can teach well'. Put another way, all our highly accomplished science teachers recognize that a deep-seated understanding of the subject matter is a prerequisite for teaching for understanding (Bishop and Denley 1997). Such humility was an attitude that featured often in our research. Not only did these teachers believe in the need for well-established subject matter understanding, but they also emphasized the need to know it in ways that could convey the same excitement to the students. It was fascinating to explore with Eric the way he uses the process of pedagogical reasoning to transform his subject knowledge base (see Figure 3.1). This story, we believe, offers a very clear model of a science teacher blending his subject knowledge with pedagogy, in the way Shulman (1987) describes.

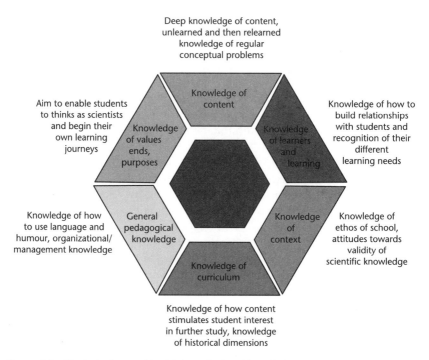

Figure 3.1 The 'spinning top' for Eric's professional knowledge.

Section 2: Relative density/buoyancy

The context

This is a GCSE class of over 30 Year 10 (14–15 age group) relatively able students, who attend a large mixed comprehensive school located in a medium-sized provincial town.

The lesson

At the time this lesson was observed the students were being prepared for the practical assessments that form part of their GCSE (14–16 age group national examination) programme. One important aspect that is examined is the ability of the students to evaluate the investigations they undertake as part of the process of scientific inquiry. Terms such as 'reliability', 'validity', 'accuracy', 'precision' and 'error' are stressed in the GCSE specification, and students are expected to analyse their work by reference to them. These ideas provide the learning framework for the lesson we describe below.

Developing relationships

Alison has only joined the school as head of the science department fairly recently and is developing her knowledge of where the main emphases in teaching about the nature of scientific inquiry have been during the Key Stage 3 (11–14 phase). A great deal of the interaction she has with the students, therefore, is designed to get to know them and to find out where they are with their thinking about science and how science works. One principle guiding much of this interaction is based on the idea that whatever the students are doing now at Key Stage 4 (14–16 phase), it should draw on, and build on, learning from Key Stage 3. This principle provided Alison with a sound basis to engage students in conversation. Now, the interest shown by Alison in all her students has meant that she has quickly established relationships with this group built on trust and mutual respect. At this point she feels able to take a risk with an innovative approach to developing inquiry skills:

> 'Relationships in the classroom. It is an element of trust between you and the students and because I'm new anyway they've had to get to know me. Firm but fair, direct parameters within which we work as a group . . .'

Establishing trust is a priority in all the highly accomplished science teachers' relationships with their students. It is a mutual understanding that through the careful and sensitive actions of the teacher they have worked hard to achieve. It is evident in all cases that it doesn't come without effort. It is significant, however, that the students both recognize and appreciate the effort and care taken by their teacher to help them engage with the subject. As a result, the teacher earns their respect.

Scientific inquiry

In a short introduction, Alison sets the context for the simple scientific inquiry she wants the students to do:

> '. . . what you are going to do today is to investigate the statement just under that first paragraph [refers to the handout]: "Do things sink quicker in fresh water rather than salty water?" '

Alison provides the students with this brief:

> It is easier to float in the Dead Sea. The Dead Sea is situated in the Middle East. All rivers and streams from the mountains that surround it enter the Dead Sea. As water flows down the mountains, it collects many minerals, one of which is salt. The only way water gets out is by evaporation. The weather and temperatures in this area are very hot.

What is different about this is that Alison has given the students a brief for this scientific inquiry which is 'designed to go wrong', as she put it. In other words, she is setting them up to struggle unless they can think their way out of it. The essence of this is that Alison knows the students will be able to collect some data, but as the emphasis of the lesson is on 'evaluation', she wants the students to explain why their data cannot answer the inquiry question.

Activity 1	Teacher thinking
Scientific inquiry: exploring the rate at which Plasticine sinks in tap water and salt water.	'They're going to look at floating and sinking. They get just a couple of lines about the Dead Sea, minerals increasing concentrations, etc. So the question I'm posing is "Do things float better in salty water?" but I'm not necessarily so much after the science, but it's skills-based. So they're going to evaluate the experiment. But I know it won't work!'
	'I was deliberately planning for the experiment to go wrong. So I knew that 10g of Plasticine would sink very quickly, I knew they wouldn't be able to time the reaction time for it to sink. I gave them free choice in planning, so I didn't tell them what to do or how much salt, because from that they would make judgements about whether the volume of water might make a difference, the shape of the Plasticine or how much salt they put in.'
	'This group now are getting much more used to not having recipes, so they're beginning to think for themselves. Well they can think for themselves, but I need to develop that further, with the confidence to say, "Here's the set up. Just go away and do it." This is a very simple one to do.'

Once Alison has indicated to the students the range of equipment that is available to them, they are then on their own to decide for themselves how to proceed:

'I'm not going to tell you what to do. The choice is yours. But what you have to do is to state the answer to that question. Just think about what the dependent and independent variables are. But what I want as the main focus today is to evaluate the data. The main focus once you have done your experiment is evaluation. On the question paper I want to consider how the results were obtained. But remember that we are always checking on the validity, the reliability, the accuracy, the precision and any sources of errors in your experiment.'

COMMENTARY

Students' understanding of the nature of science

Through the approach in this lesson, Alison is attempting to challenge students' ideas about the procedural aspects of investigative work on the basis that if they only ever follow recipes they will never engage with the problems that face any investigator. In this instance, Alison is focusing the students' attention on evidence and its quality.

Previous research shows clearly how little understanding students have of the nature of scientific inquiry. Driver *et al.* (1996), in their fascinating book *Young people's images of science*, explored students' understanding of the nature of scientific knowledge and concluded that the school curriculum is limited in promoting this kind of understanding. With the advent of the 'How Science Works' component of the new GCSE specifications, this ought to change, but as Alison's focus demonstrates the emphasis is likely to remain on procedural knowledge rather than on how scientific knowledge is created.

Is this a risk – not according to the students! When we asked them what interests them about science they were very clear about their liking for the approach adopted in this lesson. Their view resonates with many of the other students we interviewed as part of this research who also saw this kind of strategy as an important way of giving them ownership over their work and learning:

> 'Going on from what Tom said, I think I like experiments and investigations where the teacher leads us, doesn't give us a set of instructions but she gives us this, this and this, and then she gives us the independence to go off and do what we like with it and amass our own table of results and our own evaluation and things.'

> 'Make our own experiment!'

> 'And then we learn things off each other rather than just the teacher. Like today with the Plasticine.'

Risk-taking

The stress Alison places on the concept of evaluation and on the terms validity, reliability, accuracy and precision in the introduction, reflects the new 'How Science Works' component of the GCSE. It is Alison's belief that by contriving a situation, whereby the students will inevitably get poor quality (unreliable) data, they will begin to appreciate the need to focus on these concepts in order to have a framework for the evaluation of the inquiry.

This is a good example of a highly accomplished science teacher relying on her PCK to take a risk, although Alison would call it a calculated risk. Whereas beginning-teachers might see this approach as a recipe for disaster and, potentially, an unwanted source of unnecessary classroom management problems, Alison views it as a strategy to engage with the students and promote inquiry questions. Moreover, she believes she is providing the students with an intellectual challenge to solve the problem of being presented with a poorly designed investigation. As she said:

> 'In many ways I took a risk today . . . You give the pupils confidence that it doesn't matter if they haven't got the right answer. What they need to do is understand why they didn't get the right answer and what they can do about it.'

Alison's confidence is thinking this strategy will work is based on her knowledge of the students and her belief that they will both rise to the challenge and engage with it. Most importantly she knows she has the skills to be able to deal with students' questions and concerns. During the VSR Alison reflected on the students' responses to the task:

> 'So you're trying to embed an understanding that using techniques, small steps of development, to take them along the route to realizing there isn't always the right or wrong answer. It's that confidence to not worry about it and give lots of alternatives to solving that problem . . . I was trying to unpick as well what some of the students meant by dissolving and why they were stirring because they were actively doing the stirring bit. But why? And making links then with the key ideas that the energy was breaking apart the particles.'

Teaching for understanding

Alison's approach is that the students need to understand what they are doing in order to solve procedural problems. Her belief is that these thinking skills are transferable skills that can be learned very effectively in science and will be useful in many other situations that students will face as adults.

Alison's thinking about how to develop students' understanding of how science works involves the kinds of questions she poses next:

- Is this familiar?
- Is this the way we were taught?
- Does this challenge the way students solve problems?
- Does this method train students in the higher-order thinking skills they require as preparation for the scientific inquiry problems that they need to solve at the higher levels of GCSE and beyond?
- Does it produce problem-solving students?
- Is this the right preparation we should offer the students?
- How has the delivery of investigative science changed?

In response to her own questions, Alison wrote down her rationale for constructing activities to develop students' understanding of scientific inquiry. Key principles centre on the development of thinking skills and giving the students ownership over the process:

> 'It is essential that we, as teachers, should give students the opportunity to develop the thinking skills of planning and gathering appropriate evidence as well as the higher-order thinking skills of analysis and evaluation – the most difficult skills that students have to come to terms with. As adults, we all have a range of problems to solve as part of our day-to-day life. We need to prepare students for such day-to-day decision-making processes. To assist the development of these skills it is important to give the students ownership of the solutions to the problems they are expected to solve.'

For a really good discussion of the purposes of investigative work, see Duggan and Gott (2000: 60–9).

COMMENTARY

Ownership

It is over 20 years since the idea that students should engage in authentic investigative activities was first proposed (Woolnough and Allsop 1985). The argument was quite simple: when students have a stake in their practical work and are able to establish a sense of ownership they are more likely to engage with it. Moreover, if they can be assigned tasks that can be seen to be both relevant and authentic it is more likely that they will learn from them (see Hodson 1998, Chapter 10, 'Authenticity in science and learning'). Since then, and after many iterations of the National Curriculum in the UK, there is still discussion about how best to achieve this. It is clearly the case that our highly accomplished science teachers subscribe to this view, and as we can see in Alison's example, she is working hard to apply these principles to her own practice. Our evidence suggests that when students are given some degree of autonomy they will respond positively.

Developing conceptual understanding through scientific inquiry
At the same time, Alison also seizes the opportunity to help students with their understanding of scientific concepts and to use that knowledge to help solve the procedural problem they are facing:

> 'Understanding what that word "dissolving" meant. That the salt didn't disappear and where it had gone. And to get them engaged with the fact that it [the water] might be more dense so that's why it may take longer for it [the Plasticine] to go down.'

In preparing and planning for this activity Alison has used her experience not just to anticipate the many questions the students will ask, but how she would respond:

> 'What sorts of questions might the pupils ask you? In many ways they asked, "How much salt do I put?" "It's up to you." "How much water?" "Does it matter? You tell me." Some put little amounts. I wanted it to be a route of discovery for them too and they soon discovered that if they put 200 ml in they couldn't time it at all. So a lot of them put half a beaker. Would I put half a beaker? I'm not really sure. And they were asking me, because of that confidence, because they were afraid of being wrong. And you ask the question "How can you slow down so that you can make it a measurable time?" That's what I was asking some of the groups. So one group made it [the Plasticine ball] more streamlined. But when you've only got 600 ml of water, which they did, and I said "OK, you've got a real problem now," and then they made the pancake shape because they'd worked out the fact that if they changed the surface area . . . we talked about it doing the wavy movement down rather than the direct route down. So it's a case of prompting the pupils to think and get inside what was happening . . .'

For 45 minutes the students engaged in the activity trying out various approaches to get meaningful data of some kind. Throughout the time Alison moved from group to group asking, probing and prompting in order to help them solve the procedural issues for themselves. At the same time she probed their theoretical understanding so that solutions to the problem of poor data could be informed by theoretical considerations. For example, it seemed common sense to the students that it should take longer for a piece of Plasticine to sink in salt water than pure water even though at this point they could not suggest why. This, however, presented Alison with opportunities to discuss with the students theoretical concepts relating to solutions, dissolving, relative density and buoyancy. Through a process of dialogic interaction, Alison intervened with more questions:

> 'When I asked what had happened to the crystals on the floor of the beaker they came up with the idea that they'd broken up. I asked why and they came up with the fact that the water collided with the crystals and the particles had broken off. I asked where the particles were in the water. Have they disappeared? No. Where are they in the water then? And they came up with the idea that by stirring that the particles would be uniformly spread.'

Alison went on to talk in detail about interactions with the students, explaining how she tries to ensure that she builds on students' prior knowledge at Key Stage 3. Simultaneously, she is assessing constantly where the students are in their understanding so that she can decide what sorts of questions she needs to ask to get them to move forwards. Through this process she believes they can all learn:

> 'So then I asked, "What happens when no more salt dissolves?" And they came up with saturation and salt lying on the bottom. I asked how that affected the density. So you prompt the right sort of question to elicit the right responses from the pupils really. And they did give me that without me giving them the answer. So I was quite pleased because they'd obviously brought that knowledge forward. But one or two of the groups did actually say that they thought the salt had disappeared and that was one of the questions towards the end. One of the girls said, "Dispersed . . . disappeared?".'

Misconceptions

Suddenly a warning light is flashing! Alison is alert to the common misconception associated with dissolving. The student is not sure about this, so Alison has to consider the implications – is this a whole group issue or is it just an individual who is insecure in her understanding? In common with all highly accomplished science teachers, Alison is constantly making mental assessments of where the students are in their understanding and then making adjustments to her teaching in order to ensure that the students advance their conceptual understanding.

COMMENTARY
Developing relationships

Highly accomplished science teachers are inveterate risk-takers. It is as if it is an in-built part of their psyche. They live to learn, and risk-taking provides them with the fuel for learning. But they are not reckless risk-takers. Far from it. They are good judges of their classes, and know the boundaries. It is 'risk' under controlled circumstances. Over time though, they have cultivated the environment through careful relationship-building, so that students also know what the boundaries are. In these circumstances, highly accomplished science teachers know they can try things out.

Alison was talking about how she engages the students by doing perhaps somewhat quirky experiments. But we know how students like this element of unpredictability, particularly when the outcomes of scientific experiments defy common sense.

> 'You would take risks and do something a bit different, like a balloon with water. Yes, you get soaked, let's have a good laugh, but they remember and they know. I got soaked, from here to here, with a balloon, heating a balloon with water in it, and someone walked in through the door, someone being sent in from another class, I turned round and "bloop"! But the students don't forget that, and you look at the explanation. Why? . . . Lots of whacky things and very different things that would actually capture pupils' attention. But it's out of the ordinary . . . you know what's going to happen. The pupils don't know because what they expect to happen doesn't happen!'

And in Alison's view all of this demonstrates to the students that you too are prepared to join in, even make a bit of a fool of yourself. A word of caution though: *this is not about entertainment*. It is about providing students with variety, surprising them and providing the hooks which they can use to engage with the subject matter (see Flutter and Ruddock 2004: 110). And this is just part of what our highly accomplished science teachers see as important in establishing educational relationships for learning (see Bullock and Wikeley 2006: 120, and their identification of three strands to personal learning).

Sharing learning
The lesson concludes with a 15-minute plenary discussion centring on whether the students could draw any conclusions from their enquiries and if so what

trust could be placed in those conclusions. The key issues the students identified was that their reaction time was often longer than it took the Plasticine to fall.

Activity 2	Teacher thinking
Plenary: making sure the students share their learning.	'I give myself a lot of time because there I was looking at several different aspects of evaluative skills really. I always try to give myself about 15 minutes if it's that type of activity where I need to draw a lot of stuff out of the pupils and to give as many of them an opportunity of sharing what they've been discussing with one another really. With such a big class [32 students] you need that time and you can elicit any misconceptions from those types of discussion – like the salt disappears type thing.'

Although predominantly a teacher-centred, authoritative interaction (Scott and Mortimer 2006), Alison carefully teases out each of the terms (i.e., reliability, accuracy, etc.) in turn, helping the students to use them in the context of an evaluation. In other words, she aims to generalize the concepts from the students' own experience with the intention that when they undertake another scientific inquiry of this kind they will be able to apply what they have learned here to a novel situation. At the same time she also reinforces key points about the concepts of dissolving and density that she had picked up during the practical activity to satisfy herself that she is not leaving any conceptual problems unattended.

The students' view of this approach to teaching and learning coincides very much with Alison's aims to teach for understanding. As one student put it:

'Sometimes I like school science but it can get boring when it's just written work and you're not quite understanding what's going on. But when you understand it and you get the real flow for it it's really enjoyable because you understand.'

The lesson concludes neatly by Alison returning to the terminology she started out with to reinforce its importance in the formal GCSE practical assessments the students will soon be taking.

Alison's background

With a degree in biology and physical science following a broad spectrum of A levels, Alison has a wide background in science. As the current head of the science department in this school, she has also led departments in more challenging schools. However, a shortage of experienced science staff is not making the task easy, particularly with the need to change approaches to science teaching to reflect the aspects of 'How Science Works'. Alison is very much a collegial leader who believes in sharing knowledge and resources in order to give students an appropriate consistency of experience, whoever may be teaching them.

Alison's beliefs and theories (personal philosophies) about science teaching
From her time as an A level student, Alison has always had a passion for science. Her personal philosophy she describes as 'hands-on' as she considers herself to be a kinaesthetic learner and someone who really wants to help students understand the key ideas of science. Bridging the world of school science and science in the everyday world is another passion. Alison appreciates that not all students are going to be scientists, but she does believe strongly that science education provides an important skills base, both in practical terms through the use of equipment, but more importantly in terms of mental preparation. The contextualization of the science to make it relevant is vital too. One approach is by ensuring that links to science in the everyday world are always present. Another is to help students visualize abstract concepts. By this Alison means providing opportunities for students to make models that represent their understanding. She has become a strong advocate of the use of thinking frames as one way to get students to expose their thinking for scrutiny (see www.thinkingframe.com).

Fundamental to model-making and all other aspects of scientific inquiry is collaborative work which Alison makes central to the way she organizes science for her students. In the activity described above, she chose girl/boy pairings on the basis that girls and boys tend to bring different organizational skills to scientific inquiry. On hearing the students' views it was clear that learning from one another was something they had come to expect. They accepted the idea of a seating plan or working in boy/girl pairs, but argued that it is not ideal when students do not get along.

One further important aspect of Alison's belief is about teaching is her aim to teach science for understanding. One element within this is the crucial role of questioning:

> 'Questioning is crucial. Asking the right question is crucial and the ability to react instantly to a comment that pupils have made is key.'

The point here is that written work would not necessarily reveal the level of understanding of all students. Therefore, you need mixed approaches:

> 'That's why you need to get into the pupils' heads, [find out] what they understand and what they don't and what they can't visualize, can't articulate, and support that.'

Getting 'inside the students' heads' is an expression that Alison often used to convey the idea that she wants to know where they are, where they coming from, what they understand, their alternative frameworks, etc. (Driver *et al.* 1994).

Alison's professional knowledge

When asked about how she maintained her subject knowledge in science, Alison referred to professional bodies (such as the Institute of Physics and the ASE) and journals (such as *New Scientist* or *Scientific American*) which are available online. She also talked of scouring resources within the department, having a stack of newspaper articles and all kinds of texts, some dating back many years, that have resulted in the creation of her own home library. Many of the highly accomplished science teachers argued that some of the texts may not now be material you would want to use directly with students, but are sources for inspiration. A good example of such older references might be the Nuffield Combined Science programme published in the 1970s. Alison also referred to *The little giant book of science experiments* (Press 1998) which she uses as a source of quirky ideas.

Alison reflected that she was comfortable with her practice in earlier years but looking at the stark reality that she now faced:

> '. . . these pupils were demotivated, they had no aspirations, they had had teacher after teacher after teacher. Phenomenal! There was no science department when I went in there to head it up. You had to be extremely creative and look at different ways of engaging those pupils because there was no way they wanted to do science.'

Alison talked more about her professional learning resulting from taking on this struggling science department. She talked particularly of managing a culture change which focused on engaging students in science.

Without engagement, students are unlikely to feel motivated or inspired by science, leading to the inevitable consequences that follow for classroom management. For Alison, it was a challenge not just to lead by example, but to encourage a whole science department to think differently about how they should present science to the students (see Figure 3.2).

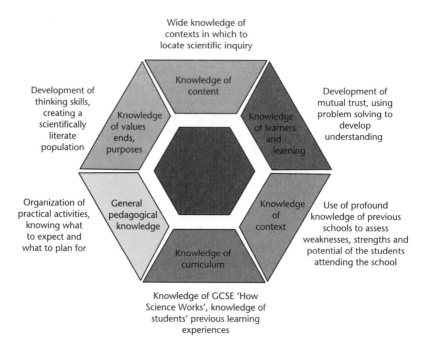

Wide knowledge of
contexts in which to
locate scientific inquiry

Development of
thinking skills,
creating a
scientifically
literate
population

Development of
mutual trust, using
problem solving to
develop
understanding

Organization of
practical activities,
knowing what
to expect and
what to plan for

Use of profound
knowledge of previous
schools to assess
weaknesses, strengths and
potential of the students
attending the school

Knowledge of GCSE 'How
Science Works', knowledge of
students' previous learning
experiences

Knowledge of content

Knowledge of values ends, purposes

Knowledge of learners and learning

General pedagogical knowledge

Knowledge of context

Knowledge of curriculum

Figure 3.2 The 'spinning top' for Alison's professional knowledge.

Section 3: Kinematics

The context

This is a class of over 25 Grade 10 (15–16-year-old) students in a mixed private school just north of Johannesburg in South Africa. This was a relatively able group although a number of the students clearly found the mathematical ideas in the topic somewhat challenging.

The lesson

This lesson focuses on the relationships of three motion-time graphs as part of a topic on kinematics. The week before the students were engaged in standard ticker tape experiments using the dynamics trolleys. In preparation for this lesson they were analysing segments of ticker tape to determine how the dots, and the varying distances between them, represented velocity and/or change in velocity. The purpose of the lesson was to develop the students' understanding of the relationship between displacement, velocity and acceleration through graphical representations. Most interesting of all was the way Aaron had conceived the lesson around the three graphs and was intending to use them as a mechanism to monitor the progress of the students' learning.

Subject knowledge

Aaron brings to this topic ten years of experience of students' difficulties regarding the interpretation of motion-time graphs. He senses that they dislike graphs largely because they have difficulty interpreting them and therefore do not understand them. Aaron believes in teaching for understanding and therefore looks for ways to enable students to think things through for themselves. He believes he has developed a way of doing this by helping the students to derive one graph from another (see Figure 3.3).

In addition to developing the students' abilities to interpret the graphs, Aaron uses the students' ability to explain the relationships of the graphs to one another as a check on the extent of the understanding they have developed with respect to displacement, velocity and acceleration.

Almost immediately after running the VSR, Aaron stopped the tape to remark:

> 'Often, through marking exam papers and just looking at the arguments, they give you weird responses in terms of what a graph is. And if we're looking at a distance(position)-time graph they'll talk about the area underneath the graph, but they have no clue that the graph doesn't actually give you any quantity – that it's specifically the gradient of the graph we're looking at to get the velocity – so they just make broad statements and generalize.'

Here Aaron is demonstrating how he is using his pedagogical content

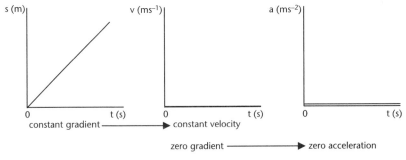

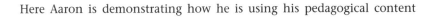

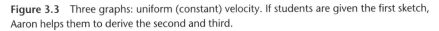

Note: s = distance; v = velocity; a = acceleration

Figure 3.3 Three graphs: uniform (constant) velocity. If students are given the first sketch, Aaron helps them to derive the second and third.

Note: s = distance; v = velocity; a = acceleration

knowledge by manipulating his knowledge of the subject matter in response to the 'weird responses' the students show. Their difficulties, misconceptions, errors or misunderstandings are, in effect, the raw material Aaron is using to develop his professional knowledge base. From years of marking exam papers, Aaron has learned that students commonly misunderstand the relationship between the area under a displacement-time graph and the gradient of the line which represents velocity.

Activity 1	Teacher thinking
Exploring the three graphs.	'Prior to this lesson we looked at the three graphs, but disjointedly. So we looked at what a displacement time graph was, how it worked, what were its properties and what you could extrapolate from it, and we looked at them in isolation. The students had never had a chance to put all their graphs together until today and looked at how we could combine them . . . They'd always looked at them separately.'
	'My thinking there in showing them the three graphs and how they relate is to bring some kind of continuity between uniform motion and non-uniform motion, accelerated motion and negative accelerated motion. Because again, they've looked at them in isolation all the time, but now I want them to put all three together to say, "This is how that relates to that, these are the properties of gradient and area that help us intertwine the graphs and bring some kind of meaning that runs through all of them." '

For Aaron, it is not good enough for students to be able to just use algorithmic approaches to solving problems in physics. He wants deeper understandings. Without those he feels no satisfaction. He wants the students to be able to apply their knowledge so they would not be fazed by problems set in situations they have not actually encountered in the classroom.

A few moments later Aaron stopped the video tape to pick up a common misconception:

> 'They see a straight diagonal line on an ST graph meaning an increasing displacement and they'll draw the same one for the velocity. When I was going around giving them the exercises that's exactly what some of them were doing. They would draw a [diagonal] straight line for the acceleration time graph that was increasing acceleration

after I'd said, "We're only limited to constant acceleration. So you should only have horizontal lines." So they don't interpret one graph in terms of another.'

Now Aaron stresses again the need to explore the unit for acceleration and how it differs from velocity. He says to the students:

'This is the unit, this is the symbol, this is how you calculate it.'

He then commented:

'They don't know ms^{-2} means metres per second squared and I think that is fundamental to understanding what an acceleration is. What does it mean to change velocity at a certain rate? I think unpacking that definition is important.'

In the previous lesson Aaron had got the students to compare visually two pieces of ticker tape, one showing constant velocity and the other showing accelerated motion, by looking at the changing distances between the holes punched by the machine. He also wanted to reinforce the idea that science has a very precise meaning for acceleration:

'When we started talking about acceleration they assumed the English meaning of this, which is to go faster. I made a distinction about what "English" says about acceleration and what a scientist means by acceleration . . . I stressed at that point that a change in velocity means increasing or decreasing speed, but also because the data quantity means a change in direction, so it's not purely moving faster in terms of speed.'

This approach is consistent with Aaron's view about teaching for understanding. He is aware of the way common usage gets in the way of scientific understanding. However, he is not dogmatic. He simply helps the students to see that words can have multiple meanings, but stresses that the scientific view has just one, very precise, meaning. Students have to know when they are talking the language of science.

COMMENTARY

Language in science – everyday and scientific usage

It is very easy for science teachers to assume that the students will relinquish their everyday usage of words and immediately accept the scientific usage. Aaron, like many other of the highly accomplished science teachers, is all too well aware that unless he makes the effort to make distinctions in usage clear, he may simply compound difficulties in learning.

It is interesting to note how Aaron brings his professional knowledge to bear on situations such as this in order to avoid words like 'deceleration' which he thinks could introduce potential misconceptions. In this way he can make a point of drawing to the students' attention how language in science is intended to be precise. For example, how much difference does an indefinite article make? 'A force is required to open the door.' 'Force is required to open the door.' Which of these statements might a physicist consider to be a more precise form of communicating the physics involved in opening a door and why?

Wellington and Osborne (2001: 17–19) in their book *Language and literacy in science education* highlight issues such as the duality of meaning in scientific terminology and offer examples, illustrations and materials that can give beginning- and early-career teachers a head start in promoting literacy through learning and teaching science.

Aaron avoids the use of the word 'deceleration' because he thinks it has the potential to be confused with negative acceleration:

> 'I just generally use negative acceleration. I don't want to even talk about deceleration and yes, they do come up and say, "Yes it's decelerating sir." I try to discourage that word as far as possible and stick to just one because you can speed up in the opposite direction and have a negative acceleration, but it doesn't mean a deceleration in their understanding.'

Aaron identifies two more problem areas that he anticipates in his teaching: the common misconception that the shape of the graph represents the path the object is taking – up a hill or down a slope or on the level; and that every graph should start from zero:

> 'I've just picked up with experience in terms of how they interpret graphs. You ask them the question, "What is the initial velocity of the graph? Zero," even though they see it on the y axis as being 10. So when they look at that 10 it doesn't make sense to them. They think it's touching the y axis and it's 0. They're not looking at the "y" intercept, even though they have a maths background.'

Aaron knows that there are more pitfalls to be addressed if he is to have any chance of helping the students understand these counter-intuitive ideas. (See Lenton and Stevens 2000 for more insights into numeracy and graphicacy in science.) Aaron addressed the next pitfall by using the dynamics trolley for a visual representation.

Activity 2	Teacher thinking
Dynamics trolley to demonstrate negative acceleration.	'Yes. I'm trying to explain to them that you can be moving forward, but you can be slowing down moving forward. So I'm trying to highlight to them that we have velocity in one direction but acceleration is in the opposite direction, and that could be simulated by someone applying brakes in the car and stopping before a robot [South African term for a traffic light].'

The VSR reminded us of Lewis Wolpert's phrase in his book *The unnatural nature of science*: 'if something fits in with common sense, it almost certainly isn't science' (1992: 11). Aaron works hard to identify contexts that can increase the relevance of the ideas and concepts and tries to help the students see that science often offers a different window on the world.

Although the early phase of this lesson is largely teacher-centred, Aaron is responding to the students' questions as they try to engage with the ideas. As well as directing questions using the students' names and allowing them thinking time, he draws out questions and fields them back to the whole class, creating an atmosphere where he hopes no student ever feels inhibited to say if they are not following. He asks if they understand and if they are 'happy' with the concepts while constantly surveying the class as a check to see if they really do 'look secure', as he puts it. Many teachers ask these questions, but it is clear from the high level of interaction that Aaron promotes that the students believe he is sincere. They recognize that he wants them to understand the ideas and is not just paying lip service to the idea of asking questions if they don't follow:

> 'I find if your relationship is good enough with them, where they actually find it comfortable to talk, that they will raise their hands and say, "I didn't get that/I don't understand the second graph/I don't understand what you're saying".'

Aaron maintains that developing good relationships with the students is all important and he works hard to involve as many students as possible. But interestingly, he is not satisfied with this very general level of monitoring the students' progress. He also studies their body language to make sure he is not misled by suggestions of 'apparent understanding'. He therefore builds in a strategy to obtain more reliable corroborating evidence of the extent to which the students are making sense of these abstract ideas (see Figure 3.4) He explains to the students:

> 'My idea is to see now whether you've understood what I've said in my previous discussion about graphs, but also to see whether you make a link between what is velocity and what is acceleration. Are you making a link in terms of what this thing is doing and do you see that acceleration is the link to velocity in terms of how fast per second it's travelling?'

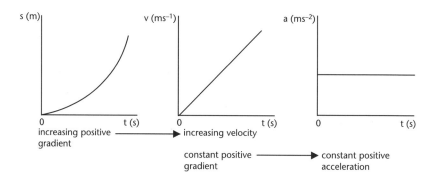

Figure 3.4   Three graphs: uniform (positive) acceleration. Students are required to derive the second and third graphs from the first.

Note: s = distance; v = velocity; a = acceleration

COMMENTARY

Misconceptions

Aaron's attention to student understanding was quite remarkable. Everything about the way he planned the lesson was built on his previous experience of student learning difficulties. He used knowledge from examinations, his experience from years of interaction in the classroom and evidence from research in science education from his Masters programme to inform the way he constructed his approach to kinematics. His knowledge of the misconceptions students commonly display was not only utilized to plan his sequencing of concepts but also used formatively to inform his interactive decision-making as the lesson progressed.

Through his own Master's degree-level research, Aaron was well aware of the extensive literature on misconceptions in science and built this knowledge into his planning (see *Children's ideas in science* – Driver *et al.* 1985 – for some of the earliest work in this field).

Aaron was at pains not to denigrate students' everyday conceptions of acceleration, but to show how scientific and everyday usage can sit side by side. He also showed how he aimed to pre-empt unnecessary confusion by, for example, getting the students to use the concept of negative acceleration in preference to deceleration.

Although a skill, graphicacy still causes many students problems. The AKSIS project jointly undertaken by King's College, London and the ASE aims to focus teacher and student attention on the interpretation of graphs (see Goldsworthy *et al.* 1999). Aaron identified the common misconception that all graphs have to show the origin and was aware of all that flows from that. He also knew that more time tends to be devoted to the drawing of graphs rather than interpretation. But he saw the potential of the graphs to diagnose issues of understanding and so aimed to place more emphasis on and allocate more time to the latter.

COMMENTARY

Monitoring learning

It was apparent to us that Aaron was using a quite sophisticated technique to monitor the students' learning through their ability, or otherwise, to describe accurately one graph and then reinterpret it in the form of another to demonstrate they really do understand. The clever part of this is that it detects 'apparent understanding' because the students would only be able to draw the final graph if they really understood what they were doing. Not only does Aaron then have some form of written record of what they have done, but through his interaction with them he can estimate the extent to which what has been drawn is an accurate representation of what the student knows.

We would draw your attention to the work of Millar *et al.* (2006) which reports on the work of the Evidence-based Practice in Science Education (EPSE) Research Network. Arising from this important programme the authors make the point that '*understanding* cannot be measured or observed directly' (p. 49). In other words, new ways to look at the consistency of student answers are needed. In fact, they follow Treagust's (1988) two-tier approach in the design of the diagnostic questions where the first tier requires the student to select a statement that best represents his or her understanding, and then a second level demands a justification for that selection. In other words, the second level is a check on the first. By the same token, Aaron has devised something very similar, although he talked of it in terms of a 'puzzle':

> 'If they can't do it I have to go back and do something differently or present it another way or give them some kind of information which is to say, "This is what you're missing. This is the link that you don't have, the piece that you're not putting in the puzzle in the right way, and let's re-orientate that piece so we can actually make the puzzle work now." So if the whole class didn't know this I would actually have stopped and said, "Let's backtrack guys. You're not getting it. You just don't understand it." '

This intuitive approach to monitoring learning is a characteristic of highly accomplished science teachers who all, in one way or another, tend not to accept simple recall responses as either valid or reliable measures of student understanding.

As a further check on student understanding, the conclusion of this lesson centred on the interpretation of a slightly more complex velocity-time graph (see Figure 3.5).

First, the students were required to describe the motion of a car by interpreting the velocity-time graph shown in Figure 3.5. Second, they were required to translate the velocity-time motion graph into an acceleration-time motion graph. Aaron's view was that if they were able to translate one graph into another for themselves then there was a good chance that they fully

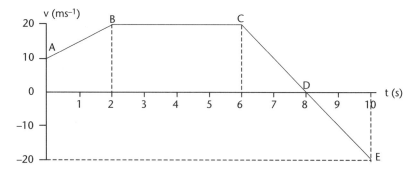

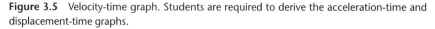

Figure 3.5 Velocity-time graph. Students are required to derive the acceleration-time and displacement-time graphs.

Note: v = velocity

understood the relationships between the three concepts of displacement, velocity and acceleration. As a yet further check on the students' understanding, Aaron asks them to translate the graph into a displacement-time graph.

Activity 3	Teacher thinking
Interpreting a more complex velocity-time graph.	'. . . if you could go one back to the displacement-time graph you're really secure in what you know, which is the other place I would go after an extended question. It wasn't one of the questions I planned to do but as we had more time I would say, "OK, let's go and try and do a displacement. How would it look as a displacement graph?" '

This approach had been refined over a number of years. Each time Aaron reappraised the sequencing of the ideas and activities so that he was sure the students could follow the logic of the progression. Ultimately he aimed to challenge them intellectually, but at the same time he is carefully sequencing the ideas so that they understand step by step. Aaron creates an environment where he gives students opportunities to succeed.

The final part of the lesson centred on Aaron consolidating the learning by asking students to explain their understanding of how the graphs related to one another and checking the concepts of positive and negative acceleration by asking the students to describe what sensations they would experience if they were in a car and being subject to these effects.

COMMENTARY

Constructivist approaches to science teaching

Not all the highly accomplished science teachers would have described their philosophy as constructivist, but there were certainly features of their practice that could be described as characteristic of constructivism. For example, the practice of eliciting the students' starting points at the outset of a topic was common. It was also common practice to recognize that the students often had their own explanations, misconceptions or 'alternative frameworks' for scientific phenomena and that they were not merely vessels to be filled with knowledge. Less explicit, however, was any overt recognition of the more social aspects of constructivism, although even then all the highly accomplished science teachers were strong advocates of peer learning and the role of language in science learning.

Probably one of the best articles to obtain to get a comprehensive grounding in constructivism in science education is Driver and Oldham's (1986) article which explores the roots of constructivism in cognitive psychology. This will take you back to David Ausubel and the famous quote, 'The most important single factor influencing learning is what the learner already knows. Ascertain this and teach him accordingly' (Ausubel 1968: 18). One has to say this is a somewhat simplistic view of the state of children's minds as it does not really take into account the social and emotional context in which the children live. Leach and Scott's (2000) chapter in 'Good practice in science teaching' gives a very clear overview of constructivism and learning in science, bringing together both cognitive and social (Vygotskian) dimensions to the construction of knowledge.

Aaron's approach of engagement through interaction with the students, was the aim of getting them to rethink and reconstruct their understandings, was initially more intuitive than one fully supported by theory. However, as he had gained experience, particularly through his Master's programme, his knowledge of the theoretical basis to what he was doing increased substantially.

Aaron's background

Aaron had good experiences of learning science at school, particularly physics, chemistry and maths, and chose to undertake teacher training immediately afterwards. He considered routes into teaching maths or computing science, but was advised by a college lecturer that he would never be out of a job teaching science in South Africa. Since graduating Aaron has taught in state schools and was head-hunted to lead the science department in his current school. He was recommended to us by the science educators at a major university in Johannesburg where he is completing a Master's degree in science education.

Aaron's beliefs and theories (personal philosophies) about science teaching

Underpinning all of Aaron's practice is his aim to teach for understanding. He takes a constructivist approach as the elicitation of students' ideas features strongly in his thinking about teaching. He likes to plan his teaching by knowing 'where the students are' in their thinking. His beliefs about teaching science suggest that unless the students are engaged they probably would not learn. He believes it is necessary to move away from the curriculum sometimes in order to have the students with you.

Aaron expressed an interesting view on the relationship between school science and science in the 'outside world'. His outlook on the nature of science is worth noting. The notion that 'science is messy' rather than cut and dried or certain gave a sense that he wants to convey to students the tentative nature of science knowledge. Above all, however, Aaron feels a strong responsibility to make the science relevant to the students and that is clearly a major driving force in the way he thinks about the way he wants to teach:

> 'I think school science is divorced from science in the outside world . . . Scientists are "messy" people. There's a lot of trial and error that happens. In class you make it sound as if it was just tried the first time and right the first time. There was no trial and error or "I had to do it 100 times before I got it right." So I think we present a false front to kids when we teach sometimes in terms of the science we have in school and I think again the responsibility is that of curriculum writers as well as teachers to bring real life science into school science or vice versa.'

Aaron is actively altering his approaches to teaching in recognition of the important changes that are going on in the curriculum in South Africa, where a focus on the relevance of science to the everyday experience of the child is seen as a key aspect of reform:

> 'Relevance is a big thing for me and I want to make it relevant as far as I can because it has so much more meaning for the kids. They are thinking about real life science lots of times and what's happening at home and [we need to] get the link between what's happening at home and what's happening here.'

Throughout our discussions, Aaron stressed the need to contextualize the science. Only then would the students engage and see science as a subject to pursue further, an important consideration in South Africa as the development of a scientifically-able population is seen as the lifeblood of economic progress.

Aaron's professional knowledge

As a teacher of ten years and with a background of teaching in different types of schools from the very challenging to the highly academic, Aaron has a wide variety of experiences to draw from (see Figure 3.6). In order to bring equality of opportunity to all schools, the government introduced Outcomes Based Education (OBE). Very recently a new revised curriculum has been rolled out which Aaron is now engaged in translating into practical action in the classroom. His philosophy of teaching for understanding and helping the students to make meaning from their science, aligns well with the aims of the revised curriculum. However, he is having to dig deep to make it work. In this comment he talks of changing his style to meet the demands of the new curriculum:

> 'Well they were interested because it wasn't a normal lesson and I think they appreciated I was willing just to change my style for a lesson.

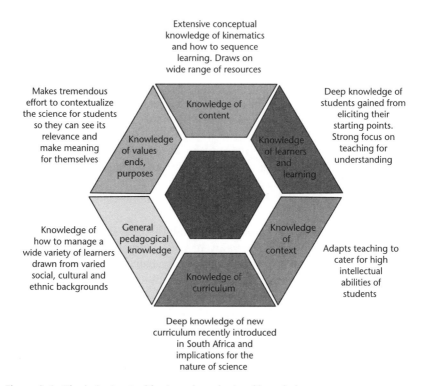

Extensive conceptual knowledge of kinematics and how to sequence learning. Draws on wide range of resources

Makes tremendous effort to contextualize the science for students so they can see its relevance and make meaning for themselves

Deep knowledge of students gained from eliciting their starting points. Strong focus on teaching for understanding

Knowledge of content

Knowledge of values ends, purposes

Knowledge of learners and learning

Knowledge of how to manage a wide variety of learners drawn from varied social, cultural and ethnic backgrounds

General pedagogical knowledge

Knowledge of context

Adapts teaching to cater for high intellectual abilities of students

Knowledge of curriculum

Deep knowledge of new curriculum recently introduced in South Africa and implications for the nature of science

Figure 3.6   The 'spinning top' for Aaron's professional knowledge.

Prior to that there had been information about what was a metal, what was a non-metal, what are the properties of metals and non-metals. Now we have to do it practically and say why metals aren't good for you, why some metals, whilst used in vitamins, are good, like iron and potassium, but why some like mercury aren't good. I think they appreciated that they could let their hair down, get into groups, discuss their points and present it back to the class and it gave them a topic of debate. So we used their English skills, speaking and oral skills, and I had to make a decision, together with them, about who debated best.'

It is worth noting how Aaron is introducing the students to the concept of 'argumentation' and assisting them to develop persuasive arguments by marshalling evidence to support specific claims. Much has been written in recent times on how to promote argumentation in the science classroom (Erduran and Osborne 2005; Simon *et al.* 2006). It is worth taking time to explore these approaches and to understand the basis on which learning in this way is predicated.

4 Biology

In this chapter we look closely at three teachers, Emma, Iain and Derek, teaching mainstream topics that involve concepts in biology. The topics featuring in these lessons are enzymes and the digestive system, looking at cells and in-vitro fertilization, topics that happened to be the ones being taught by our highly accomplished science teachers at the time we negotiated to visit. In other words, there was no deliberate choice being made to choose one topic or another.

Once again, we are not trying to suggest that what follows is how to teach any particular topic. Our focus is solely the professional knowledge of these highly accomplished science teachers, how they acquire it, how they develop it and how they use it.

Section 1: Enzymes and the digestive system

The context

This is a class of over 30 Year 8 (12–13-year-old) students in a medium-sized, mixed comprehensive school located close to the centre of small town in the UK. The students are drawn quite widely across the area creating a relatively broad social mix.

The lesson

For the past week or two the students have been looking at the digestive system. In the previous week they were introduced to the concept of enzymes when modelling the gut, but this week they are going to look in a little more detail at how enzymes work. The key ideas that the teacher, Emma, wants the students to concentrate on in this lesson are projected on the screen (see Figure 4.1):

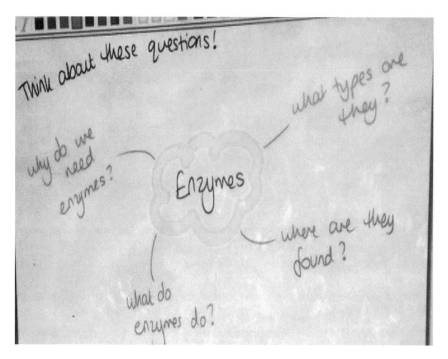

Figure 4.1 Emma's preparatory questions presented on the electronic whiteboard.

Enzymes
Think about these questions!

- Why do we need enzymes?
- What types are there?
- Where are they found?
- What do enzymes do?

As the students enter, their attention is directed to the e-whiteboard where Emma has presented the key questions. She says to them:

> 'Today we have to think about those four questions. If you need to speak to someone else in order to help you, that's fine. I want you to think while I take the register. You don't need to do any writing.'

'Training' the students
At this point in the VSR, Emma establishes her belief that discussion should be a normal part of classroom practice. She talks of 'training the students' to engage in discussion and enable them to gain confidence so they are more

likely to contribute to the lesson. In this one short statement, Emma highlights her view that peer-peer interaction is a key aspect of learning, but that it will only happen if she actively encourages it while at the same time avoiding demotivating and pointless writing activities.

Activity 1	Teacher thinking
Starter activity: four questions written on the e-whiteboard.	'I think it's quite a good thing, especially to train the kids that when they come in there will be a series of things they can think about or look at to remind themselves . . . So those questions were up there and were barely referred to really but were a stimulus to start them thinking.'
	'I quite often say to them that they don't need to do any writing, it's all about thinking. But also I'll say, "In order to help you think you might have to talk to someone about it" simply because I find children are so sociable, they want to talk about their learning.'

COMMENTARY

Training the students

This idea of 'training' the students is common to all the highly accomplished science teachers. In one way or another they all aim to be absolutely clear about their expectations but they believe the way to do this is by establishing routines.

Quickly students will come to know the behaviours expected of them leaving the highly accomplished science teachers with more freedom to support the learning they are trying to promote.

Emma is no exception to this and finds ways to ensure that the students know how the routines will work:

> 'I think it's quite a good thing, especially to train the kids that when they come in there will be a series of things they can think about or look at to remind themselves.'

Emma is training the students to become accustomed to the idea that discussion is a normal part of classroom practice. She talks of training the students so that they know it is not discussion of what was on TV, but discussion that allows them to gain confidence in contributing to the lesson. Ultimately, it is all about helping students to build self-esteem. Arguably, the idea of 'training the students' is a behavioural characteristic of a teacher. It is worth looking at the Hay McBer (2000) report on teacher effectiveness which highlights a number of behaviours (e.g., having a clear strategy for pupil management, of which establishing routines is one) which are said to characterize effective teachers.

Through student talk, Emma also aims to build the confidence of every student in his or her ability and willingness to respond to questions in recognition that, with support from their peers, students are less likely to believe they will make fools of themselves:

> 'If I can I set the starter to simply think and talk about something they will do. I find with a lot of classes that they almost don't know how to think about answering the question unless they talk to someone, because you'll say to them, "Think about that," and they'll go, "Yes," and when you call on them to answer it they can't. They know the answer, and you know they know it, and they know they know it, but unless they've actually said to someone, "Well I know it . . ." "What is it?" . . . "Ugggghhhh . . ." and then that person has helped them. It's easier for them to do it in pairs.'

Framing the learning and establishing goals
In addition to giving the students the four organizing questions to think about, Emma also clearly sets out what the main activity will be, 'We are going to make a model showing how enzymes work.' She argues against writing up learning objectives or outcomes, but makes it clear what the students will be doing and what she expects them to learn as a result of doing the activity:

> 'So it's not the learning objectives as such: "all of you will be learning the answers to these questions", because it's more than that. But that's where they're aiming. And they need something to measure themselves by that is simple, although I'm trying to measure it more by "How much explanation are they giving? Are they using key words? Connectives?" '

The choice of the four organizing questions is deliberate to provide a link with the previous lesson in addition to giving the students a sense of purpose.

Emma had already introduced them to the concept of enzymes and was automatically expecting them to refer to what they had written previously. The concept of conceptual progression, i.e., looking back and looking forward to earlier and future work, is strongly represented in her thoughts. Put another way, Emma takes an holistic view of the learning across the whole series of lessons and works out what part in the bigger picture each lesson will play. In addition, to ensure students get a sense of continuity and progression, she uses the framing questions as the mechanism by which students can get a measure of that progress as well as obtaining a sense of achievement and fulfilment.

The phrase 'continuity and progression' may have become something of a cliché, but highly accomplished science teachers in fact strive to achieve this through their planning. No single lesson is an island. Highly accomplished science teachers create a learning framework for the students so that by the time the topic is complete they can see the whole picture and how each lesson contributes to it. Emma's phrase of 'looking back and looking forward' sums this up nicely.

Students' writing

Another point to note is the emphasis Emma places on the nature of the writing she expects of the students. Her approach is parsimonious. For Emma, a student's exercise book is an important record that complements texts and revision guides. Writing is therefore used sparingly, intended as a representation of a student's active processing of information rather than an alternative text containing material copied from the board or other sources. Thus, any material that is put in their books has to be both original as well as something that contributes to the 'story' of what the student has learned. As she said:

> 'I didn't make them copy it out into their books because that wasn't what I was looking for. It was just a hint to point them in the right direction. I was more interested in what they could do, for themselves and in their groups – create the answers to those and many more questions while talking about what the enzymes are doing inside their body.'

Once the students were oriented towards the main focus of the lesson, Emma made a link to the next activity which was designed to make the transition from digestive system to enzymes and how enzymes work:

> 'What I'm going to do is to ask you to make a model of how enzymes work. And the model is up to you – in small groups how you do these models. But first of all I'd like to do a little bit more reminding about the question we were talking about last lesson.'

Engaging the students

The question being referred to was the perennial myth about chewing gum and what happens if you swallow it, 'Does it stay inside you forever?', a good question to exercise a group of 12-year-olds! It worked effectively as an attention grabber and led the students smoothly into a short animation captured from a website which looked at digestion and what happens to chewing gum.

Activity 2	Teacher thinking
Animation.	'One or two [students] mentioned that when you swallow gum it stays inside forever or four or five years and a lot of them went, "Yes, I know this for a fact." So many people have said this, and I wouldn't say it was a misconception, but perhaps a bit of an old wives' tale. I thought we should bring it up in this lesson. The other thing I find about it is that this is more of a starter in a way because it did a lovely recap of the digestive system, which hopefully they all knew. And it mentioned enzymes, and then answered that question they'd been asking about the previous lesson. So it tied in so nicely I couldn't not use it. Again, it set the focus of the lesson.'

Forays onto the Internet can offer rich pickings for ideas to engage the students in contexts they can relate to. Emma is steadily building up a bank of resources chosen carefully to achieve learning through engagement. Her underlying belief is that it is necessary to help the students remember by using what she calls 'a little hook'. She has noted in various assessments that where she used a 'hook' the students can tell her much more about it. To most teachers this is hardly surprising, but it is the *choice* of hook that matters. Emma calls them snippets, material that is just long enough to capture interest, but not long enough to switch them off.

Once the animation finishes, Emma draws attention to the key ideas that would be useful through the lesson. She then refocuses the students on the purpose of the lesson – modelling how enzymes work, before saying:

> '. . . in your books . . . and we are going to put there some of the key words you might want to use when you start doing this model of how enzymes work'.

Developing a vocabulary

It is Emma's belief that without the vocabulary or the knowledge and understanding of words that help to connect ideas, you cannot expect the students to be able to write any kind of explanation. And explanations for Emma are the stuff of science:

> 'My philosophy of science is that I'm really keen that what the kids will have is, yes, this foundation of knowledge and being able to explain and having all the background information. Knowing facts and stuff and all that stuff, but they can explain things. They can look at something and go, "Well I think the way that this is working is . . ." And they can draw on that knowledge but can explain things. It's all about linking ideas and applying knowledge.'

For the next few minutes Emma draws out the words and terms the students know are associated with the digestive system and captures them on the tablet PC. She uses an example of a model of how enzymes work projected on screen from the PC.

Activity 3	Teacher thinking
Questioning students using an example of a model of how enzymes work projected on screen from the PC.	'I get them to do a bit of writing of key words; when they look back in their book and when I'm talking about "I want you to explain this . . . make sure you are using these key words." '
	'So any key words or phrases, important learning points, I either just give it to them like that, and then we work on processing and modelling information so they understand it and can recall it more easily because they've got that understanding.'

At this point, Emma is getting the students to engage with how the words look (i.e., the shape made by the pattern of ascenders and descenders), how they are links to one another (e.g., protein and protease) and how they are spelt. She says to them:

> 'Here are our key words. If you remember the last lesson all the different foods that contain carbohydrates, like starch, are broken down by

enzymes like amylase into glucose or sugar. For proteins – protease. Look, I'm going to highlight the ending again [highlights "ase" signi- fying an enzyme]. Anybody know the name of the enzyme that breaks down fat. If you think about and posh fat ladies – liposuction! It begins with "lip" and that links with fat.'

Active processing

Like all highly accomplished science teachers, Emma is not satisfied with being a provider of information – she has learned to orchestrate and sequence a set of activities so that students have to process actively the information she provides. In other words, she is not satisfied for the students to be passive recipients of the content; she creates the circumstances where they are required to have to do something more with it. In this case, she wants them to manipulate the information and use it in the construction of a model, the main activity in the lesson.

It is common for teachers to talk of 'getting the students to think' but this idea of 'active processing' recurs time and time again in Emma's articulation of her beliefs and is clearly evident in her practice. Gradually Emma helps the students to assemble sufficient information to be able to construct a picture of how enzymes work. For a group of even relatively-able 12–13-year-olds, this is quite a challenge. The example, however, gives the students a target, but without closing out a range of other alternatives. Metaphors for enzyme action, such as 'chopping up' and images of 'teeth' provided through the earlier ani- mation and the example model shown, via the computer, give the students sufficient ideas to allow them the chance of completing the task. In fact, Emma herself criticizes the example she had shown them and rejects it as not having any intrinsic value other than providing the basis for discussion. Moreover, from experience she now recognizes that without the students having established any ownership over it, this model would have little value as a learning tool.

Modelling

The process of 'modelling' plays a central role in how Emma believes children can best learn science. She had considered using static representational models to assist with the concept of long chain molecules (such as carbohydrates) being broken down in smaller constituent parts, but experience has led her to believe that this way students are less likely to engage in thinking actively about the process of enzyme action.

From past experiences using representational models, Emma has learned that students do not necessarily distinguish between different types of particles. Although 12–13-year-olds might cope with the fairly simple idea that large food molecules, such as starch, can be broken down into smaller ones, she considers that molecular models can cause as just many learning problems as

Activity 4	Teacher thinking
Modelling.	'I was going to use Molymods to model these [enzymes] . . . And the reason I thought I wouldn't do that is that Molymods are only a representation of atoms, and we use them to build up molecules. I thought! . . . I started saying to them . . . "This is glucose" when glucose itself is made up of atoms. I thought, "This is really going to confuse them", which is why I decided to use paper [i.e. to make models.'
	'With atoms, particles, cells, they mix up these things all the time and there are so many misconceptions you almost can't say they're misconceptions . . . almost cast-iron beliefs.'
	'I want them to do the modelling so they can think more deeply about what's actually happening, what the enzymes are doing.'

they are intended to solve. As a consequence she believes strongly that she can achieve much higher levels of engagement if the students have to find ways themselves to represent the ideas being discussed, and, most importantly of all, that in getting them to do that, the students have to be thinking. In fact, she sees 'modelling' as helping them visualize what is happening as well as a way of getting them to process information and ideas. Emma's view is that if they are having to transform text into visualizations then they will have to think, and if they are thinking then there is a better chance they will be learning.

Teacher-student interaction

While the students are engaged in the activity Emma moves swiftly from group to group around the class in order to promote active learning by asking probing questions, suggesting prompts or asking for explanations or ideas. Some examples Emma used were, 'Which of these are the red blood cells?', 'You just said carbohydrate, did you mean protease?' and 'That's good, but how could you improve that bit?' Emma constantly uses the opportunities provided by the modelling activity to make communicative interventions in the learning. During the 20 minutes the activity lasted Emma's interventions were dialogic, interactive and focused on the subject matter. In other words, most of her time was focused on conceptual development as she encouraged the students to talk about what they were learning with her and with one another, but with very little time devoted to management issues or reference to other content.

And all the time Emma is prompting the students to use the vocabulary she spent time establishing beforehand and making sure the students who tried to describe the action of the enzyme in terms of 'teeth' did not believe what they were suggesting represented reality in any sense:

> 'They're all going to be saying enzymes have teeth because when they watch that one [animation] with the teeth they're going to think that. But that same group had the ones with the blood cells, so they said, "Here come all the food particles, they're really small now because they've been chopped up by the enzymes, into the blood they go and here come the red blood cells to take them away" and I said, "Are the red blood cells carrying the food?" "Yes." "OK," and I left it at that and a bit later said, "How have you changed it?" "We're not sure the red blood cells are carrying the food." And I thought thank God for that! I would really have had to correct them there.'

As well as working hard interacting with the students, Emma continues to promote peer-peer interaction as she did at the start of the lesson, only now she is aiming to initiate reflective thinking. Her approach involves encouraging the students to use the newly-introduced vocabulary to discuss the modelling, getting them to reflect on one another's responses and helping them revise their ideas.

Monitoring learning

In addition to engaging with the students to direct their learning, Emma also uses the opportunities to monitor learning and diagnose misconceptions or misunderstandings. She is well aware of the dangers models pose for learning and that student acceptance of the scientific view could well be compromised by unquestioning adoption of the analogical features of a model. This, of course, is the downside of modelling, but the advantages perceived by our highly accomplished science teachers are that these strategies constitute really good opportunities to challenge errant understanding, as well as being excellent opportunities to encourage students to examine their own thinking in situations where there is cognitive conflict. Emma acknowledges how metaphors used to help in the description of enzyme action (such as chopping or cutting up) can cause real problems of their own, particularly when students interpret them literally. But as she says:

> 'But there again I quite like it when they go off on these tangents because you really find out what they think.'

COMMENTARY
Misconceptions

In common with the other highly accomplished science teachers, Emma's knowledge of likely misconceptions within the subject matter is a central part of her professional knowledge base. Most science teachers are well aware of misconceptions and plan to account for them in their teaching and the students' learning. The knowledge of likely misconceptions and the design of activities to reveal them through the students' thinking is an important and recurrent feature of highly accomplished science teachers' practice.

The literature on the deep-seated nature of children's misconceptions and alternative frameworks is vast. Driver's books *The pupil as scientist* (1991: 24–31), *Children's ideas in science* (Driver *et al.* 1985) and *Making sense of secondary science* (Driver *et al.* 1994b) are essential reading.

Emma's use of 'modelling' represents an interesting strategy for taking a diagnostic approach to monitoring students' understanding in science. She has developed her practice to contrive opportunities to ensure she is able to gain access to what the students think, for example where she caught the students talking about 'how the molecules just shrink and get into the bloodstream'.

Reflective discussion

As an incentive to complete their models, Emma informs the class that she will make three very short videos of the models using a webcam attached to the portable tablet PC. This is a strategy that has grown out of a combination of Emma's beliefs about the role student talk plays in learning and her enthusiasm for incorporating information and communication technology (ICT) into her teaching. These short videos form the basis of the plenary session:

> 'I've found that if I just video their little explanations or record their voice and then play it back to them, quite often to the whole class, they will often pick up for themselves what they want to improve and what mistakes they've made and how that can improve their own explanations. Previously I've only done a voice recording with a different class of their answer to a question and then when we've watched it back asked the whole class to pick up when they've noticed that that person is using a key word or connective and what connectives they're using and what key words.'

COMMENTARY

Using ICT

All the highly accomplished science teachers were active users of ICT in one way or another. However, their usage of the technology was never indiscriminate. For example, Emma selected animations and models of scientific phenomena, but saw them as opportunities to develop students' critical faculties/thinking skills by providing a framework for the students to critique them.

Futurelab (www.futurelab.org.uk) is one of many sources that highlights ways that ICT can be used to engage and motivate students. On this site, Jonathan Osborne offers a comprehensive literature review of the role of ICT in science education (Report 6) while Wellington (2000: 195–225) provides a critical overview of the ICT in science landscape, highlighting the dangers involved in using material without appropriate evaluation. For an introduction to the pedagogy underlying a range of strategies incorporating ICT in science teaching, see also Hennessy et al. (2003).

In our research, the highly accomplished science teachers always made it clear that the use of ICT had to have a demonstrable purpose and shied away from using it simply because there is a government agenda to incorporate ICT into teaching. Emma's incorporation of ICT was very much oriented towards promoting discussion with the students. The use of the webcam as a neat way to capture students' work for further discussion is a novel strategy.

In previous years, Emma has tried an approach using material drawn from other classes, but has now found that students are much more engaged by looking at their own work. Perhaps this is hardly surprising, but the strategy does have to be handled with some sensitivity to avoid the possibility of students ridiculing one another's efforts. It's at this point that Emma believes she can extend learning further by getting the students to be critical of what they themselves are proposing, not from a negative stance, but on the basis of how they think they can make improvements. Essentially, Emma is promoting the development of a set of attitudes towards science with the idea of always being able to improve and refine ideas at the pinnacle.

Activity 5	Teacher thinking
Plenary: critiquing the webcam videos.	'. . . at the end we totally pick them apart and say, "How do we know this is happening?"'

Activity 5 (*cont*)	Teacher thinking
	You've shown the shape like this, the enzymes are doing that. And I also want to start asking them more complicated questions because I'm pretty sure they can cope with it. "What do the enzymes do then? What do they do when you're not eating?" Ask those kinds of questions to get them really thinking about it. I think the more you find problems with it the more robust they will make their own model.'

Once more, Emma is utilizing strategies that encourage students to critique one another's work, and thus engage in another form of 'active processing'. In this comment Emma reports her interaction with the students as exemplifying the type of interaction she is encouraging students to have with one another. She also implies that more teacher-centred approaches would not provide the conditions for such interaction:

'I was quite happy that they were all pretty much on task for the whole lesson, which is brilliant, and secondly, coming up with really interesting points. When I walked around one or two of them said, "We're going to have it in the stomach and then the small intestine. Can we have it in the large intestine?" And the person next to them said, "No, there'll be nothing left then will there?" "Oh forget that then Miss." And I thought, "Yeah, that's what we're aiming for." And I think in groups that's much, much more likely to happen than if I had them working alone or as a whole class with me talking at them. You just couldn't field that many questions.'

In further reflections during the VSR, Emma reasserted that this approach is more powerful than simply telling the students the information because the thinking required, combined with the peer-peer interaction, is more likely to lead to understanding. Another central tenet in Emma's philosophy has come to be the goal of teaching for understanding. It is much more satisfying because the focus of the teaching is on student thinking (meaningful learning) rather than information retention (rote learning) (Ausubel 1968); it is about deep processing rather than surface processing (Entwhistle 1988).

COMMENTARY

Social construction of knowledge

In both the modelling process and the reflective critiquing during the plenary Emma stimulates the students to construct knowledge for themselves. By exploring different perspectives, they come to recognize that knowledge creation is a complex process of working and reworking ideas until there is some consensus. Of course Emma recognizes the potential dangers of this strategy, so her interventions are designed to steer or point the students gently in directions that are going to be fruitful.

Through the process, however, students begin to appreciate the often highly provisional nature of scientific knowledge. Just as importantly Emma is building their confidence (and self-esteem) to feel that they all have the potential to contribute. Everyone may be challenged to justify their idea, but nobody is ridiculed. They all have time to share ideas. In these ways they make meaning out of the content of the lesson.

A very readable article by Duit and Treagust in the *International handbook of science education* (2003) explores the development of a view of learning that includes constructivism and social constructivism. For another perspective an early article by Driver *et al.* (1994a) provides some excellent exemplars of student-student interactions, illustrating how knowledge may be socially constructed in the classroom.

Emma's background

Emma is an advanced skills teacher. She came into teaching following a degree in chemistry and chemical technology and a short spell in research in the pharmaceutical industry. The decision to train for teaching, as with many science teachers, arose from early experiences of being asked to train others in the workplace. In her analysis of her practice through the VSR process, instances of the use of 'explain' and 'explanation' abound. It would seem that the motivation to teach science comes strongly from Emma's concern not only to be able to explain scientific phenomena herself, but to help others use science knowledge to be able to explain phenomena for themselves:

> 'At the moment people who are influencing me are talking about real world science. And they'll say this thing about *Daily Mail* [UK tabloid newspaper] syndrome, where people read what's in the papers and take it as given, even though they might subconsciously have the

knowledge to explain that it is incorrect. It might not be science, it may be to do with statistics or maths or geography, but they do actually underneath perhaps have that knowledge, but it's their explanation skills and reasoning and questioning skills and picking problems and flaws in the argument skills that are not there.'

Emma's beliefs and theories (personal philosophies) about science teaching

This leads us to what drives Emma's approaches to teaching. It is clear that she has a desire to develop students' thinking skills so they are not only scientifically literate at a functional level, but critically literate, in order to prepare them for their role as citizens in a democratic society and so that they are not unduly swayed or misled by the rhetoric and sensationalism they will meet in the popular media.

Given her background in research, Emma is well placed to draw on her professional experience to construct authentic learning experiences for students. To achieve this Emma strives to demonstrate the relevance of the work to her students:

> 'So at Key Stage 3 I don't find the kids will argue and say, "Why is this relevant to me?" but it doesn't mean you shouldn't try and make it relevant. A lot of the time it's easy I think to make it relevant. The lesson today is on enzymes, so it's about their body, so there is relevance there because we're finding out about what happens to the food in our bodies, and they are interested and do want to know in most cases.'

Highly accomplished science teachers like Emma are not just interested in relevance; they look for *contemporary* relevance, issues arising which students might see or hear in the news. Their desire is to have a 'cutting edge' feel about what they do, not just to engage, but to excite the students. The enthusiasm in their presentation of this knowledge is designed to be infectious and to capture the students' interest.

However, engagement is not the same as involvement. Real involvement requires intellectual participation and that entails engagement with the material at a critical level. In recognition of this, Emma has developed approaches that demand more of the students than perhaps she might have looked for earlier in her career. Her philosophy centres strongly on this notion of students having to do 'something more with the information'. Steadily her beliefs and theories about how children learn are shifting the development of her practice towards one that encompasses the promotion of reflective thought. As we have suggested elsewhere, the idea of doing something more with the knowledge fits well with all highly accomplished science teachers' views that students must be given appropriate opportunities to be active learners.

Emma's professional knowledge

What have we learned about Emma's professional knowledge from this analysis of her practice? Emma herself was not at all sure whether what she knew could legitimately be called professional knowledge. At first, she was somewhat dismissive, referring to it as 'experiences' but agreed that there were things she knew which derived from learning in other situations. In other words, perhaps there were things she knew that could be said to be more than just experiential knowledge. What is the difference between learning from experience and the acquisition of professional knowledge? Learning from others is an important source of professional knowledge for Emma. Whether it is from colleagues, from people in the local education authority/board who have influenced her in connection with her activities as an advanced skills teacher, or from her own work in the world of ICT, learning and applying that learning to her own teaching is fundamental to her reflective thought (see Figure 4.2):

> 'I pick up learning theory. I pick up things and flit around . . . but there's too much for me to do. But I'm much more interested in learning and application and all that "processing" – all what you could call

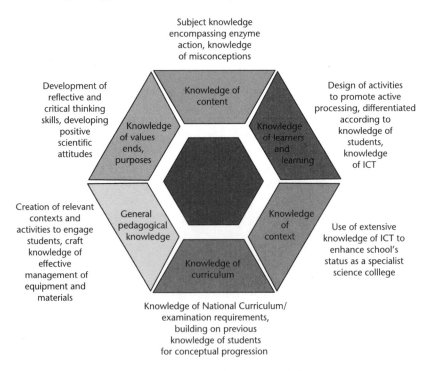

Figure 4.2 The 'spinning top' for Emma's professional knowledge.

the "science of learning". And I'm much more interesting in that than a lot of the content I have to teach them.'

Interestingly, Emma is perhaps a little different in that it seems to be the students' learning that characterizes her passion for teaching, rather than the science, as with most of the other highly accomplished science teachers. Emma by her own admission is not someone who begins with theory and attempts to apply it to her practice. Despite suggesting that learning theory is what most interests her, Emma works hard to maintain a subject knowledge base that she can draw from to provide students with relevant and interesting contexts:

> 'Professionally I have to make sure I keep up to date with things and I'm on mailing lists for things like the Wellcome Trust, I get *New Scientist*, things like that . . . I'll skim through and quite often, in fact I'd say every week, there's something that I'll see or get electronically that has relevance to one of my lessons that week. It's lovely when you can bring something in and say, "Look, this was dated two days ago and here I am teaching you about it." '

It is fascinating to see how Emma brings together different knowledge bases in order to create activities that will achieve her educational goals. To achieve this, she brings together different knowledge bases through her pedagogical reasoning.

Section 2: Looking at cells

The context

The context for this lesson is a private medium-sized girls grammar school, located in an urban area of Northern Ireland, that draws students quite widely from the surrounding districts. The class that provided the basis for observations and discussion was an able group of 25 or so 14–15-year-olds.

The lesson

The lesson is centred on a simple practical task that asks the students to look at their own cheek cell and follows the procedural guidelines recommended by the Institute of Biology for handling or working with human tissue. The practical will be familiar to all biology teachers and probably to most teachers of science. The activity builds on work done the previous week that was designed to develop the students' skills in using standard optical microscopes.

Classroom management

Like all the other highly accomplished science teachers, Iain establishes simple routines with the students relating to health and safety, storage of their coats etc., in order to create a strong sense of order. He thinks through the management of the practical activities carefully in his mind before beginning, to ensure that he would not create unnecessary problems for himself at a later stage. Over the years, for example, Iain has learned that unless he prepares the students ('trains' them) to use the microscopes effectively a lot of time will be wasted in non-productive activity as he knows they will struggle to get anything of significance (other than air bubbles!) into the field of view.

Purposes

So much of what is taught in science today follows prescribed schemes of work, be they developed in-school or from commercial or other sources. As head of the science department, Iain is responsible for producing such documentation. However, he retains a strongly objective- (or outcome-) driven approach in his teaching that ensures he maintains ownership of the teaching and learning process:

> 'I would still go through the process, although I wouldn't write it down any more, of what are the learning intentions? What would I like the pupils to come away with at the end of this lesson? What experiences would I like them to have and what skills would I like them to develop? *Then it's a case of devising activities, resources, delivery styles, methods, which allow those things to be addressed.'*

Common to all the highly accomplished science teachers is that their decision-making about learning is objective-driven. For Iain the operative word is 'devising'. Activities are not selected because they are specified but because they can be utilized and/or tailored to achieve specific learning outcomes (see Gott and Duggan 1996: 800). Included within this is the selection of activities designed to promote student engagement. This lesson was supplemented by material chosen precisely to do just that:

> 'I always try to create a bit of variety so that they aren't doing the same thing, unless it's practical work, for any length of time. So I'd use animations quite a bit, or DVDs, CD-ROMs. I'd use simple models, and keep the models very simple . . . and try to use analogies that make some sort of sense [i.e., ones that students can relate to].'

Establishing a context

Iain immediately sets the scene for the students by reminding them of an event that had hit the headlines quite recently. Baby Carrie was a child abandoned in awful circumstances. The authorities used DNA tests to help establish possible parentage. Coincidentally, some students knew quite a lot about the event. It acted as a hook that immediately gained the interest of the rest of class.

Activity 1	Teacher thinking
Introduction.	'If you can establish the links you will make the whole experience more worthwhile and enjoyable and therefore they'll hang in longer and therefore they'll begin to see the relevance of school science to everyday science. I find in biology it's not that difficult.'
	'When I thought about this in the preparation of the lesson I thought, "How could you get them to think about the fact that there are cells that are accessible in the body that you can actually get at?" And I came back to a baby's body that had been abandoned at the local leisure centre. They named this unknown baby "Baby Carrie" and they went round all the females in the area and took cheek swabs to test the cells.'

Building a repertoire of stories and anecdotes, but more importantly, knowing when and how to use them to engage students in learning is central to Iain's thinking about how to capture and retain the students' interest. The ability to transform his knowledge in this way we would suggest is representative of his PCK. Iain talks of:

'. . . having something just at your fingertips every time you have a particular topic. And you're able to draw on two or three examples at that particular time because then they [the students] become engaged very quickly as well.'

COMMENTARY
Making the science relevant

No one would claim it is anything new to try to find ways to help students connect with the science they are being taught. Without doubt, making the science relevant was seen as a key feature of good science teaching by the students we talked to. Iain looked for opportunities for the students to make local connections either through his research or through local events that the students might recognize.

Either way he sought to contextualize the material he was teaching. Coincidentally, the UK government also thinks this is important as it believes a science curriculum disconnected from everyday life is a science curriculum that will fail to yield the scientists of the future (HM Treasury 2004).

So what guidance is available to teachers to help with this? Although almost 20-years-old, Douglas Newton's book *Making science education relevant* (1988) still offers useful advice to help you think about how you do this.

Undoubtedly the best solutions lie in the teacher's own professional knowledge and experience, where stories, anecdotes and links to other branches of science provide the stuff to engage the students. How good is your history of science? How good is your knowledge of scientists and their lives? How good is your knowledge of related technological applications of scientific concepts? How good are you at enabling the students to see 'why'? How good are you at drawing on student culture?

At this point Iain wants to get the students thinking about the nature of the cells they are going to observe under the microscope. Here he uses what might be called his 'craft' knowledge (Doyle 1990). Others might call it 'tricks of the trade'. It's knowledge that simply helps teaching run smoothly:

> 'Just roll your tongue round the inside of your cheek. It's nice and smooth, and the reason that it's smooth is there are thin layers of cells and these cells are arranged together like crazy paving. These cells are flattened so they form a big sheet. They fit together very, very neatly and they are very thin. They form sheets, but they'll be thin enough for the light to pass through. The image will be magnified and you'll be amazed to see these microscopic building blocks.'

Using an analogy to suggest the cheek cells look like crazy paving is designed to help the students get an image of what they are going to be searching for through the microscope. Iain also displays a digital image of the cheek cells a previous class had prepared. He is well aware of the problem that observation is not independent of theory; it has to be guided by something, and if students have no concept of a cheek cell, they would not know what they are looking for. The images of crazy paving and building blocks should be sufficient to give them a clue.

COMMENTARY

Using analogies

When we talked to students about what makes a good science teacher the answer always included something about being 'good at explaining'. Analogies included as part of explanations often save words and offer a richness and insight that can allow students suddenly to get the idea. Paatz *et al.* (2004: 1066), in an article that theorizes the nature of analogical thinking, offer a very clear statement about how analogy can develop understanding, 'Analogical thinking is a process of enriching a person's knowledge about an unknown target domain by using his/her knowledge about a base domain.'

In this instance the analogy is a simple one, to give students a visual picture of how the cheek cells tessellate and create a very thin but smooth layer. The analogy also offers students the opportunity to suggest how the analogy fails. Clearly, if they can do this, it will give Iain an idea of the security of their understanding of the nature of cheek cells.

An article by Taber (2001) in *Physics education* very helpfully distinguishes between analogy, metaphor and model with respect to their uses in teaching. Analogy, for example, uses the idea of being 'just like' something else. Put another way it is about 'making the unfamiliar familiar' (p. 223). Taber, however, warns of the dangers that lie ahead if these approaches are used indiscriminately. If, however, you want a simple introduction to using analogy, the *ASE guide to secondary science* is an excellent starting point (Wood-Robinson 2006).

Iain also knows that he has to reinforce the technique for searching a microscope slide that he started the previous week, knowing how much time can be wasted if he does not do this well. He reminds the students of the sequence of operations that will ensure that when they swivel the high power (×40) objective lens it will be in position directly above a few cheek cells that were located using the lower power objective:

> 'In the past, when I've sent them [the students] off, having done the same sort of introduction and they've gone looking for cheek cells, they've actually been looking at them but had no idea they were looking at them! [See commentary on theory-dependent observation on page 92.] So there was no way they knew where to start from and you'd spend the whole period just adjusting every single person's microscope.'

Having captured the students' interest, Iain brings them together at the front of the class. As with other organizational techniques, this process has been carefully routinized and is certainly not an invitation to the students to make a fast rush to the front. However, Iain stresses the importance of having the students 'close' to him. By this he means in close proximity so that he can settle them and maintain control:

> 'I just find the closer you get them to you the longer you can keep them together. I would . . . get them in close and extend those five minutes and get it to a point where it holds together . . . Within ten minutes the danger is that . . . they're closer to each other as well and it's easier for them to be distracted.'

Some years ago Iain said he had a made a decision to invest a little more time in the introductory demonstrations in order to ensure students were clear both about the purpose of the activity and what to do.

Activity 2	Teacher thinking
Demonstration: how to prepare a slide.	'It was a big conscious decision a few years ago to take more time with introductory demonstrations and to do them much more slowly than I would in the past. After lots of experiences when you send people away, thinking you've explained what you want them to do, you suddenly discover only half of them have any idea what they're supposed to do . . . You think, "I want to get this all done because I want to get them doing this thing," and in fact the time you invest at this stage is probably worth it because they set off with some sort of notion of what you're trying to do.'

Through experience, Iain has discovered ways of doing things – he refers to this as 'just a few tricks he has picked up over the years'. This is, perhaps, another example of his 'craft knowledge' in action (Doyle 1990). He explains to the students what to do but, he says, it is all to do with the pressure you apply in rolling the cotton buds across the surface of the slide to spread the cells out:

'What you are trying to do with the cotton buds is roll the cells off. Roll the bud gently back and forth on the slide. And you'll have no idea whether you've been successful or not because they are transparent.'

Iain still balances this time investment in the demonstration with the possible loss of interest if he keeps the students waiting too long. In this instance the demonstration showing how to spread the cells and stain them takes about 8 minutes so that students were into the main activity 15 minutes after the start of the lesson. By keeping these aspects short Iain makes sure he maximizes the time available for interaction, which is when he believes he can make the most impact.

Activity 3	Teacher thinking
Looking at cheek cells.	'I've begun to think a little bit more about the balance of lessons, in terms of, particularly, the activity part. I think now they [the students] have to be active, they have to be involved, and even if that's not a practical activity they have to be in discussions and questions and thought processes and going off at tangents and just generally contributing.'

This point about involvement is important, because interaction with the students is central to Iain's beliefs about teaching. Involvement is more than engagement. His message is clear and strong – student contributions lead to them establishing ownership over their learning and results in greater enjoyment. We return to this again later.

Throughout the practical activity Iain moves around the groups – but not at random. From his knowledge of the students, their abilities and their attitudes, he knows the sequence of visits that will ensure all students will be successful:

'... what I've got to do is get as many people to be successful initially as possible. Hence take the time with the demonstration and then for those people who aren't initially successful we need to get as many of them as possible to see the cheek cells in as short a period of time as possible.'

COMMENTARY
Theory-dependent observation

Knowing what to look for when manipulating an image under a microscope is easy for science teachers who already have a theoretical framework in place to enable them to assess what they see. Iain points out that beginning-teachers often do not realize how important this framework is and leave the students guessing what they are expecting them to see. ('Is this it Miss?!') Students have always had a knack of being the 'experts' at finding the air bubbles trapped under the coverslip. This idea does not apply just to microscope work, but to all areas of science. Scientists rarely make observations without some theory lying behind them. We are choosing to observe because we have some idea about what we expect to see. This, of course, is the same thinking that lies behind the emphasis placed on making predictions in scientific inquiry. For an excellent introduction to the nature of science see *What is this thing called science?* (Chalmers 1999).

Over the years much has been written about the relationship between theory and observation. Hodson's (1990) article in *School Science Review* seeks a complete review of practical work in science and explores this issue in some detail. Also, Chapter 2, 'Learning to observe' in Driver's (1991) book, *The pupil as scientist*, examines the issue from a theoretical perspective and offers some very nice examples of how children do not see quite what the teacher expects.

Finding the cheek cells is a problem-solving exercise. As Iain moves from group to group he takes the opportunity to interact with the students and build relationships. He describes it as a case of 'getting to know them and what they'll accept and knowing how they will react'. It is also a chance to guide them in their drawings. Translating an image under a microscope to a piece of paper can be a hugely difficult task for many students unless the theoretical ground is prepared for them.

Iain manages the interaction in order to get the students thinking. Ostensibly, he is concerned about the students' ability to manipulate a microscope. However, for him this is also about consistency of teaching style, about asking students for their thoughts and not simply instructing them. He knows he can do it in a few seconds, but how is he going to foster ownership and independence through an approach that just tells them what to do?

> 'The bit I left as a problem-solving exercise for these girls, I might well have tried to solve those problems before we start with weaker girls and say, "If you can't see these immediately, think about them, think about the diaphragm, think about the lens position, about cleaning the object because that may be where your problems lie." '

The students see it this way too:

> 'He knows who everybody is and goes round in a practical and talks about what you're doing and why you're seeing certain things.'

> 'And he goes over it and over it till it's drilled into your head.'

> 'He makes sure you're having fun in a way.'

Throughout the VSR, Iain stressed how this kind of knowledge, knowledge of students, their abilities, aptitudes, attitudes, interests, is key to all his decision-making, whether it is in the planning, during the lesson or afterwards as he evaluates the outcomes:

> 'You really have to make an effort to get to know individuals and get to know the dynamics of particular groups of students to the point where you almost have to get to know bits and pieces about the individual that are nothing to do with teaching them biology, but something where they know you have an interest in them.'

Once Iain is satisfied that every student has seen what he wants them to see, and that he is sure the simple techniques he is teaching them have been accomplished, he completes the lesson by bringing them all together to 'tie things up', as he puts it. By referring back to the digital images he had projected earlier, he refocuses their attention and reinforces the messages about what is expected in the drawing, (e.g., scale, features). While his classroom talk can be properly described as interactive/dialogic, according to Scott and Mortimer (2006), he also tries to make his questioning in plenary sessions interactive as well. As Iain is in control of the talk, (this is a teacher-centred activity), this might best be described as somewhere between non-interactive/authoritative and interactive/authoritative (Scott and Mortimer 2006). First of all, Iain makes this point:

> 'I find it not particularly successful saying "Does anybody know? Can anybody tell me?" I'll always identify the person who is going to answer the question before the question is asked. So, "Laura, I want you to tell me, Kitty, can you tell me?" I just think it gets their attention reasonably and it also gets everybody else's attention because they think they could be next!'

Too often, he sees his less experienced colleagues running into difficulties using the 'Can anybody tell me?' approach. He sees it as a recipe for chaos as it encourages calling out unconsidered responses. By using names and offering 'thinking time' he can keep students tuned in for longer. In addition, Iain tailors his questions based on his detailed knowledge of the students:

'I would do a lot of questions and answers and I would tend to target the questions to specific pupils by name, and in the case of doing a lot of that, they [the questions] would be very much differentiated. So the people who I would perceive to have more problems, or find it more difficult, would get much more straightforward closed questions. But the "better" people might be stretched with something a bit more open-ended.'

COMMENTARY

Questioning

Questioning is such an important part of any teacher's work that it deserves some considerable attention. Principally, questions should promote engagement by being inclusive. In the case of science you have to be careful because so much of the questioning can revolve around simple recall of factual material. The teacher may feel a great sense of excitement and inclusion, but promptly forgets that the students only participate every now and then and feel neither excitement nor inclusion! For a practical introduction to questioning in the science classroom look at Wellington's (2000) book *Teaching and learning secondary science*, which categorizes questions into different types according to the mental operation required.

In describing his practice, Iain explained in some detail his approaches to questioning and what he believed it should achieve. First of all you have to know students' names, and that accords with Iain's feelings and values about gaining trust and respect. Second, you have to use them and draw students in. As he puts it, the 'good' ones may be shy and hesitant, 'You need to try and build up their self-confidence.' This returns us to the idea of contributing where contribution leads to engagement and involvement. Once involved the students are encouraged to be active intellectually and we are then, as Iain puts it, in an 'upwards spiral'.

Iain's background

Iain was recommended to us by colleagues from the local higher education institute for whom he acted as mentor to beginning/pre-service science teachers. In their view, he provided a model of a science teacher who could articulate the thinking underlying his practice and use that to help others embarking on new careers in the profession.

After a taking a broad-based degree in the biological sciences, and a number of years working in a research environment while working for a PhD, Iain made the leap into teaching principally because of the positive experiences he gained from supporting undergraduate students, 'I much preferred the demonstrating to the research!' He is now leads the science department at the college.

Wishing to set an example to the students about his own authentic involvement in real science, he continues to be involved in some locally-based research into competition between native red squirrels and the ubiquitous grey squirrel.

Iain's beliefs and theories (personal philosophies) about science teaching

As evident throughout the pre-interview and the VSR, Iain recognizes the dilemma facing all science teachers; How do you educate all students to be scientifically literate while at the same time be preparing the scientists of the future? Making science enjoyable was the central feature of Iain's approach because it stemmed from a core value; that students should feel involved in their science education. To achieve this, he saw it as his role and responsibility to ensure he provided opportunities for students to be active in their learning:

> 'I think it probably improves the chances of learning and definitely improves the chances of it being enjoyable and them having the impression that it's worthwhile because they've contributed more to it ... It's an upwards spiral ... enjoyment and motivation link it together. That's certainly been my experience.'

Although this lesson was about the acquisition of a specific skill set to do with using the microscope, Iain talked more generally about learning. He believes students have to process ideas and concepts actively, not just encounter them by copying them down. The result is that since beginning teaching ten years ago, Iain has steadily shifted his thinking about pedagogy from just meeting the demands of an overtly assessment-led curriculum to include a greater focus that centres on student learning. He calls it a philosophy of 'not teaching to the test'!

Through hard work and experience, Iain is now highly confident of his command of the material he teaches. He talked of almost having to relearn A level and even starting from scratch in some areas in order to teach it. Consequently, he now believes he has the knowledge and the experience to offer students a better learning experience by creating an interactive-dialogic environment where he can both engage with them and mediate the content at a conceptual level.

Gaining ownership leads to another plank in Iain's theories about learning, that of relevance. Relevance is perceived by students when everyday knowledge and scientific knowledge are linked through whatever it is being studied. Leach and Scott, in *Good practice in science teaching* (2000: 41–3), make the distinction between the two very clear. Ownership, for Iain, only comes when students are assisted to see this relationship through what they are being taught:

> 'It goes back to this notion . . . are the learning experiences worthwhile? If the delivery is good and relevant it has to be linked to everyday science . . . they'll hang in longer and therefore they'll begin to see the relevance of school science to everyday science. I find in biology it's not that difficult, but most aspects of school science you can relate to what's happening outside.'

Iain's professional knowledge

What has Iain learned during ten years of teaching, what are the significant knowledge bases he has developed and how do they interact (see Figure 4.3)? Throughout the research, Iain emphasized how regular and systematic evaluation of his teaching has resulted in change and improvement in practice. Iain wrote, 'I reflect on every lesson and evaluate the effectiveness of resources, practical exercises, questions and teaching strategies'. In addition, he talks through his thinking with colleagues on the basis that a collegial approach to professional development often generates new and alternative ideas that do not emerge through personal reflection alone.

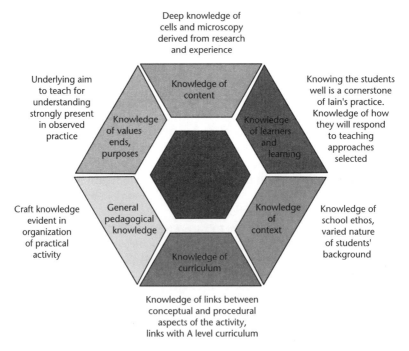

Figure 4.3 The 'spinning top' for Iain's professional knowledge.

According to Iain, making the science relevant and making the links with the everyday world of science does not come without hard work and he is critical of teachers who do not do it:

> 'I think the thing is to recognize that those are the links that you want to try and make. I just feel that some people haven't done that initial step, but once you realize that, if you can relate school science to science in the real world then it's actually a better experience for the pupils . . . That's the first step and then you start to become much more aware of things you might want to use from newspapers, TV programmes, textbooks, radio programmes, or resources that are pro-duced from our examining boards . . . I'll stack that away somewhere and use it at some stage in the future.'

To keep up-to-date, Iain reads extensively, be it science texts or journals, such as the *School Science Review* or the *Journal of Biological Education*. An advanced certificate in education focusing largely on science education taken a few years ago provides a strong theoretical background for his pedagogy of science teaching. He also makes a point of searching the popular media for stories and ideas.

It's difficult to separate out any one aspect of Iain's practice as being more important than another. They are all interrelated and combine to produce an approach to learning and teaching science that, for Iain, represents what he has learned through experience and hard work. He summarized his philosophy as:

> 'Be there on time, well organized and enthusiastic – know your stuff, keep them active and try to give them a laugh at some stage. Reflect and evaluate – note the changes needed. Every lesson is a step on a long journey of discovery!'

Section 3: In-vitro fertilization

The context

This is a class of 24 (somewhat challenging), Year 10 (14–15 age group) students in a large mixed 11–18 comprehensive, in a small rural town in the UK. Special care has to be taken to cope with two of the students who are occasionally excluded from school for behavioural reasons.

The lesson

This lesson forms one of a series that is concluding a module of work cover-ing human reproductive function. In previous lessons the students had encountered the menstrual cycle, contraception and fertility. Within the curriculum (specification) there is considerable scope to explore socio-scientific issues. In this case the lesson is designed to give the students an opportunity to examine the issue of in-vitro fertilization (IVF) and consider the scientific and social reasons that can determine who is considered eligible for IVF treatment and who is not.

Given the nature of some of the students in this class the opportunity for student-teacher confrontation is considerable. As an advanced skills teacher, Derek often observes other science teachers and notes how easy it can be to create a bad atmosphere at the very beginning of a lesson. Derek sees entry into the classroom as a critical time to manage the students' behaviour positively. His experience has led him to devise a strategy, that he uses here, involving a combination of taking the register with a simple, ready-prepared starter activity, to create a calming, emotionally neutral atmosphere.

Engaging the students

Once Derek has clearly directed the students to their seats he says:

> 'I would just like you to read the paper in front of you about IVF, and do what it says at the bottom and highlight anything you don't understand. If you understand it all, you don't need to highlight anything. And if you want to add anything at the bottom, if you already know about IVF, test-tube babies, or anything else you have heard, please do so. You have one minute, 34 seconds . . .'

. . . and uses a remote control to switch on student-friendly background music timed to stop in one minute and 34 seconds!

Activity 1	Teacher thinking
Starter activity: reading a simply expressed IVF fact sheet.	'To engage the kids I gave them something to be doing while that [taking the register] was happening. So there was something there for them to be getting on with.'
	'. . . when they come in there's going to be a piece of paper with some information about IVF in front of them in a picture and they're just going to sit down and read that information and maybe highlight and write down something they know about it. It's just getting them thinking about IVF, which is a difficult process'.

Activity 1 (*cont*)	Teacher thinking
	'. . . it's recapping perhaps what we thought we'd covered yesterday a little bit. It's an engagement [activity] and gets them thinking straightway. And to a certain extent, I think it gets their confidence up because my questioning is all "Do you understand that guys?" '
	'. . . you give them a particular time frame to do something. You don't just say, "I'd like you to read that." [I say] I'd like you to do that and it's going to take you one minute, 34 seconds, and then we're going to stop it. So I think it's a way of getting the kids to focus and also choosing odd time scales as well. If I give a kid five minutes to do a task, why not give them four minutes 20 seconds or six minutes 30 secs, because five minutes is too loose. Everything takes five minutes or six minutes!!'

The concept of 'training' the students is evident in Derek's practice. In this instance, he uses a rather unusual technique of providing music to keep the students on task. Derek has been training the students to accept that when the music is playing they should be on task, but when it stops they should be listening.

Building student confidence
The task is a simple one on purpose – it is 'do-able' for all students. In the VSR Derek said:

> 'It's very easy to give kids a starter activity which ruins the lesson because they sit there and say, "I can't do this. I haven't got a clue." '

Building up students' confidence and self-esteem is central to Derek's philosophy. He wants to challenge the students through the lesson, but not so much at the start that they feel they cannot do it. He expanded this view, pointing out how giving the wrong kind of starter activity to the wrong group can actually be counterproductive:

> 'If they can't do it it's a pointless starter because it doesn't challenge them, it switches them off straightway! I don't think we should be trying to challenge the kids in the first minute, we should be trying to

engage them. So giving them something that's a real challenge in the first minute, I don't think works. It might for top set kids, and kids you're pushing forward, but not for kids who have generally low self-esteem or aren't confident about their intelligence or their science. By giving them something they don't understand in the first two minutes, you might as well give up!'

The starter activity is all about 'engagement'. Derek wants the students with him from the start and he wants to know a little more about what they know about IVF by asking them to identify any terminology or concepts they do not understand. He also seeks to engage with them further by getting them to clarify their own questions. Once he has built the initial foundations for discussion the chance for progress is greater, particularly when he can use this information to inform his decision-making during the course of the lesson.

Precisely one minute and 34 seconds later the digital timer on the iPod halts the music and Derek calls for the students' attention and summarizes the IVF process, highlighting a few key points. This is Derek's first opportunity to interact properly and to make use of the students' questions about what they understand and what they would like to know more about. Within a minute or two he switches the screen to a PowerPoint slide that states the objectives for the lesson.

> 'So what is today's lesson? Objectives are up there. I've reviewed the process of IVF. So within five minutes we can tick it – IVF, it stands for in-vitro fertilization.'

Derek asks if the students know what 'in-vitro' stands for. One student says the word 'glass' and another chimes in, for a moment of revelation, 'Ah, so that's where test-tube baby thing comes from.' Derek had deliberately contrived his first objective to be easily achieved early on in the lesson, as part of his strategy to raise all the students' self-esteem. If they could meet with early success, they could be successful later in the lesson too. This was a chance to show the students they could learn, and it was an opportunity to say to them, 'Well done', and help them establish a positive view of their own ability to learn:

> 'A lot of teaching is about tricking kids into learning, I think – making them feel as though they've achieved something when they don't realize they've achieved it. If you work hard to achieve something and you achieve it you feel happy. But if you've done absolutely nothing as far as you're aware and you've still achieved and someone is telling you you've achieved, it's a great success. So by ticking off one of the objectives in the very beginning, I think is quite good.'

COMMENTARY

Raising student self-esteem

As part of developing his relationship with this class, Derek sees the raising of student self-esteem as an important ingredient. This is not, of course, peculiar to science, but it recognizes that science is often perceived by students as a difficult subject. Derek works from a premise that these students need visible evidence of achievement if they are to feel they can succeed. This belief is in common with many of the other highly accomplished science teachers who also try to set achievable goals while appreciating the need to challenge students intellectually. Another device Derek uses appeals to the students' sense of maturity. By giving them the opportunity to engage in the discussion of grown-up issues (in this case, IVF) he not only has the chance to raise their self-esteem through the demonstration of his trust, but can, in addition, demonstrate to them how an understanding of science is important where other people's futures are concerned. He called it 'giving them a sense of grandeur'.

Simulation

The short introduction to the lesson gets the students focused on IVF as a process. The bulk of the time, however, is allocated to a simulation activity that presents six cases of childless couples and requires students working as a group to act as a decision panel determining which couples should be prioritized for IVF treatment. The simulation aims to utilize the students' science knowledge and to engage them in reasoned decision-making.

Activity 2	Teacher thinking
Simulation activity. Derek's thinking about modifying the resource pack.	'. . . but the process of how IVF works in a laboratory is not the objective of the lesson. That's a vehicle to get them to talk about how people make decisions about the ethics of who gets and doesn't get IVF. The fact is they need to understand a little about IVF to get there.'
	'I chose not to give them any of this information [indicating genetics data that was supplied]. There's a thing about the genetics involved and I chose not to do that.

Activity 2 (*cont*)	Teacher thinking
	Genetic screening! That's obviously moving it forward a bit. I didn't want to do any of that really. I just used the family scenarios and adapted them to this group. So some of the facts of IVF are really not as useful to them as others.'

To provide the structure of the simulation, Derek obtained a commercially available resource pack from an in-service training session he had attended. However, he modified it so that (1) he could have some ownership over the material, and (2) so that it better suited the students' needs. In doing this, Derek made decisions about how best to manipulate the content to engage the students and to provide them with what he felt they needed to know for conceptual development. Interestingly, he also decided not to include some content on genetic screening. There was a danger here that explanations of this content could lead to a loss of focus in the lesson. Nonetheless, Derek expressed a concern that the students must still have a good foundation of 'science fact' if they are to be able to make decisions and justify their choices of which couples should receive priority for IVF treatment.

COMMENTARY

Science education for citizenship

Derek's choice of material as a vehicle for teaching the content of the curriculum resonates with his view that he also has a role in developing a scientifically-literate population for life in a technologically advanced society. The dilemma for school science is that not all students will go on to have careers in science, but they will all be citizens in a society who have a say, not least through the ballot box. For all highly accomplished science teachers, their concern is that whatever else the population's view is, it should at least be a scientifically informed view!

Since the introduction of the new GCSE curricula in science education at Key Stage 4 (14–16 age group) in England, opportunities to address science education for citizenship have been more plentiful. For many beginning- and early-career teachers the issues can be uncomfortable both in terms of the content and from a management perspective. Derek certainly found it easier to manage when the topic had a strong science base and it was clear that other highly accomplished science teachers used the science as the framework for discussion. Teaching controversial issues is nothing new in science education, but using socio-scientific topics as vehicles for teaching both the conceptual and procedural aspects of science is generally recognized as complex. To develop a repertoires of teaching strategies, Ratcliffe and Grace (2003), in their book *Science education for citizenship*, offer ideas, approaches and learning strategies underpinned by theoretical perspectives which support the process of pedagogical reasoning.

Derek quickly distributes a fact sheet on IVF he has created to support the simulation. He stresses again how the information on the fact sheet is necessary for the decision-making process:

> 'Firstly you need to know what the science is. You need a bit more information about how IVF works, why it works, who it works for, who it doesn't work for and some of the facts surrounding IVF. We're going to do that – I'm going to give everyone a fact sheet. When you get it, have a little read and I'll talk about some of the facts in a little more detail, because this will help you discuss it further in your groups in a minute.'

He gives them 30 seconds to begin reading and also gives them a very simple goal for the activity:

> 'Now you have to decide which three cases [of cases A–F] you are going to put forward for IVF treatment. So you are going to have to tell three "couples" they are not going to be able to have it, and you've got to decide how you are going to make that decision. There's no right or wrong way of deciding – it's down to you discussing the merits of who should have it.'

Before he sets them going he has a final advance organizer – their groups and where they sit. Derek has thought very carefully about this. Using his knowledge of the students he has decided on the groups. He uses the screen to show them:

> 'You need to know which groups you're in and where you're going to sit . . . We are going to have four groups and they are going to be in the four corners of the room. So we will have a bit of a furniture moving exercise . . .'

There is nothing unusual here other than the fact that Derek has manipulated everything to ensure he can engage productively with the students and promote learning. He knows that with the wrong group composition, without well-organized seating arrangements to encourage discussion and without easy-to-access information this activity would collapse. As a safeguard to ensure he captures the students' ideas, Derek hands out one more piece of paper prepared for the students to rank the cases and to display their reasoning.

Dialogic interaction
The bulk of the lesson now involves Derek deploying his skills in asking, probing and prompting, spending just enough time with each group to ensure they always have a goal and remain on-task. He uses his knowledge of the students, their personalities and characteristics, to promote and maintain group interaction:

> 'I have given Jasmine a bit of responsibility there. I'd spent too much time there and it was kind of obvious that I'd said everything I needed to about working as a group and discussing it and I needed to go and speak to some other groups and check they were OK, so as I walked away . . . I looked at Jasmine and Sam and said, "Jasmine, you're going to need to take control here and get these guys working with you," and so she immediately felt it was a bit of praise and responsibility.'

All the time Derek remains acutely aware of what is going on in the room and whether students are on-task. He pointed out how his vision has developed compared with newly-qualified teachers he has worked with in recent times and his own experience starting out ten years ago:

> 'They don't even see things. You talk about having eyes in the back of your head – I still remember when you first get into a classroom and you're first teaching a lesson you can only see what's straight in front of your eyes. It's like tunnel vision.'

As one group looks like finishing more quickly than he anticipates, Derek intervenes to work through their reasoning with them. His questions, probes and prompts put them back on track with some new ideas to consider. In the VSR Derek explained his approach with the students:

> 'I play devil's advocate here . . . I tried to express the opposite opinion . . . I was just trying to get them to discuss it a bit more and think about it in a bit more depth.'

COMMENTARY
Promoting student discussion

The reasons that highly accomplished science teachers all promote peer interaction through group work are diverse, but common to all of them is the belief that discussion promotes better learning. Another reason they adduce for promoting discussion is that it provides the circumstances for developing students' critical skills by 'getting them to think'.

Discussion, though, does not happen just by putting students into groups. First, all the highly accomplished science teachers think carefully about group composition and the structure they provide to ensure clear educational goals are always in sight. Second, they are effective in their role in supporting discussion. We believe our research shows that their practice has much in common with Scott and Mortimer's (2006) analysis of meaning-making in the science classroom. These teachers use carefully chosen prompts, probes and questions to generate what Scott and Mortimer call dialogic/interactive discourse. According to Scott and Mortimer, 'dialogic' means that there is a high level of interanimation between the teacher and students and that all ideas generated by the students are acknowledged, shared and discussed (see p. 611).

Derek is sensitive to the problems of students apparently 'constructing knowledge' within their groups, particularly if it results in misunderstandings. Although he would not have described his interventions, his prompts, probes and questions as 'dialogic/interactive' this is, in effect what he is doing through his belief that the students should develop their critical faculties so that they have the capacity to appraise the outcomes of their discussions.

For a full and readable analysis of the nature of discussion in the science classroom we suggest you look at Mortimer and Scott's book (2003), *Meaning making in secondary science classrooms*.

By his actions the students have come to know Derek's style of interaction. They know he will talk to them as adults, respect their opinions, would not be shocked (if they try to shock him) and will show he enjoys being with them. As a result the tenor of discussion is calm and positive where the students are keen to discuss their ideas with him as well as seek his opinion for deeper understanding. The students themselves readily supported discussion as a strategy that can help them learn:

'I think that's quite good because everybody gets to voice their opinion and you know what everyone else is thinking and you can say what you think.' 'You get involved.'

'Plus if you're stuck on something you've got the rest of the group to help that one person or two people with that question.'

'I think it helps as well in that you can make more friends in the lesson who you don't normally get on with.'

The level of emotional and intellectual support offered through group work encourages many students, who perhaps might not normally show interest or even behave disruptively, to participate. It also provides Derek with good evidence to involve students in their learning more often in this way. Interestingly, the stronger science base to this simulation also made Derek feel more comfortable compared with an earlier experience when he had tried one that focused on the topic of legalizing cannabis and had 'less science' in it to support the discussion:

'Something like a debate on legalizing cannabis – I don't think there's as much science in there as the debate about IVF treatment for example. I think it is a little more social citizenship type perhaps . . . When we start talking about the effect of global warming on the environment, that's driven by science and evidence and the opinions and decisions the kids make have to be driven by evidence.'

Plenary

After 30 minutes Derek recognizes the simulation has reached a point where extending it would invoke the 'law of diminishing (educational) returns'. He 'reads' the class, but knows now that the success of the lesson will hinge crucially on the quality of the reasoning the students can offer to support the three cases they have prioritized for IVF. He has used the time efficiently to interact with all four groups several times, but he now sketches an outcomes table (see next page) on the whiteboard. This was a late decision, but Derek had been musing for a little while now how best to collect and analyse their decision-making. There were two reasons for Derek doing this, (1) he can give the students a quick visual insight into how their choices differed, and, more importantly, (2) he can provide himself with leads for questions.

With a close eye on the clock, he points the remote control at the iPod. The students are suddenly aware the music has stopped and look up towards Derek who has positioned himself strategically. Immediately, he says to them:

'All eyes this way – these are going to be the most important eight minutes of the lesson for a lot of people, because it's a chance for you to say who you chose and why. And it's a chance for the rest of the group to listen to those decisions – not to comment, not to shout out, but to listen. And the whole point of the lesson is about actually making decisions based on scientific evidence and judgements.'

Activity 3	Teacher thinking
Plenary discussion.	'I always leave more time than you think. You think you need 5 minutes and I always leave 15 minutes because by the time you've got in there and explained it, it takes longer than you think.'
	'. . . when I said it was the most important bit of the lesson, I was kind of fibbing [lying] to a certain extent because the most important bit as far as I was concerned was the process they'd just been through in the last half an hour as they were discussing and in their groups talking together. That was the object.'

Derek asks the groups in turn for their choices and writes them up. The students are fascinated as the matrix provides them with plenty of food for thought – Case F, the only one they had all prioritized, was the gay couple, and no one prioritised Case B.

	A	B	C	D	E	F
1			X	X		X
2				X	X	X
3			X		X	X
4	X				X	X

Derek makes a point about how what follows in the plenary has significance for the students and their GCSEs. He explains to the students what examiners will be looking for when they test their understanding of topics such as IVF:

'As far your GCSEs are concerned – in your exam you may be asked to write a reason why someone should or shouldn't receive IVF. You have to think about what we've done today. Write reasons – you can't just write, "Because they're young." Think of reasons. Think of what you have discussed in your group. Back up your decision with evidence.'

The new science specifications (curricula) in England place an emphasis on the role of science in society. Derek says that although he is not particularly used to teaching in this way, as an advanced skills teacher he has been involved in providing continuing professional development (CPD) on the teaching of controversial issues. But now, he says, 'I guess it seems a little more real now that we're meant to be doing it!'

Towards the end of the VSR Derek was asked to reflect on the extent to which he felt he had been successful in achieving learning. His response focused largely on the development of transferable skills, although he had sufficient evidence from the early part of the lesson, and his interaction with the students, to feel confident that they could all state what IVF was:

'It was very good. The discussions the kids were having and their engagement and what they were saying, the opinions coming out, were excellent, I would say. If you give them a role-play situation they're fine ... For that class, that was outstanding ... but if you know the group of kids and how they behave at other times of the week, even within this classroom, they were outstanding. We form a good relationship.'

One student comment, taken from the group interview conducted a short while after the lesson, summarized neatly a wider view across the class:

'You're actually hearing what's going on and you're not reading it out of books, but actually thinking yourself. I learnt more today doing that lesson and all the other things about the NHS [National Health Service].'

Derek's background

Derek began his working career as a marine biologist. Like many other science teachers who emerge from the world of research, involvement in an esoteric and often small research communities influenced his decision to turn to teaching, particularly as he found that he was good at explaining ideas and concepts. In his own words:

> 'I guess I knew I had some sort of gift for making the complicated easier. I figured at the time that was what teaching was . . . So I did teacher training and discovered that I was quite good at it really and I enjoyed it and it was quite fun and the kids responded pretty well to me.'

Teacher training provided a new set of challenges which, to a large extent, Derek felt he was tackling on his own. These, however, provided him with a set of unique learning experiences which would appear to form the foundations for the development of his professional knowledge base and may have much to do with why he has become an advanced skills teacher.

Derek's beliefs and theories (personal philosophies) about science teaching

Rather than defining Derek's philosophy by what he says, it is perhaps more helpful to infer where he is coming from via his practice. For example, the effort he put into getting 'engagement' was enormous. Engagement was part of a package that cannot be teased apart from 'developing relationships'. He has a nice way of expressing it:

> 'It's not about the teacher dictating to the kids all the time and the kids just acting like sponges, because it doesn't work like that. It's about the teacher knowing what they want from the kids, the kids knowing what they want from the lesson. And it's like a two-way thing.'

Knowing the students well is fundamental to Derek's approach. If this knowledge is secure, Derek can also take risks ('all singing and dancing' as he phrases it) as he too is a firm believer that risk-taking is an important tool for teacher learning:

> 'I've made those decisions and I know it's Period 3 on a Tuesday and I know the kids and what they're capable of, and know what level to pitch it at. So how then do I plan the lesson? Starter, main task, plenaries, or is it going to be something different or something all singing and dancing? A lesson that's didactic/cut and paste/textbooks open and copy this and that? How is it going to be? I guess my main driving force is that I want to make it so the kids learn something and what they learn is something I want them to learn, they have fun and it's not boring and it doesn't allow them to misbehave. In other words, it's engaging enough for them not to be out of control.'

Highly accomplished science teachers see that the content of the lesson and students' behaviour are inextricably linked. Simply put, if you do not make the effort to engage the students then the chances of them misbehaving, or looking for alternative opportunities to digress, to engage in unwanted behaviours, etc., are far greater. You should not be surprised if they do not co-operate in quite the way you hoped. Highly accomplished science teachers apply this equally to 'good classes' where the students will tolerate poor planning and teaching. They see it as their *duty* to make the material engaging. In fact, the thrill of teaching comes from the students' responses.

Derek's professional knowledge

Without question, Derek sees himself as a continuous learner! And he remains astounded by science teachers who do not want to admit that they do not know something. The view he professes to the students when he finds himself in this position is, 'Because I'm a teacher it doesn't mean I know everything. It means that I'm learning.'

More generally it seems to us that highly accomplished science teachers are very comfortable with the idea that they are not perceived by students as the fount of all knowledge. They accept they cannot know everything, but, by the same token, they know they have the skills to find out, and they know that when they do they have a level of scientific understanding that allows them to make sense of whatever it is they do not know. If they can find out from colleagues, that is a bonus. It also gives them an opportunity to show, even if they are regarded as experts, that they too are fallible and still willing to learn from others. Such collegiality is a key to their success.

The willingness to learn is of course the key to the development of a profound subject knowledge base. Derek is somewhat dismissive of his subject knowledge base:

> '. . . there's a difference between subject knowledge and delivering it. I don't see the subject knowledge bit as important as the delivery bit. It's the delivery and the kids picking up that knowledge, which is 99 per cent of my job I guess.'

We would argue here that, what Derek is really getting at is, his ability to transform the subject matter into material that can be accessed by the students. He expresses this more explicitly:

> 'But I have to manipulate knowledge all the time I guess. But that's all about lesson planning and structure and how to get kids to engage in the knowledge you've got I suppose. I mean this is what I do all the time I guess.'

In the extract below, Derek tries to articulate what he believes his knowledge base for teaching is:

'That knowledge has come from I guess knowledge of the syllabus and of the assessment of what I think they're going to be tested on and what they actually need to know. Most lessons have learning outcomes which are in lots of ways unachievable, let's say. So let's use the reflex action for example. How do kids learn all that in one lesson? I don't think they can. So what bits am I going to get them to try and learn and what bits aren't I? I suppose that's my starting point. That comes from a knowledge of syllabus, assessment and where it falls in the bigger picture, and my experience of teaching the course. So then I think, "OK, I want them to learn this, this and this. How am I going to get them to do that and engage them in the first instance? When they walk through the door how am I going to get them on task or to listen to me or sit down and get their bags away?" A lot of those decisions probably come from my knowledge of the class – the kids sitting there, their ability, their range of abilities, their behavioural abilities, their concentration abilities. It's my knowledge of the individual children that I'm teaching and how I think they, as individuals

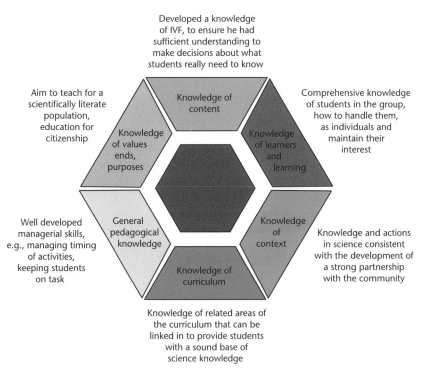

Figure 4.4 The 'spinning top' for Derek's professional knowledge.

or as a group, will respond. It also comes down to the time of day and sequence or time of year, etc.'

Coincidentally, this is precisely the kind of thinking and behaviours that the certified NBPTS teachers engage in that Berliner (2004) refers to in his article documenting pedagogical expertise. Their knowledge starts from their knowledge of the learners and their circumstances. Every pre-active decision is thus highly contextualized in that previous experience is the lens through which all new knowledge is viewed and processed.

Although Derek wants to ensure he engages the students, he knows that the curriculum itself is the foundation on which he has to build. Essentially he is using his knowledge of the content, the curriculum, the students and general pedagogical techniques to decide what will work best with a particular group. This is the creation of his personal, professional knowledge (see Figure 4.4).

5   Chemistry

In this chapter we look closely at three teachers, Isabel, Ursula and Orla, teaching mainstream topics that involve concepts in chemistry. The topics featuring in these lessons are atomic structure and bonding, reactivity series and drugs, and are the topics that happened to be the ones being taught by our highly accomplished science teachers at the time we negotiated to visit. In other words, there was no deliberate choice being made to choose one topic or another.

As in Chapters 3 and 4 we are not trying to suggest that this is how to teach these topics. Our focus is solely on the professional knowledge of these highly accomplished teachers, how they acquire it, how they develop it and how they use it.

Section 1: Atomic structure and bonding

The context

This is a class for 28 Year 11 students (15–16-year-olds), in a mixed comprehensive school on the edge of a large city in the UK. Although this is a top set there is quite a range of ability with the majority of students predicted to get grades B and C in their GCSEs but some possibly D grades.

The lesson

The students are moving into a revision phase in preparation for GCSE examinations and they have been revising their chemistry. For this lesson Isabel wanted to have some space for a 'kinaesthetic' lesson to consolidate revision on atomic structure and bonding. The previous lesson reviewed ionic, metallic and covalent bonding, and this lesson was intended to act out structures and bonding to provide a more concrete experience. The lesson took place, therefore, not in the normal classroom but in the drama hall.

Once the students were in the hall, Isabel asked them to sit on the floor so that she could tell them about the lesson. Her learning outcomes were expressed in terms of BATs ('be able to's) on her lesson plan. She would normally have the lesson objectives written on the whiteboard in her classroom but here she needed to tell the students.

COMMENTARY
Learning styles and preferences

There was a lot of interest from the highly accomplished teachers in trying to identify and respond to individual learning styles, particularly using the popular VAK (visual, auditory, kinaesthetic) approach often associated with 'accelerated learning' (Smith 1996). While the theoretical basis for some of the ideas being advanced is somewhat vague, there is some evidence from neuroscience to support VAK and for Howard Gardner's multiple intelligence theory (2006). In the case of Isabel's teaching, the idea of providing kinaesthetic reinforcement stems from her interest in using drama in her lessons. Of the three 'learning channels', the kinaesthetic is probably to most under-represented outside the performing arts or physical education. Although science is a very practical subject, it does not mean that it fully exploits kinaesthetic opportunities. Practical work emphasizes using the hands but other activities can involve more of the body and provide learners with opportunities to be creative and experimental. Another reason Isabel may be keen on these activities is that they engage the students affectively as well as cognitively. We are only beginning to get a full understanding of the linkage between the emotions and learning but it is clear that emotional engagement combined with intellectual engagement can result in learning which is firmly rooted and stable (Jensen 1998). One student commented about the modelling activity:

> 'But with covalent bonding I don't think I'll ever forget it, no matter how old I am, I'll never forget how to do that.'

The discussion with Isabel after the lesson revealed some of her thinking about this lesson. For many teachers, this might have been seen as a high-risk plan but, through the development of a relationship with the group, she did not see it that way. She has extended her range of pedagogic skills through contact with the drama department in the school in order to learn how to manage these activities more efficiently.

At the start of the lesson, while the students were coming in, Isabel had quickly stuck up large labels around the hall reading, for example, 'Ionic' and 'Lattice'. The lesson was very well prepared and materials were always on hand where required. The students did not need much introduction to this

Activity 1	Teacher thinking
The first activity in the lesson was a game called 'Move to answer'.	'They've done a lot of sitting doing stuff and I want to recap what they know and so I want them to get up and move . . . I'm going to see straightaway if they understand electronic configuration, the ionic bonding and transfer of electrons, covalent and sharing, the properties that these types of bonding create.'

activity as they had played this game before, which simply involved Isabel asking questions requiring them to move to the appropriate label.

The first question, or rather statement, was:

'OK, I am a gas.'

The students moved quickly to the 'Covalent' label. It is interesting to note Isabel's phrasing of the statement which is a deliberate use of 'I am'. This personalizes the situation which the students are acting out – they are being a gas or whatever as they move around the hall. The next questions were also dealt with quite easily:

'I am diamond.'

'I am formed between metals and non-metals.'

During the activity Isabel positioned herself where she could observe the whole scene and she was carefully watching where the students went. Students knew which of their peers might be relied on to know the right answer and could just move with them. The next questions were a bit more demanding and were fired quite quickly to keep the students moving and thinking:

'I conduct as a solid and a liquid.'

'I conduct when molten and in solution but not as a solid.'

Although Isabel had a pre-prepared list of questions, her choice from the list was in response to how well the students seemed to be able to answer. The final questions required a bit more thought:

'The bonds that hold me together are strong forces of attraction between oppositely-charged particles.'

'I have free electrons which can move over my structure and allow me to conduct electricity.'

While the students were moving around the hall, Isabel was still noting their responses and using the observations diagnostically. Before moving on, she was keen to give the students this bit of feedback:

'OK . . . that was really interesting . . . because what you've shown me is that you know a lot of stuff really well but some of the higher-level stuff about relating properties to the structure of the compound or molecule . . . we need to spend a little more time on that.'

This was signalling something to herself and to the students about their strengths and an area which required further work. Isabel saw this initial activity as a 'starter' but clearly it had a purpose in checking on prior learning as well as getting into the main content of the lesson. After the lesson, in the VSR interview, Isabel reflected:

'. . . there were bits they were very, very confident about and bits they got right but were less confident about and bits they are just clueless on . . . their inability to comprehend water as a small covalent molecule was interesting and they were confused by graphite as well. But interestingly they thought graphite could have been ionic and that could have been because of its ability to conduct electricity . . . I've basically put up stars against the questions that they had no problems over so I know I can go back and go over those particular bits with them.'

The need for reinforcement is an important part of Isabel's view about revision. Students need more than one opportunity to revisit topics and possibly more than one way of doing so. Very clear instructions are characteristic of Isabel's teaching. She needs to mark the transition from one activity to the next. Here, moving into the next phase of the lesson, she does it simply by telling the students to move to the middle of the space in the hall.

The next phase of the lesson was a recap on atomic structure as a precursor to extending the activity to modelling bonding. Isabel had brought a set of bibs with her – the sort of thing used in PE lessons to identify teams:

'I've got 30 vests and that's something I've gone and bought myself . . . Bibs give them a certain amount of freedom. It's not me . . . it's the bib . . . you realize how they can use them in different ways to manipulate, the way they can have the blue side, the silver side, the red side. It gives them that freedom to be able to think in different ways of how to express themselves.'

Activity 2	Teacher thinking
'Modelling' atomic structures and electronic configurations.	'It's more thinking about atomic structure . . . I started off doing the basic atomic structure . . . they needed to get into how they were working as a team and how they could involve everyone, rather than a core of people just doing the same thing again and again, leaving people sitting on the side.'

The students were given a few minutes to work out the structure for their atoms:

> 'OK . . . three, two, one . . . quiet. So . . . start with Group 1 . . . Group 1, you were doing boron . . . are we ready, three, two, one, OK?'

The use of the 'three, two, one' device worked well with the class and is a routine that Isabel uses regularly with them.

Students in Group 1 move round showing the orbits of the electrons around a central student in a silver bib representing the nucleus in the boron atom. The point of the modelling was to emphasize the electrons moving around the nucleus in two orbits. Isabel is aware of the limitations of the model but here is just concerned with showing an inner orbit with two electrons and the outer orbit with, in this case, three electrons. She asks to explain what the group is showing. She is a little concerned about the involvement of all group members and gives them this bit of feedback:

> 'I love the way you've got the different colours for the different shells of electrons, I loved the fact you've got them moving in different directions . . . it's clear that you've got that, but how could you have used the other the people . . . think about that for the next one you do . . . using more of the group is better because everybody knows what's going on.'

The second group perform their atom (carbon). Again, a student is asked to explain what the group is showing. And again, the question is asked about involving the whole group:

> 'OK, same groups I'd like to do . . . atomic structure . . . this group, magnesium and this group, aluminium.'

Isabel does not intervene in the group discussions, leaving the students to decide for themselves how to create their models. Overt looking at her watch and giving time checks has the effect of keeping the groups working and under pressure. The skill of the highly accomplished teacher is to be able to get the balance right here – too much time and there is the risk of the students becoming disengaged, too little and they are not able to meet the set targets:

> 'OK ... three, two, one, stop ... can you watch over here please? Which element were you doing? Aluminium? And what was its electronic configuration?'

The students are all able to respond to the question and give the correct response. The group then performs its model of aluminium with Isabel taking the part of one of the outer electrons.

COMMENTARY

Security vs. unpredictability

The highly accomplished teacher needs to provide a secure learning environment for students; a safe environment within which they can express not only when they do understand but also when they do not. This requires the building up over time of relationships and routines. On the other hand, with routine can come boredom and predictability. Creating the right balance between security and predictability presents a challenge. We have discussed risk-taking elsewhere in this book (see p. 37). The notion we are presenting here is that of the 'calculated risk' – trying to build in an element of uncertainty and unpredictability into lessons to keep the students guessing but at the same time having sufficient trust in the teacher that this is worth going along with. It can be tempting to 'play safe', particularly when working in unfamiliar territory, but part of Isabel's approach is to avoid normality and to give each lesson some element of challenge in this way. Her students appreciate this. When asked how this lesson compared with a 'normal lesson', one of her students said:

> 'The thing is though, to me that wasn't really an abnormal lesson because getting taught by Miss T, there isn't anything "normal" after a while ... After being taught by Miss T for so long you kind of get used to it.'

Getting the balance right is not easy. There is a rather surprising relationship between stress levels and cognitive efficiency. It's not just a simple inverse proportionality where, as stress levels rise, cognitive efficiency decreases. That might be true at higher levels of stress but a healthy level of stress or stimulus improves cognitive function. The right amount of stress can induce what psychologists refer to as a state of 'relaxed alertness' which is recognized as being a desirable starting point for us to learn effectively. Feeling comfortable with and trusting the teacher may reduce stress but this element of unpredictability which Isabel's students recognized just keeps them alert and anticipating something interesting and even exciting from her lessons.

Reflecting on this part of the lesson in the VSR interview, Isabel said:

> 'I actually spent a lot of time chatting to the drama department, who I've done some work with, about how they get students to get started, [and to] stop and I'm not very good at bringing it in all the time, but trying to get them to watch one another.'

Having satisfied herself that the students have a clear idea about how to represent electron orbits, Isabel is ready to move into the next phase of the lesson.

Activity 3	Teacher thinking
Modelling bonding between atoms.	'I had actually initially decided that half of them were going to do a different ionic one and I changed my mind . . . because I was keeping an eye on the clock and seeing the time going and realizing that this would probably be the way of doing it. Getting that half to do one lot of bonding and the other group to do a different thing.'

As before, Isabel pays attention to the lesson transition linking Activity 2 with Activity 3. She says to the students:

> 'OK, so we've a good idea about electronic configuration and atomic structures. Now, can we put that together when we do bonding? Now for this you are going to need to work as two separate halves of the group to come together. So our first one, we're going to do is lithium fluoride – so I want you guys to think lithium and you guys to think fluorine and then we're going to bond you.'

Before getting the two atoms to 'bond', she needs to check that they have got the structures right. She asks about the atomic structure of lithium and what it 'wants' to have (in terms of completing an electron shell):

> 'A full outer shell – is it going to be easier for lithium to gain seven [electrons] or lose one?'

Isabel appreciates the risk here. Attributing 'wants' to inanimate objects is obviously a distortion but she has presented this to students in previous lessons as a way of explaining what happens during the formation of an ion through the gain or loss of electrons. There is a tension here between the precise use of language and being able to present scientific knowledge in a way that can be more easily assimilated.

Next she asks them to consider the electronic structure of fluorine and what it 'wants':

> 'A full outer shell . . . is it going to be easier for it to lose seven or gain one?'

So the students can then act this out:

> 'One electron from here needs to move across to the seven over there . . . What is being formed here? . . . An ion . . . good . . . what charge does it have? How many positives? . . . One . . . good . . . and what's been formed over here? An ion . . . what charge? Minus . . . how many minuses? One . . . OK, good. Now what happens between the positive and the negative? . . . They attract . . . Go on then – attract, attract, attract!'

The questions here are almost rhetorical but the students respond in chorus until given the instruction to move. The dialogue may not convey the building of dramatic tension here. The instruction at the end releases that tension and allows the students to act out the bonding with one 'electron' moving from the lithium to the fluorine atom. The emotional engagement is an important part of what Isabel is trying to do here. She has strong beliefs in the use of drama in her teaching to help students 'feel' what is going on.

Whereas Isabel chose not to intervene much with the groups when they were doing the ionic bond, she was more active when thinking about covalent bonding in methane and moved between the groups, checking they knew what they were doing. Making judgements about when to intervene and when to stand back is an important part of the skill of an accomplished teacher. The temptation is to want to help the students by guiding them to the correct response but this may reduce the thinking required. Here the decision was to listen to the groups from close-to rather than observing them from a distance in order to be aware of the quality of discussion:

> 'We've got carbon here – how many [electrons] does carbon have in its

outer shell? . . . Four . . . how many does it want to have in its outer shell? . . . Eight . . . If it's not going to get rid of any, it needs to share. How many hydrogen molecules will it need to share with? . . . Four.'

The next step was to get the four hydrogen molecules to move up to the carbon atom. The students moved around with the 'hydrogens' placing themselves around the 'carbon' nucleus, with electrons paired up with the carbon's electrons:

> 'OK – hydrogens need to explain to us what's going on. Who are the silver people?'

Here Isabel is referring to the silver vests identifying the nuclei of the hydrogen atoms:

> 'They're the nucleus . . . so we still need to have the nucleus there but is the nucleus going to be right next to the electrons? . . . Little bit further, maybe further behind them? . . . The electrons themselves, nice to see people arranged in pairs so we can see what's going on. So we've got the sharing there – why's hydrogen happy?'

The students answer that it is 'happy' because it has a full outer shell. Attributing emotions like happiness to atoms is of course inaccurate but, as before, Isabel has made a decision to use this language to aid understanding. The important thing for the students is to be able to explain what is happening during covalent bonding. If thinking about the atoms being happy or sad helps with those explanations then perhaps the end justifies the means.

COMMENTARY
Models and modelling

The next activity involved more modelling. Having used themselves to model atomic structure, the class moved on to using molecular modelling kits. We have discussed modelling before (see p. 34) and made the distinction between a model and a simulation, although many teachers will use the terms synonymously. Isabel uses models and simulations extensively in many topics in her teaching. She views them as being particularly important for supporting students' learning about things which they cannot see (like atomic structure or enzyme action in the digestive system). Students need to appreciate that models are only analogues of the phenomena that they represent. The same applies to other less concrete analogies we might use in our teaching (see p. 89). When we talk of the circulatory system being like a domestic central heating system, what do we mean by 'like'? Not that it has copper pipes and water flowing round inside. Our comparison is limited to it being *similar*: something is being pumped through different circuits allowing an exchange process to take place. (Although, of course, there is a big difference between heat exchange in a central heating system and gas/nutrient exchange between blood and tissues.) It is important that students appreciate that, in these examples, 'like' does not mean 'the same as' or 'identical to' but rather 'similar to' or 'sharing some features with'. We may need to be explicit about explaining to students what we mean when we say something is 'like' something else to prevent misconceptions being created or reinforced.

Activity 4	Teacher thinking
Testing knowledge through a quiz about atomic structures using model kits and then drawing out chemical formulae.	'. . . it was more about knowing that ammonia is NH_3 and water is H_2O. So for me it was more looking at formulae because these are terms which come up in the exam paper a lot and they've got to actually know what they are.'

The students are told that they are going to work in teams to make some molecular models and then bring them up to Isabel – points will be awarded for the first team. The students do not need much instruction about using the kits because they have had previous experience of their use, although Isabel is keen to make sure they remember to use the correct colours. She starts with carbon dioxide. The first group is unsuccessful but the second group makes a correct model. The first group then has another go but is still wrong. The third and fourth groups are correct and finally the first group gets it right. The choice of carbon dioxide was intended to estimate the students' recollection of having done this before, thus it was not intended to be too hard but also not too easy by having to cope with double bonds.

Perhaps a rather odd choice comes next, as water is easier, but Isabel wants to vary the challenge. All four groups seem to be able to do this straightaway:

'OK, the next one I want you to do is ammonia.'

Buoyed up by their earlier success, one group is very quick to respond but have the wrong central atom and are sent back. The other groups gradually come up with correct solutions.

'Next one . . . hydrogen gas.'

All four groups seem to be able to do this successfully.

'Next one . . . methane.'

Despite having modelled this in the previous activity, one group has to have three goes, but the others are more successful.

Although the next part of the lesson is a continuation of the quiz, Isabel creates a break here by packing away the kits and doing some other clearing up. This can be very useful as a way of giving a bit of brain 'downtime' while at the same time signalling a change in activity. With all the tidying up done, Isabel begins the second part of the quiz which involves drawings of structural formulae. The first one, potassium bromide, is easy for all four groups. The next one, however, lithium oxide, proves more difficult and all four groups get it wrong:

> 'Right . . . look at your periodic tables, you've done this. You know how to do it – crossover rule, hint!'

Isabel decides to just drop a hint while at the same time encouraging the students by reminding them that they have done this before. Two groups get the right answer after a couple more attempts but the other two seem to be stuck:

> 'Right, we're going to stop that one there . . . can you listen please . . . we've forgotten our crossover rule – look at the group that they're in . . . remember our five stages – symbol, charge, crossover, ratio, formula . . . you guys did this about a week ago and were really good at it – crossover rule, five stages.'

At this point Isabel feels that she needs to stop this particular example to remind the students of the five-stage process they had been taught (but were not applying) to work out the formula. Isabel feels it is worth one more go and gives what is perhaps the most difficult example that the students need to know at this level:

> 'Let's try another one and see how you do . . . What is the correct formula of aluminium oxide?'

After some time one group does work out the right answer but Isabel knows that this is something for further work in class.

After the lesson, Isabel was still surprised at the students' response:

> '. . . we did a whole lesson on the crossover rule and writing out

formulae of ionic compounds and they so got it . . . We went through these five steps and they were absolutely fantastic and now they just couldn't do it!'

Isabel's plan for the lesson was slightly disturbed by this problem in understanding and she needed to make the decision to stop although she had intended to go on to some more complex material.

COMMENTARY
Reinforcing learning

There are some interesting questions about where and when learning takes place and how to make it last. The contrast is made between superficial and deep learning and highly accomplished teachers will want to ensure that they are teaching for the sort of understanding associated with deep learning (Entwistle 1988). Timetables artificially divide learning into lesson-sized chunks, often of one hour or less. When we consider the difficulty many students have in understanding concepts in science, it is doubtful that deep learning can be achieved in the relatively short time available in a single lesson. *Reinforcement* of learning plays an important part in the overall process and the highly accomplished teacher will need to think of ways to present knowledge differently to not only recall previous learning but to try to deepen it. Whether overtly constructivist or not, our highly accomplished science teachers saw learning as an active process for learners to construct their own understanding of science concepts and sought out ways to help them do this.

Revision time presents another opportunity to provide further consolidation after initial learning, but revision can often be just 'going over' the topic again. Before this lesson Isabel had already spent some time in class reviewing atomic structures and bonding in a more conventional way but she now wanted to know if the students really understood so thought of a different way to get them to test out their knowledge. Teaching for understanding (Newton 2000) is something we have mentioned before. For further reading in this area, see the references in Chapter 3 (p. 39).

With only about ten minutes of the lesson left, it is now time to make the transition into the last part of the lesson. The students clear away as instructed and form a circle in the open area of the hall.

Activity 5	Teacher thinking
Quiz with an inflatable question ball.	'It was a little bit of fun. Some of the questions are directly related to what they've done and some were going back over some very basic Key Stage 3 knowledge of elements, which was quite nice . . . The whole idea is getting them to listen to one another because the same question could come up again . . . And I suppose just also bringing them back together as a class to end the lesson because they'd been in these little groups. I feel sometimes it's quite important to bring them back together before I finish the class.'

The final part of the lesson is a game with an inflatable question ball:

'We've got two others in the department already and then I saw that one at the ASE.'

Isabel has found that even Year 11 students enjoy doing a question and answer quiz:

'. . . this is an elements ball – there are 96 questions . . . so, when you catch the ball you answer the question that is under your left thumb . . . so whichever question, for example, that one's 75, "The force that holds atoms together is called a chemical blank", you need to give the missing word, or choose a, b, c or say true/false . . . now you're going to be listening to everyone else.'

The conduct of the quiz is very smooth with the ball being thrown fairly sensibly across the circle. Isabel is on the outside checking answers. Occasionally Isabel needs to intervene and get other students to answer. Not everyone in the class has a turn before Isabel signals the end of the lesson.

Isabel's background

Isabel is an advanced skills teacher. She did a degree in pharmacology and started to do a PhD but ran out of funding and completed an MSc instead. She comes from a family of teachers but that had led her to a 'Never, ever!' view about becoming one, but eventually she was persuaded to apply for a PGCE. This was a very positive experience and she enjoyed both the university part of the course and being in school. Her university tutors and the teachers involved in her training were good role models for Isabel; their love of their subjects, their concern and support for the trainee teachers and their ability to inspire interest were key qualities she recognized from the outset. The move to advanced skills teacher was initiated after Isabel was first appointed to her present post and she clearly enjoys the challenges and opportunities that this status carries, with its requirements to not only work in her own school but also beyond it:

> 'At the moment I'm spending a lot of time in primary schools . . . So that's amazing because it really helps me understand where the students are coming from that I'm getting in Year 7. So it's phenomenal when you look at what primary schools do . . . So that's helped me quite a lot. I'm still nervous around it and still don't know it all, but certainly when I go into schools I make it very clear that they're the specialists and I'm there to help in any way I can.'

Isabel's beliefs and theories (personal philosophies) about science teaching
High on Isabel's list is the quality of the relationship with the students and their response to the subject. Feedback from students is also important:

> 'Just kids saying goodbye to you on the way out so they view you as a person and they want to say goodbye to you and "Have a nice holiday" or whatever. They want to know a bit about you and they're not doing it in a distracted way but because they're genuinely interested.'

It is difficult to get feedback about learning if the students are not actively engaged. The desire for active engagement also lies behind Isabel spending time with drama teachers to learn new ways of working with her students to develop their confidence, their social skills and their self-esteem. Both drama and her enthusiasm for kinaesthetic learning are linked with Isabel's belief that such activities encourage creativity:

> 'Not everyone in the department does kinaesthetic learning. It's just something I became really interested in. I'm very interested in creativity in lessons and if they're sat down at the desk how can you make that more creative for them to learn, because it will interest them and they'll enjoy it.'

Isabel's professional knowledge
At the time of working with Isabel, her immediate concern in terms of her professional learning was knowledge of content, focusing on new GCSE courses and particularly the 'How Science Works' component. Having studied

pharmacology at university, some aspects of chemistry and biology were well-grounded but Isabel quickly appreciated the need to develop her subject knowledge in physics, and in chemistry and biology as well. Even after several years teaching, Isabel appreciates the need to be constantly updating her subject knowledge. She recognizes that it is not just a question of getting the information. There is also the important job of translating it into an accessible form for students:

> 'Then it's going home and trying to absorb all that information, highlighting it or editing it on the computer and then thinking about how I can best get that information to the students.'

Isabel works with colleagues in the department and there is some sharing of resources but she feels it is her responsibility to do a lot of the ground work herself. She regularly attends the ASE annual meeting every January and has collected a lot of ideas and materials from there. She also takes whatever local opportunities arise to visit other schools and interact with local authority support staff. This all takes time but she believes that there are direct benefits to her teaching (see Figure 5.1).

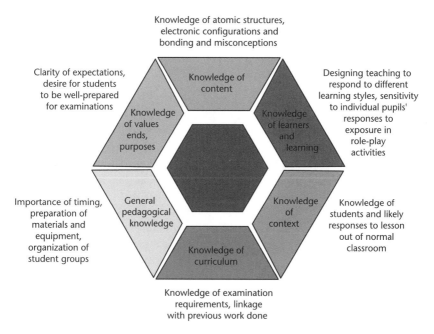

Figure 5.1   The 'spinning top' for Isabel's professional knowledge.

Section 2: Reactivity series

The context

In this instance, the class comprises a small group of around 12 Year 10 (14–15 age group) students, who mostly have learning and behavioural difficulties of some kind. It takes place in a small rural town in an extremely large mixed comprehensive that attracts over 2000 students from around the area. The school is a specialist science college in the UK and is recognized nationally as a model of good practice for science teaching.

The lesson

This lesson focuses on the concept of chemical reduction within the context of metals and the industrial processes associated with metal extraction. It is the second of several designed to enable students to appreciate the properties and uses of different materials, the differences between metals and non-metals and how metals are extracted from their native ores. The integrating theme which provides the sequence with conceptual coherence is the reactivity series of metals. Although Ursula introduces the concept of 'reduction', for this group her principal aim is to consolidate the development of a relatively limited conceptual framework for their GCSE science, where the main idea is that important industrial and domestic materials are extracted from natural materials mined from the earth:

> 'My lesson objective is just one very small bit within my big picture but if I just go in and do one lesson on a one-off on iron, yes at the end of the lesson they perhaps could say it to me [i.e., that the iron comes from the Earth]. But actually in a week's time that will be gone. What I'm interested in is at the end of Year 10 and beyond these students have these concepts embedded. And therefore I need to keep returning to them to keep building and linking.'

A constant theme in Ursula's discussion of her practice is the notion of 'building and linking'. She refers to the big picture within which a broad range of concepts must fit. Her job is to help the students see how this jigsaw fits together. Students are reminded at every opportunity about what they have done before and how what they are doing now will prepare them for what comes next, as this short interchange illustrates:

> 'OK – this is out task for today – this follows on from the last lesson. It's all about [pause] . . . if you've got a metal that's joined up . . . you can take away the metal by "reducing" . . . [pause] . . . that's the key

idea from last lesson, "reducing the oxide". When we say "reduce", what do we do to the metal oxide? . . . When we reduce it? What do we do? What do we take away from the metal oxide?'

A student responds with, 'Oxygen!'

'Excellent! Oxygen. We are going to take away the oxygen from the metal, but only if it's less reactive than carbon – remember from our reactivity series?'

At this stage the questioning is led authoritatively by Ursula. She is well aware the students would not necessarily be able to recall the key ideas from the week before, so she wants to set the scene for this lesson by being absolutely clear about what they were learning then and what they are going to use today.

COMMENTARY

Integrative theme

The idea of having some kind of integrative theme running through the lesson, and/or sequence of lessons, is common to all the highly accomplished science teachers. In this case, the theme is the *reactivity series* which Ursula uses as a point of reference each time she gets the students to think about how easily a metal can be extracted from its ore.

Highly accomplished science teachers typically conceive their teaching of a topic from an holistic perspective which implies that they aim to achieve the learning goals through a series of lessons where each lesson plays a part but is not necessarily an end in itself. They tend to take an overview of the learning and work out what part in the whole each lesson will play. This way of conceiving the learning through a series of lessons, rather than a more atomistic approach, enables the teacher to link ideas, concepts and episodes to show students how they are related. Moreover, by having a clear longer-term conceptual framework comprising one or more integrative themes helps to ensure students get a sense of their progress and achievement. Have a look at Wynn and Wiggins (1997), *The five biggest ideas in science*, for more ideas about the big ideas (integrative themes) in science.

One way to do this is through concept mapping, a metacognitive process that allows you to map the learning territory, keep the 'big idea' in mind and determine what the key learning routes are. There are many articles and books on concept mapping. Perhaps the one to start with is Novak and Gowin's (1984) *Learning how to learn*, which explains the theoretical roots of concept mapping in cognitive psychology.

Getting off to a good start

All the highly accomplished science teachers had their various ways of establishing routines for their students. Often they called it 'training the students', a shorthand for getting the students accustomed to their expectations. Ursula is no different:

> 'At the start of the lesson, what I do with all my groups is put their books out. One of the things is that I teach in different rooms, so by the fact that I do this it means I don't have to make them learn a new seating plan. So it helps with how they adapt and what I tend to do is that I'll do two lessons to my seating plan and then they do one lesson where they choose where to sit. Today, I put them into their friendship groups so that they wouldn't decide to have a "moment" on me.'

Behind this is another principle of Ursula's approach. Apart from ensuring she knows all the students by name right from their first meeting, she wants to get to know them as individuals:

> 'Yes, I am interested in each of them and go on the basis that if I treat them as adults then we're going to treat each other with a certain level of respect and that's going to contribute to our classroom climate.'

Potentially a difficult group, these students responded positively to Ursula's relaxed and relatively informal conversational tone, either when she elicited their starting points through her questioning or as she circulated around the groups during the practical activity. At all times a strong sense of emotional support was there in the classroom so that students were unafraid to check their understanding about the concepts or about what they were supposed to do.

COMMENTARY

Science and special needs

Students with special educational needs have a right to a science education as much as any other students. The practical implications when the students themselves perhaps pose a health and/or safety risk to others for behavioural reasons means that beginning- and early-career teachers might well restrict what they might otherwise do. There will never be a strategy for all occasions. Ursula's approach in these circumstances, however, is to get to know the students well, aim to establish mutual respect and design activities that address their needs. Other highly accomplished science teachers adopt broadly similar approaches on the basis that if you do not know the students well, planning for them is almost impossible.

Most searches to find materials to support teaching in this area lead to the Inclusive Science and Special Educational Needs website (www.issen.org.uk). To understand more about how you might transform your knowledge for students with special educational needs, journals such as the *British Journal of Special Education* or the *British Journal of Support for Learning* often address issues in science (e.g., Bell 2002) that can provide theoretical support to actions in the classroom.

As soon as the students enter the room, Ursula is prepared for them and the starter activity is set out for them. In this case it is a simple activity designed to reinforce learning from a previous unit of work, but also to act as lead for this lesson's work.

Activity 1	Teacher thinking
Starter: assigning metals to objects in photographs.	'So the idea of getting the starter out is that as other students come in the task is up on the board, so I'm not going to have to repeat myself lots of times. Once I've got enough students in there I can just focus them towards that. So we have started anyway, but it means that they come in, we're going to start work.'
	'The starter I used was based on the idea of knowing the difference between metals and non-metals and from the previous module, where they had to do materials and their uses, they struggled in terms of being able to define them. They look at something and actually being able to find the material has been quite a challenge for them. So we were just having a very short practice on that, but some of the things are going to be made of iron so that gave a lead in for us for the lesson.'

Once the group is well underway with the activity, Ursula gives them a time limit and expected outcomes for the activity in order to make the transition to the next phase:

'The other thing I do is a lot of timings. So I'll say, "We'll spend two minutes on this," just trying to engender an idea that actually we haven't got too much time and we'll move on, to try and keep the pace.'

Once the given time has elapsed Ursula moves on with another routine that gets the students efficiently to the front:

'Right, could you please bring yourselves to the front. Not your books, just your body and chair.'

At this point in the VSR, Ursula stopped the tape to explain why she wanted to move the students and how she went about it with different groups:

'Because this group is so small it's easy just to say "Bring yourselves up" but certainly when I'm going to show them something or take them through something I want them up close and personal. So I think it's worth the potential risk of them wandering off in that transition moment to actually have them up near me. And it increases the interaction between us.

With a larger group, then I'll ask for them to come up one row at a time. If I've got three rows I'll bring up the second row and then the third will come and sit on the desks. So all of them get a different place to go to.'

Conceptual development

Once the students are settled at the front, Ursula establishes the conceptual background they need to make sense of the practical activity. However, she is realistic about what the students know and understand. She knows they know the words element, compound and mixture as labels, but not as a 'means of interpretation' (Sutton 1992). This practical activity, therefore, has the potential to provide concrete examples of all three concepts:

'Going back to their concept of atoms, elements and compounds it really doesn't exist, although they know the words and they can state definitions, but they don't really understand what's going on. So part of that observation is: "Do we really know that iron oxide is different to iron?" Actually, because they were able to observe and say, "Iron oxide isn't magnetic, whereas iron is," it's hopefully supporting them in their idea of compounds being different to elements.'

COMMENTARY

Language in science

So much of science for students is about learning terminology, new words, some of which seem familiar and many which do not. Students may use terms such as atom, element and compound, but as Sutton rightly points out, words, if they are only labels, will not be associated with any level of understanding. In *Words, science and learning* (1992) Sutton argues that if words are to have meaning then they should also be used by students as a means of interpretation. It is also worth looking at Sutton's chapter in the *International handbook of science education* (2003).

With these students, Ursula is very circumspect about making any assumptions regarding what they understand even when they use the correct word. Evidence of student understanding comes when students are able to use the words in different contexts or when they use them to contribute to explanations of other concepts or phenomena.

With this group, the aim of bringing the students to the front of the class is twofold, (1) to remind the students of the chemical principles underlying the extraction of copper which they had done the week before, and (2) to demonstrate the technique for the practical activity.

Activity 2	Teacher thinking
Demonstration.	'The definition of reduction we used last lesson was the idea that reduction is removal of oxygen. Each time we looked at an oxide we looked at how we were going to "take away" the oxygen and "add it" to the carbon. So a change I've made for this group is that with other groups we might look at things like carbonates. But with this group I stuck solely so that they could see it was an oxide just to keep that one factor as a constant . . . Here we're looking to reinforce from the last lesson "taking away" oxygen using carbon.'
	'Another thing about this group, because these students have communication difficulties, is that I do very few practicals with them where I give them a sheet of instructions. I tend to do a show and do.'

Ursula continues to remind the students of the events of the previous week in order to make clear connections with the practical activity today. Again she acknowledges that the students may not have understood the chemistry the first time around, but now she can stress the similarities, as this extract from the lesson transcript shows:

> 'This is what we're going to look at this lesson. We are going to look at the experiment with iron oxide. But before we do that, let's just remember last week's experiment. We're going to do something a bit similar. In last week's experiment we started off with copper oxide. Remember the experiment ... What's going to take away the oxygen?'
> [Pause]
>
> 'Carbon.'
>
> 'Carbon. We mixed it with the carbon, because the carbon is going to take away the oxygen. We heated it. What did we use to heat it in?'
>
> 'Test tube.'
>
> 'We used a test tube. OK. I want to do a similar experiment today, but iron is more reactive than copper. So is it going to be easier or harder [to take away the oxygen]?'
> [Pause]
>
> 'Harder.'
>
> 'It's going to be harder. So we've got to be a bit smarter this week, because last week it just worked.'

Carefully Ursula guides the students to where she wants them to be, but she is very conscious of the closed nature of the questioning and the danger that she is merely getting them to guess 'what's in the teacher's head'.

> '... they're really struggling here as they're desperately playing "Guess what the teacher's thinking".'

On the screen, Ursula projects further examples of reactions (word equations for the reduction of zinc oxide and tin oxide) that illustrate the chemical principle of 'reduction' and which reinforce the idea that it is possible to predict how difficult the reaction might be if you know where the elements lie within the reactivity series relative to carbon. Once she has established the pattern Ursula demonstrates and talks about the technique for carrying out the main practical activity, to be absolutely sure they know the operations they are going to be doing:

> 'So here's my set-up. Notice that I've got two Bunsens. I want twice as much heat this week. So, we are not going to use test tubes, because it's going to get too hot. So we are going to use these, these bottle tops. This is what we're going to heat it in. And we are going to heat it very, very strongly. First of all we are going to mix it [iron oxide and carbon powder in a test tube]. We're going to put the mixture in here [in the bottle top]. It's going on top of the gauze, and it's going to have another bottle top on top.'

Practical work
This is an illustrative activity designed to achieve the principal learning outcome. There is no investigative aspect. Its purpose is simply to provide students with a concrete model of metal extraction that shows that iron (an element all the students recognize) comes from a completely different material, an orange/red powder that they commonly call 'rust'. Ursula takes them 'back' to last week again.

Activity 3	Teacher thinking
Extracting iron from iron oxide.	'I really want to take them back to last week and see how much they remember and therefore how much we can build on because it is going to be a similar experiment. I really want them to get the idea of copper being really easy to extract and can they remember that moment when they found the copper bits.'
	'The bigger picture in this module "Reactivity" is just one aspect for this lesson, this idea of the extraction of iron. But that's building on all our concepts of depending on its reactivity, it's going to go through a reduction reaction and the only reason it can do this is because of the reactivity. So we're having to use those ideas but I want the students at this point in time at the end of this lesson to be able to say, "Iron comes from iron something"; iron oxide would be good and that's where we get this very important metal from. We know about iron. We know what it's used for. That's what I want them to get.'

In talking about her beliefs about how best to teach science, Ursula says that the incorporation of practical work is vital if students are going to remember their science. In this case the scheme of work did not specify any practical other than an activity to make a model of the blast furnace. Like all the other highly accomplished science teachers, Ursula interprets the scheme of work as a loose framework rather than a straitjacket. Given the nature of this group, Ursula thought it unlikely that a paper model would capture their interest and therefore looked for alternatives. An opportunity for students to heat something with two Bunsen burners had a much better chance of engaging them even if it was only for a few minutes. Once she had emphasized the various safety aspects and how to hold the base of the second Bunsen to direct its flame obliquely onto the bottle top covering the mixture, the students were underway.

COMMENTARY

Learning by doing

Both students and teachers valued participation in practical work. For the students it was the tag they used to remember things. For teachers it was part of the process of getting them involved. Students tended to associate doing things with learning. The highly accomplished science teachers, however, were far more sceptical. 'Learning by doing' is a phrase known to any teacher, but in science there is only limited evidence to suggest that doing results in learning. In fact, sometimes it can lead to confusion if its purpose is not absolutely clear to the student. We might remember Driver's (1991: 9) reinterpretation of the common aphorism, 'I do and I understand', often invoked in support of practical work, to 'I do and I am even more confused!'

Ursula makes it a priority to ensure that science is perceived by students as a practical activity. She is very aware of its potential to engage the students but, by the same token she is equally aware of its limitations. Science educators such as Derek Hodson and Jerry Wellington have written at length about the role of the practical and the extent to which it can promote learning in science. Hodson's article in *School Science Review*, 'A critical look at practical work in school science' (Hodson 1990: 33–40) is still an important reminder to think carefully about what we expect to achieve by asking students to do practical activities. In particular Hodson makes the point that we should be clear what we are trying to achieve. Are you intending the students to learn about science or learn about doing science? Wellington's book *Practical work in school science* (1998) provides a comprehensive review of practical work from a number of perspectives.

Even though the activity lasts only 15 minutes, it is Ursula's main opportunity to engage with the students. Her relaxed and informal conversational style enables her to be dialogic in her approach, getting the students to explain to her their ideas about what they think is happening to the mixture of powders between the bottle tops (Mortimer and Scott 2003). As she talks to them she uses the terminology in context, so concepts such as element, compound, mixture, reduction, reducing, reactivity series, more reactive, less reactive, energy, metal oxide, ore, metal, and so on, are all dropped into the classroom talk to encourage the students to use them too. As much as the purpose of the engagement is to teach, it is also to learn – to learn about what the students are learning:

> 'Something I try and do when I'm talking to the students is I tend to work completely through the questions but then [I do a] back up afterwards. I very rarely tell them a straight answer when they want help. I'll try and break down the question for them so that then they can get into it and build it up so we then get an answer; at that point I'll probably repeat their answer to them to make sure that we've really got the idea formulated. But I want them to think it through, even if they're stuck.'

Still keeping to clear time frames, Ursula identifies a specific outcome to signify the end of the practical activity and the start of a whole-group discussion. In this instance she wants the bottle tops to be left to cool and certain pieces of apparatus to be tidied away.

Consolidation

By bringing the students to the front once more Ursula signifies that she wants to share their observations and give them an opportunity to test the magnetic properties of the materials.

Activity 4	Teacher thinking
Testing the magnetic properties of the materials.	'To reiterate from earlier, there were several purposes to this activity. One is that I want the material to cool down, so I need them in their seats, not standing there waiting, but also we've got another chance to reiterate the concepts and contents of their observations. I haven't worried about writing out the experiment because that's not important.'

Earlier she had established with them (a 'heads-up', as she called it) that iron was a ferromagnetic material and therefore, if the extraction process works, then the presence of native iron should be detectable with a magnet. Ursula explains that as the bottle top is made of steel, which is also magnetic, the students need to transfer the cooled contents of the bottle top to a piece of paper and then move the magnet under the paper. The students are asked to predict what they would expect to see and are given a short worksheet to complete that summarizes the main learning points.

For the last few minutes, the students test the products of their practical activity for iron and Ursula takes a final opportunity to get around all the groups to commend them on their efforts and check once more what they have learned from the lesson in order to decide how to proceed in the next lesson. For Ursula this was assessment for learning in practice:

> 'I would say that when I started teaching and was first setting lesson aims and objectives the only thing I really was considering was actually how I was going to achieve that particular part. Now it's what they can say to me that I'm interested in and actually what is it they can say to me that they can then actually use and apply. At that point I know whether my teaching has been successful.'

The idea that what matters is what the students can say to Ursula is an important one to consider. According to the Hay McBer report (2000) this is what effective teachers do – they listen to students and they plan accordingly. Given the emphasis Ursula places on making links with previous work, getting a really good grasp of what's been achieved in this lesson is crucial for planning the next.

Ursula's background

Ursula entered the teaching profession straight from university after completing a degree in biology. While teaching she also undertook a further degree in physics. Within a short time, she took on the role of head of science in a challenging mixed comprehensive school. Ursula has been known to us for many years both as an expert teacher and a highly skilled mentor of trainee science teachers. Her abilities have been recognized by the Office for Standards in Education (Ofsted) who describe her lessons as inspiring and enthralling and by teacher training institutions because of her ability analyse and articulate her practice.

Ursula's beliefs and theories (personal philosophies) about science teaching
The philosophy underlying Ursula's practice is a complex mixture of beliefs, theories and values. Taken together they add up to a highly caring approach

that recognizes students as individuals who need to be motivated and encouraged to learn how to learn. In fact, some of Ursula's very early positive experiences of school shape the way she works with students. Influential teachers both at primary and secondary school demonstrated their interest in her and this is the approach she now emulates with her own students:

> 'When I was at secondary school, the teachers who influenced me most were the ones who took an interest in what I was doing and cared for me, and I think that's had a real impact on my decision on how I work with the students.'

Both from observing her practice and talking to her, it is clear that Ursula sees science as a practical subject which students learn best when they are doing it. Learning by doing, of course, is a common philosophy to which many science teachers would subscribe, but Ursula combines this with her desire to teach for understanding on the basis that without understanding the students will do no more than rote learn. This can be seen in the next extract where Ursula emphasizes the practical side of science, but then stresses the importance of developing the students' thinking skills:

> 'My lessons tend to be very, very practically based and for me most students, particularly low ability, who learn through doing as well, I include as many practicals as I can ... The practicals also give the students a real motivation factor because I want to do things which are fun because I want to maintain interest instead of pounding it into them. And I want the students to learn by thinking. It's changing now but so much science was "learn this bit, learn this fact, churn out this fact" ... But I want them to have as much understanding as possible so they can put it into context and really think it through.'

Ursula's professional knowledge

Ursula sees her role as one that should make science relevant to the students' own lives and believes that they should be learning science as a part of a being a citizen, but she also recognizes that students have exams to pass. She works hard to develop her own science knowledge to achieve this. However, her approach is not one of cramming them with knowledge/facts which she might just have acquired herself, but one which aims to lay a conceptual framework into which new knowledge can be incorporated over a period of time. To Ursula this is vital because it is the glue the will hold the sequence of lessons together:

> 'With this group I wanted to make it a lot more concrete for them so they were going to do the practical and my key point was this idea of

heating with carbon to extract iron. That's what I really wanted them to do, so I wanted that theme to run through the lesson with just that end point which I'm going to pick up on next lesson of the blast furnace and how it works. So I wanted to introduce the idea, but lots of little things to keep coming back to the process of reduction, not so much the word. I wanted the understanding there of what was going on in the system.'

Knowledge of, and knowledge about, the students is a determining factor for Ursula in deciding how to create the learning experiences for them. Ultimately she is flexible and prepared to take risks ('take a tangent', as she calls it) in order to enable them to learn and for her to learn as well (see Figure 5.2).

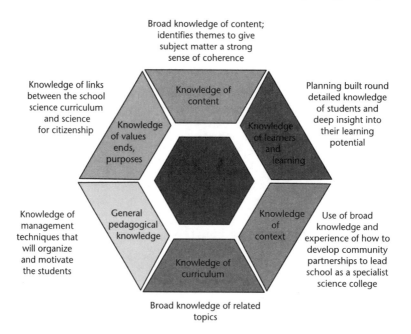

Figure 5.2 The 'spinning top' for Ursula's professional knowledge.

Section 3: Thalidomide, stereochemistry and how science works

The context

This is an upper set of 24 Year 10 (14–15 age group) students drawn from across the city in an 11–16 age band mixed Catholic comprehensive school in the UK. It is a well motivated group of students as they have opted for all three sciences rather than a combined programme and have also chosen to do an Advanced Subsidiary (AS level) in science for public understanding.

The lesson

This lesson is part of a series that introduces students to the effects of drugs on the human body. In this lesson the drug thalidomide (marketed as a sleeping pill called Distaval in the UK in the 1950s and 1960s) is used as a way of helping students engage with the processes involved in developing drugs before bringing them to the marketplace. Orla's principal aim is to help the students work through some of the issues involved in testing the safety of 'medicinal' drugs before they are advertised and sold on the open market. She is using this as an opportunity to address the 'How Science Works' requirements of the new GCSE syllabuses introduced in the UK in 2006.

Involvement

Fundamental to Orla's approach to teaching is a belief that she must 'get the students involved'. She begins by showing two images of babies suffering the teratogenic effects of thalidomide as a result of their mothers having taken Distaval as a treatment for morning sickness. Orla is well aware of the potential sensationalism of showing pictures of babies with such deformities but believes she has established relationships with this group that will allow her to explore the possible causes in such a way that the students will treat the topic sensitively.

Activity 1	Teacher thinking
Starter activity – capturing interest and getting some discussion going.	'I was a bit worried when I found that first photo, whether it would be too sensitive.'
	'I think I would definitely do that again, show the picture, not for the shock value, but I think it's enough to focus them, because they are quite shocking pictures, but it's enough to prompt them without giving them any more information. This class certainly came up with all the ideas without any prompting.'
	'In terms of general techniques it's something I'm certainly trying to do more of – get every child involved. Rather than saying, "There's a picture, hands up," I wanted them to have a bit of thinking time to come up with something and work in small groups and also for every group to feed something in, so they were all involved and not just Georgia, Ed and a couple of others who might tend to dominate.'

COMMENTARY

Engagement and involvement

Engagement (capturing the students' interest) is an important precursor to involvement where the latter implies that students are actively engaged in their own learning. Orla aims to have the students engaged, participating and contributing and thus involved. As she said in relation to the first activity, 'The idea was that everyone would have to engage and think about it in some way.' However, Orla does not think about 'engagement' or 'involvement' in isolation from the context. She creates the activities based on her sound knowledge of the students in the class, her knowledge of the environment and her knowledge of the resources and materials that are available to manipulate.

A way forward suggested by Gilbert (2006) in *Science education in schools: issues, evidence and proposals*, published by the ESRC-funded Teaching and Learning Research Programme, includes a specific reference to the 'engagement' of the students:

> More research, development, and teacher education are needed on how to increase students' engagement in science education. Priorities include classroom organisation, a changed approach to written work, and an increased focus on the on-task talk that is part of the core of learning science. There should be a strong emphasis on 'assessment for learning'.

Clearly the issues raised in this document are an important part of Orla's agenda for stimulating learning in her classroom and are evident in the practice of all the highly accomplished science teachers we observed.

Although having been a science teacher for over 15 years, more recently Orla has steadily tried to develop a framework for interaction in her classroom where discussion is the norm and where all students are encouraged to participate. Her framework aims to avoid a few vocal students dominating the talk and to prevent the less articulate students from feeling they could be setting themselves up to have their self-esteem or confidence undermined in full view of their peers:

> 'While you are sitting in your pairs I want you to – just look at the pictures – think about what caused this to happen to these children. Two minutes – just chat and then I'll ask you to feed back your responses. They are a little upsetting, these pictures. They are two babies.'

The introduction was very short, but this group is used to Orla's style and knows what is expected of them. Precisely two minutes later she says:

> 'OK That's two minutes. Let's go round and get a flavour from each group. Let's see what ideas you came up with. If you had lots of ideas, just give one so each group has a chance to add something.'

The students volunteer their ideas and Orla collects them on a white-board, praising them for their appropriateness. In our research it was clearly evident that these highly accomplished science teachers find ways to give all students opportunities to contribute, particularly by using strategies that give them time to think before the are expected to answer. Often highly accomplished science teachers use group work, or pairing, or some kind of sharing to give students time to consider their responses so that they do not feel threatened or exposed by the situation.

Orla goes on to present a little of the background history to the tragedy of thalidomide but encourages the students to intervene and ask questions along the way.

Learning framework

By offering a brief history of the inadequacies of the processes of drug development in the past, Orla gives the students a way into ask many more questions later in the lesson. She then switches to a PowerPoint slide (see Figure 5.3) showing the organizing framework for the lesson. This framework is important as it provides her with opportunities both to monitor learning as the lesson progresses and to evaluate her own teaching.

As a chemist, Orla recognizes possibilities to make links with other areas of the science curriculum that will follow next year and introduces the group to something of the chemistry of thalidomide. But she says, 'At this level, you don't need to know this depth of detail.'

- How many drugs are developed each year?

- How are they tested?

- What problems might there be when you are testing a new drug?

- How can we prevent those problems causing the tragedies we see here?

Figure 5.3 Learning framework.

Subject knowledge

Based on her knowledge of the group, Orla has made a decision to introduce some detail about the chemical structure of thalidomide even though she knows they would not need it. She switches to the molecular structure on screen and explains that the thalidomide molecule is one of two enantiomers and these molecules are non-super imposable mirror images of one another. One enantiomer, the (S) form is the active form, i.e., the teratogen. Unfortunately the inactive (R) form is readily converted in the liver to the active form. Orla believes it is important to provide the students with hooks or activities that they will remember which in turn will help them recall the science.

Orla said she introduced the information about the different isomeric forms of thalidomide as 'an interest thing'. Because she was confident she knew the aptitudes of the students, she felt this would play well with those that were stimulated by this kind of chemical knowledge:

> 'We could have covered the knowledge in ten minutes but they wouldn't necessarily have remembered it and understood why and they wouldn't have got the process. That's what it's about – broadening that part of it. Certainly with your average group I wouldn't have put this bit in, but several of these [students] are likely to go on to do science A levels and might see it in their lessons in the future and go "Oh yes, I remember that." '

However, knowing that not all might show the same enthusiasm, Orla devised a simple activity to provide a 'memory hook'. She reiterated that as long as they got the idea of the two forms, that was all she was after. The activity had two simple parts, one based on smell and the other on touch. Orla's reasoning was that she was appealing to the kinaesthetic learners, those learners who like to learn through a more hands-on approach, physically interacting with materials.

Activity 2	Teacher thinking
Exploring enantiomers: (a) smelling aromatic herbs, spearmint and caraway (S)- and (R)-carvone respectively, (b) trying to put a left-hand glove on the right hand and vice versa.	'There's no obvious practical with thalidomide! But I think I heard from a colleague that caraway and spearmint are enantiomers. So it's a little aside that is just of interest to them. Again I think that's important. More and more we're moving towards starters that have no linked lesson, which is an odd thing to do

Activity 2 (*cont*)	Teacher thinking
	. . . because you wonder if you're wasting time. If I want to get them to learn about this doing something different – but it's just the bigger picture again. Making a link!'
	'What a lot of kids will remember from that lesson are the gloves. If they're kinaesthetic learners that's what will stick in their heads.'
	'It sounds ridiculous trying gloves on, but it wasn't until they put the wrong glove on the wrong hand that I think they got the idea that they're structurally the same. I think that did get the point across well. I'm pleased with that model which was fairly simple but it worked really well.'

Modelling

Orla saw this practical approach as a kind of modelling which 'gets the idea into their heads much better'. Unlike a letter 'A' for example where the mirror image can be superimposed on the original, a left hand glove cannot be fitted (comfortably) on a right hand, i.e., it is non-superimposable. Orla recognized the apparently trivial nature of the idea but:

> 'It's that practical demonstration – not for every type of learner, but I would say the majority. If they can see something in action, they will understand that better and remember it better than if they'd just been told. I would say my ideal way, if possible, is to have a model that they then explain. For most kids that's the ideal.'

This episode reveals something of Orla's underlying beliefs. As she pointed out, she could of course have simply provided the information, but she decided to go to some length to break up the lesson and provide opportunities for more open and relaxed discussion about the nature (stereochemistry) of the thalidomide molecule (see Figure 5.4). This is all part of her broader strategy for enabling students to create a mental framework needed for the location and retention of new knowledge. Before we say more about this, we continue with a little more of the lesson.

While the students are smelling the herbs, and trying to guess what the

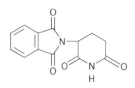

Figure 5.4 Thalidomide molecule.

caraway seeds are, Orla moves between the groups. The interaction is inter-active/dialogic (Scott and Mortimer 2006) in nature, giving the students an opportunity to ask the questions they have been thinking about for the last 20 minutes or so, and to enable Orla to ask her own. Her questions are more targeted to exploit her knowledge of the students and to attend to their particular interests and characteristics. In this way she continues to ensure they are actively engaged in thinking about the issues the story of thalidomide has raised with regard to the safeguards built into drug development. This also enables her to draw out aspects of the way science works.

COMMENTARY
Assessment for learning

Creating opportunities within lessons to interact with the students is fundamental to the practice of all highly accomplished science teachers. For Orla it enables her to make judgements about the quality of the students' learning. Based on her knowledge of the students' abilities, aptitudes and personalities, Orla uses open-ended questions of the type that invite students to reveal their thinking about the nature of science. Her interactive approach welcomes students' alternative ideas which she explores with them. Such interaction is genuinely dialogic (see Mortimer and Scott 2003; Scott and Mortimer 2006). But not only does it help Orla with gauging where the students are in their learning, it also allows her to use it as a yardstick to assess the effectiveness of her teaching.

For more ideas on approaches to assessment for learning we suggest you explore the 'Inside the Black Box' series of booklets published by the NFER and Marshall *et al.*'s (2005) booklet, *Science inside the black box*, which outlines and explores a range of techniques designed to promote assessment for learning in science. Additionally, the chapter on formative assessment by Black and Harrison in *Good practice in science teaching* (2000) also sets out the principles of formative assessment and offers a range of ideas and strategies on how to learn from your students.

Active processing

From the outset of the lesson, Orla was insistent that if the students wrote anything down, it should be brief and focus only on what was important. Of course, for many students deciding what is important is a major challenge. As a result many tend to scribble down everything, with no attempt to be selective. During the VSR, Orla identified that 'training' her students to acquire this transferable skill of learning how to learn is one of her underlying educational goals:

> 'With this class I'm trying to instil note-making into them, not very successfully so far! They're terrible copiers. A piece of information and they want to try and write it all down. I'm trying to develop this skill of picking out key points because the sixth-form college that most of them go on to say that their study skills are generally awful. They're spoon fed. So I don't want to just give them a worksheet, but also I don't want them to write everything down.'

Orla does not see any value in dictating notes to students, or other approaches that do not involve them in any thinking (i.e., 'active processing'). During the lesson she gave the students pointers about significant events in the thalidomide story, but also used their questions to help them make bullet points in their notes:

> 'Well I think in terms of their learning they need to be "active" in some way. Very few will just hear it and remember it, so they need to do something to embed it. If they're just writing and scribbling so frantically they might as well not bother. They're not thinking about it. If they can go through the thought process of reading the slide, picking out what's important and writing that, that's going to embed in their brain much better than copying all the facts or not writing anything down.'

COMMENTARY

Active processing

A characteristic of all highly accomplished science teachers is the emphasis they place on students 'doing something more with the knowledge' and 'getting them to think more for themselves rather than getting me to do it for them'. As another highly accomplished science teacher said, 'The processing is when they properly internalize it.'

The term 'active learner' is one commonly used to represent this idea, but the evidence we have suggests that for highly accomplished science teachers 'active processing' requires a level of intellectual engagement which they support through the activities they design for the students in the way that Orla does. Put another way, it is one thing to have a philosophy of 'students being active learners', but it is another to provide the students with the means to be active in their learning.

Duit and Treagust's chapter, 'Learning in science – from behaviourism to social constructivism and beyond' (2003) in the *International handbook of science education* provides a thorough review of learning theory and the concept of 'being active', and how this idea might be understood and translated into practice. Richard White's (1993) classic book *Learning science* offers a psychological model for science learning, and provides a theoretical rationale for what these teachers are doing.

Maintaining the intellectual challenge

Orla is not intending to leave the students without 'hard' information to work from, so towards the end of the lesson she distributes a facts and figures sheet about drug development and testing and gives them some relevant newspaper articles to scan. Orla worked hard to locate appropriate articles. The thinking behind this is that matching the material to the strengths and abilities of the students will maintain their involvement. Talking later to the students they commented on what impresses them:

> 'Well you can tell when a teacher likes what they're teaching and when they don't. You can tell when a teacher is interested. I don't know what it is about them but they get into their subject.'

> 'They get really happy . . .'

> 'Enthusiastic.'

> 'Yes.'

> 'They're genuinely interested in it, rather than just doing it just to teach.'

It is perhaps not surprising that these highly accomplished science teachers appreciate the perceptivity of their students and that just as they try to read their students, they know the students are also trying to read them. Hence it would be really exceptional for one of these science teachers ever to pull the rug from under their own feet by apologizing for an apparently boring bit of physics or biology. They know they are going to be onto a loser if they sell the students short. So they 'make the effort'.

Monitoring learning

Orla has a simple activity based on the initial learning framework that she uses to draw the lesson together. In fact she admits it is something of a compromise in that it recognizes what will be assessed at GCSE. As the awarding body (examination board) expects students to know something of the timeline associated with the introduction of Distaval and its effects, Orla created a simple 'cut and stick' exercise involving a series of factual statements that had to be reassembled into chronological sequence. The activity required some deductive thought on the part of the students in that they had to use the information they had gathered through the lesson to be able to make judgements about the chronological positions of the statements. Although not ideal, it did mean that Orla could make some judgement about the quality of the learning taking place in relation to the organizing framework.

Activity 3	**Teacher thinking**
Cut and stick exercise to monitor learning.	'The learning objective isn't just thalidomide, but much more globally what was learned from that and I suppose I should have done a bigger plenary to come back to that slide again and those four bullet points and say "Have we done that? Are you happy now that you know a bit more about the scale of it? The number of drugs that go into testing and how they get tested and how they come out the other end?" I think they did get that.'

Orla was not complacent about the evidence for learning but felt on reflection that perhaps she could have done more to assess the extent of the learning. She was satisfied with the limited information gained from the 'cut and stick' exercise, but took greater pleasure from the positive attitudes the students displayed both as a group and individually to the issues raised:

> 'I was pleased. They showed an interest throughout. And from what they said they were taking it all on board and were happy. Certainly all the ones who did the cut and stick exercise got it completely right. So yes, I would feel content with that. There are bits I might tweak and add or take away. But I was happy with that.'

Orla's background

Orla comes from a teaching background. At school she was inspired by a chemistry teacher who 'just explained things so well'. For some years she has been heading up a very successful science department. She is committed to involvement in pre-service education and enjoys working with and supporting beginning science teachers. Orla was recommended to us as an exemplary practitioner by fellow science educators working in the local authority.

Orla's beliefs and theories (personal philosophies) about science teaching

The concept of the students being 'active' is central to Orla's philosophy of how students learn. The term 'active' does not simply mean 'hands-on' (particularly as all too often 'hands-on' can be synonymous with 'minds-off'), it means cognitive engagement where the products of one aspect of the work have to be translated or transformed intellectually by the students into other forms that can be used as indicators of the extent to which learning may have occurred.

A second aspect of Orla's practice that underlines her approach to teaching is the action she takes to establish effective relationships with the students:

> 'The best teachers engage with children. And where I see poor quality teaching, it's usually not actually the subject, it's just that the teacher doesn't form the relationships that are essential. Within science teaching I suppose it's a similar thing about engagement. There has to be a point of interest that you grab and it's different.'

One further dimension of her philosophy is her belief in ensuring the students appreciate the purpose of their learning. In other words, if they have to ask the question, 'Why are we doing this?' she knows she needs a rethink:

> 'That group . . . this morning are obviously able children, articulate and fairly interested, but even with them, if I just went in and said, "We're going to do atomic structure and there it is on a piece of paper" you wouldn't grab them. There has to be that link as to why they're learning it, why it's important, why [they should] bother.'

Orla's professional knowledge

Since Orla has been teaching science she has built up a wealth of professional knowledge relating to the subject matter. However, this knowledge base has been developed through her own efforts rather than any strategic approach to professional development offered through the profession itself. With regard to centrally provided CPD, she rather pithily noted its generic orientation:

'. . . we did a large section on behaviour for learning in science. I don't want to know about behaviour for learning in science, I want to know about science!'

The lack of science subject specific CPD has been a criticism of the provision of professional development for some years (see Roberts 2002). Orla therefore spends some considerable time undertaking her own independent research rather than relying on anything supplied as a standard resource within a scheme of work or any commercial source:

'Most weekends, if I see anything that looks relevant, anything to do with science – sometimes as a starter, I'll just bring in the Sunday paper and say, "Right, take a page each and find something to do with science on there." And do it really wide. But with this it seems so obvious that there's bound to be something relevant. So I cut them straight out [articles on thalidomide] and laminated them and copied them for the class. But I keep my own library of anything looking useful. These are all recent articles.'

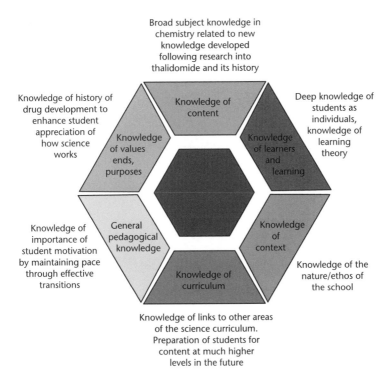

Broad subject knowledge in chemistry related to new knowledge developed following research into thalidomide and its history

Knowledge of history of drug development to enhance student appreciation of how science works

Deep knowledge of students as individuals, knowledge of learning theory

Knowledge of content

Knowledge of values ends, purposes

Knowledge of learners and learning

Knowledge of importance of student motivation by maintaining pace through effective transitions

General pedagogical knowledge

Knowledge of curriculum

Knowledge of context

Knowledge of the nature/ethos of the school

Knowledge of links to other areas of the science curriculum. Preparation of students for content at much higher levels in the future

Figure 5.5   The 'spinning top' for Orla's professional knowledge.

Coupled with some generic professional development activities, Orla sees her professional learning occurring largely as a consequence of her commitment to reflective practice. With a philosophy underpinned by a value system that centres on helping students to learn how to learn, her transformation of subject matter results in lessons designed to involve the students. We might refer to this, like Cochran *et al.* (1993) as 'PCKnowing' because what we see is Orla engaged in a process that involves her drawing on and combining aspects of these various knowledge bases (see Figure 5.5).

6   The nature of science

What do we mean by the 'nature of science'?

In Chapter 3 we considered Alison's scientific inquiry lesson which was designed to 'go wrong'. She set up a simple investigation on floating and sinking where the students were asked to find out how the amount of salt dissolved in a beaker of water would affect the time a piece of Plasticine would take to sink. This was nicely set up in the context of the commonplace observation that it is easier for a person to float in the Dead Sea than in ordinary sea water or indeed in fresh water. The suggestion was made that this could possibly be to do with the amount of salt in the water and that was what the students were to investigate – 'Do things sink quicker in fresh water rather than salt water?' The students were in Year 10 (14–15-years-olds) and would have had previous experience of relatively simple investigations like this where they were asked to plan and carry out an investigation – generating hypotheses, identifying and controlling variables, taking measurements and drawing conclusions. They were certainly familiar with the idea of 'fair testing' which is part of work in this area at younger ages from primary school.

However, in this investigation, by subtly but deliberately restricting the equipment available, the students were unable to get reliable, and therefore valid, results because the beaker was not tall enough. What was the teacher doing here? She did tell them at the outset:

> '. . . remember that we are always checking on the validity, the reliability, the accuracy, the precision and any sources of errors in your experiment'.

But she gave no hint that they might have problems. It might have been a high-risk strategy, leading to the students becoming frustrated and even annoyed that they had wasted their time on a pointless experiment. Alison handled this skilfully to show them that there was a point and that, in future investigations, they could apply their learning. Alison had planned to get the students to think like scientists – to face the same issues real scientists face in their research to ensure that their measurements are accurate and precise, and to consider sources of error so that results (and the conclusions drawn from them) are reliable and valid. The aim of the lesson was to give some insight into the 'nature of science' – the essence of the subject itself, what characterizes science both as an intellectual pursuit and an important part of our culture.

Robin Millar's paper on 'Towards a science curriculum for public understanding' (1996) endorsed the importance of the school curriculum addressing this area so as to meet aspirations for students becoming scientifically literate. It is not just a question of them knowing about science, but knowing science itself – this is what we (and others) mean by the 'nature of science'. Millar's paper and the subsequent *'Beyond 2000'* report (Millar and Osborne 1998) laid the foundations for the latest version of science in the National Curriculum (certainly as far as secondary schools are concerned) and it now incorporates some elements of the nature of science, which we will consider in this chapter.

The extent that it is possible in school to incorporate this aspect of learning in science has been hotly debated but let us examine for a moment how the nature of science has been dealt with in the school science curriculum. The introduction of the attainment target known as 'Sc1' – 'Science Investigations' – in the National Curriculum goes back to the first version in 1989. Prior to that time, practical work had often been seen in terms of the development of experimental skills but less frequently in putting those together into whole inquiries. The inclusion of Sc1, as a defined area of the curriculum both in terms of teaching and assessment, was a distinctive feature of the new (as it was then) National Curriculum for Science. The model for investigations underpinning Sc1 was based on that used by the Assessment for Performance Unit (APU) for assessing practical work in science through national surveys in the 1980s, and has been criticized for representing a rather stereotyped view of how scientists *really* work and how scientific knowledge is generated. Putting that issue on one side for the moment, the significance of the inclusion of this area within the National Curriculum was that, for the first time, something had been done to attempt to link 'school science' with 'real science' in terms of presenting a model for students in school of what happens in university, industry and research laboratories – to give them a taste of what it is like to be a scientist.

Teachers who were around at the time will remember that the first version of the National Curriculum had 17 attainment targets. We have already mentioned Sc1 but Sc17 was significant here. Sc17 was entitled 'The Nature of Science' and was intended to provide young people in school with further insights into the world of science not only in the present but by looking at the development of scientific ideas in the past and how they influence our thinking today. In effect, Sc1 and Sc17 provided an introductory course in the history and philosophy of science and there was a lot of debate at the time (and has been since) about how appropriate it was and how it should be taught. With the rationalization of the National Curriculum in 1992 and a further reduction of the number of attainment targets from 17 to 4, Sc17 disappeared as a distinct entity and it is interesting to see it rising phoenix-like from the ashes in the latest GCSE courses as what is now called 'How Science Works' (see below).

This is a brief account of how the 'nature of science' became part of the National Curriculum. It is not just an issue in the UK – attempts have been made worldwide to introduce elements of the nature of science into the school curriculum. It is not a new issue either: Derek Hodson, writing in 1991, reminded us that John Dewey had said, as far back as 1916, that understanding scientific method was more important than acquiring scientific knowledge. Anyone wishing to read more about the nature of science in science education should read the excellent book edited by William McComas (1998) which reviews a wide range of 'rationales and strategies'. It is not our purpose to explore these in detail here but it might be helpful to list what McComas *et al.* (1998) present as being a consensus view of what it might be desirable for students to know about the nature of science, drawing on eight science standards documents from around the world:

1 Scientific knowledge, while durable, has a tentative character.
2 Scientific knowledge relies heavily, but not entirely, on observation, experimental evidence, rational arguments and scepticism.
3 There is no one way to do science (therefore, there is no universal step by step scientific method).
4 Science is an attempt to explain natural phenomena.
5 Laws and theories serve different roles in science, therefore students should note that theories do not become laws even with additional evidence.
6 People from all cultures contribute to science.
7 New knowledge must be reported clearly and openly.
8 Scientists require accurate record-keeping, peer review and replicability.
9 Observations are theory-laden.
10 Scientists are creative.
11 The history of science reveals both an evolutionary and revolutionary character.
12 Science is part of social or cultural traditions.
13 Science and technology impact each other.
14 Scientific ideas are affected by their social and historical milieu.

Even if we accept this list of objectives, there are still some big questions about when and how these different things might be addressed in both the school curriculum for students and in the teacher training curriculum for teachers. We will now go on to examine to what extent we believe teachers have engaged with the nature of science and these issues concerning the history and philosophy of science.

The impact of beliefs about the nature of science on teacher thinking

It is our experience that few science teachers, certainly in the UK, receive any notable instruction in the nature of science either as part of undergraduate science degrees or in their postgraduate teacher training, where time for such things is lamentably short. Even those who have continued from undergraduate studies to postgraduate research degrees in science are unlikely to have studied 'scientific method' as distinct from using it. For many, the uses of the terms 'hypothesis', 'theory' and 'law' will have developed tacitly through their teaching experience (particularly with Sc1) rather than though a more explicit exposure to the ideas which McComas and others have suggested are key points of agreement about what it is desirable for students to know, as listed above. Terms like 'inductivism' or 'positivism', or 'the hypothetico-deductive approach' are likely to be unfamiliar to most teachers who have not studied the history or philosophy of science.

Nancy Brickhouse (1990) suggested that science teachers who are consistent in their beliefs about the nature of science are consistent in their approaches to classroom instruction and that, in effect, their belief systems are important factors in determining how they teach. Most other research (e.g., Lederman 1992) has yielded broadly similar findings. We believe that science teachers' syntactical knowledge of the way science works (i.e., their grasp of how science knowledge is constructed) will shape their reasoning and decision-making and thus their approaches to transforming what they know into activities and learning experiences for students.

Individual teachers will have constructed their own implicit theories about how science works and about the nature of science from their own experience of science through study and research, and through their experience of teaching. Thus, students moving from teacher to teacher through their school careers could experience quite different and potentially conflicting images of science and how it works. This might be particularly evident in teachers' varying approaches to conducting scientific inquiries which may be inconsistent and contradictory according to the particular belief system they hold.

Even with our highly accomplished science teachers, only one had engaged in any formal study about the nature of science through courses or other exposure to ideas about the philosophy or history of science. Their knowledge base about science in terms of content knowledge was very strong but, for many, the demands of the new science courses they were being asked to teach raised issues about their own knowledge in this area. We would now like to go back briefly to three of these teachers to see how both explicit learning about the nature of science and implicit theories influence their practice.

Eric and models

Like most science teachers, Eric had received little instruction in the history, philosophy or nature of science. As a beginning teacher he would accept that his views were naïve. But over the years the combination of his reading and experience caused him to change and develop his understanding. His views on the nature of science led to some significant changes in his practice. Nowadays he is much more circumspect about leaving the students with the impression that the knowledge science produces is certain.

Eric's explanation about his use of models give us some deep insights into his grasp of the nature of science. He took an instrumentalist perspective and made it clear to students that a model could be used merely as a device to aid understanding. In other words, he was not suggesting to them that the model was representing reality or some version of the truth. Coupled with his depth of subject knowledge and his knowledge of the students, this approach allowed Eric to take them on a journey of discovery, whetting their appetite and giving them an intellectual challenge.

Central to the lesson, featured in Chapter 3, was the use of a model to simulate the process of radioactive decay. Eric was very clear about the limitations and dangers of using his model. As someone involved in teacher training he had seen how the use of models can create more difficulties than it is intended to solve. During the VSR following the lesson Eric pointed out:

> 'You don't want to be in the position where the model is so confusing that it takes away from the idea you're trying to teach in the first place. I've seen several trainee teachers trying to teach electricity with series and parallel circuits, passing sweets around the room. And the model is so complicated that actually it doesn't help the pupils at all. They don't know what's going on. So I've talked to trainee teachers about only using the model up to a point and then simply abandoning it. Don't try and stretch the point too far because it's not going to help the students at all, and they'll actually end up with misconceptions of the model itself. I think I thought very carefully about this radioactivity model and that it wouldn't do any of those things. I don't think there were any pupils in the room who seriously believed that there were arms and legs throwing out little bits of nucleus. So it wasn't confusing in that sense but I have seen models that can confuse the issue.'

Compared with when he started out as science teacher, Eric had substantially developed his knowledge and awareness of the practice of using models as aids in the learning of science. As he said in the pre-lesson discussion:

> 'I think when I started teaching I felt science was fact and that everything I read was the truth. I was quite happy to go along with that philosophy and teach it to pupils. I've read about this, I've got quite a bit of evidence here and this is the fact of the matter and I'm telling you this is fact.'

We suspect the awareness of our highly accomplished science teachers of issues concerning the nature of science knowledge (i.e., epistemological issues) is somewhat greater than most science teachers, given the extent to which they indicated how it influenced their decision-making. In this excerpt Eric had stopped the tape and described how he uses the planetary model of the atom with the 14–16 age group:

> 'The theory is developing and still is and so I made a decision at that point also to go way beyond GCSE and start talking about quarks, even though there's no need for them to know it from the point of view of the syllabus. But I think there's every reason for needing to know it from the point of view that the model they have in front of them at the end of GCSE is not the final model. And it's simply that . . . it's a model to help our understanding and is not the definitive view of the atom. It's not the Sun with some planets orbiting around it. It's not that at all. We don't know that at all but here's an idea that will help us to understand it and that model is still being developed.'

We discussed conceptions of models and modelling earlier (see p. 34). The use of models has featured in many of the lessons considered in this book. It is perhaps one of the characteristics of highly accomplished teachers that they see the value of using them in terms of supporting students' learning, even if their understanding of theoretical frameworks for modelling in science is more limited. These teachers think carefully about the models they use, understand their different purposes and, importantly, their strengths and limitations.

Emma and 'right answers'

Emma's lesson and the associated VSR offers an insight into her views about the nature of science. Within the modelling process she is using, Emma helps students develop their attitudes towards science. One message in particular is that science knowledge is constructed in the scientific community:

'If you've led them the right way and there aren't any misconceptions there they'll have modified their model so that it does fit with what the accepted reality is in the scientific community and then when they get their SATs [national tests] question they'll go, "Right, I'm not 100 per cent sure but I'll go back to what I know and I'll be able to build up a model to answer this question." '

Another attitude she fosters is one that suggests that the science knowledge is not always certain, i.e., that in science there is not necessarily always a right answer (as opposed to a range of possible alternatives) when it comes to explaining things. When talking about her views on the nature of science, Emma alluded to the previous lesson where the students were conducting food tests:

'There were two or three groups that hadn't got the "right" [expected] results and we spent as much time probably discussing that and coming up with reasons why one group may have got different results to everybody else than we did about the food test. Quite often though the students will say, "Well if everybody got this and they didn't then it must be wrong," and I say, "Well you don't know 100 per cent." '

Highly accomplished science teachers are circumspect about conveying an image of science that suggests that it produces a fixed body of knowledge. They tend to shift the focus to the evidence and make the case with the students that more reliable, statements can only be made as the science is better understood.

Iain and scientific inquiry

Some indications of Iain's views, of the nature of science, came through clearly in the VSR as he reflected on the restrictive nature of the way that some of the scientific inquiry work was being driven by assessment demands. He also alluded to his use of models and analogies and how they helped to develop students' understanding of theory.

Investigative work is one area Iain believes students can do authentically and achieve ownership over. But he sees a tension between inquiry that sets the students a problem where they have little theoretical background, and inquiry that utilizes, for example, a more conventional hypothetical-deductive approach:

'One of the big problems we have ... because if you go for a very novel investigation then they have very little they can draw upon for their hypothesis but if you do something like the enzymes they have

> lots of theoretical knowledge which they can draw on to give them a
> very good hypothesis which they can then test.'

In fact, Iain argues for a skills-based approach for the earlier age groups so
that more complex inquiries are then not thwarted by the students' failure to
display the appropriate manipulative and intellectual skills necessary to take
on more sophisticated and authentic inquiries.

Although Iain bemoans his inability to come up with a wide variety of
analogies to illustrate his explanations, he believes implicitly in their value in
providing a 'window' on the idea or concept. When it comes to models, however, he stresses their importance in helping the students visualize what is
going on in scientific processes:

> 'Physical models – things I would use a lot are very, very simple
> models for sometimes quite difficult concepts. Things like enzymes – I
> would get a big blob of Blu-tack to get a three dimensional blob and
> push a couple of things into the surface to form the active site and
> have the enzyme with the substrate molecule. Something as simple as
> that has actually helped them visualize what's going on. Or a perfect
> example is copper wire. They find the level of organization of protein
> structure difficult, so I would get a piece of wire and just mark it with
> different colours to represent amino acids and wrap it around a pencil
> to show secondary structures and folding it for tertiary structures. A
> very simple model, but I think it gives them a better understanding
> than showing them some of the three dimensional reconstructions of
> molecules.'

All three teachers touch on elements in McComas' list although it certainly could not be said to be a guiding framework. It is possible to see items 1,
2, 3 and 12 in these brief examples.

How implicit theories influence practice

In other interviews with teachers, some of the objectives came through clearly
in the way they talked about scientific inquiry. For example, objective 1 in
McComas' list about the tentative and provisional nature of scientific knowledge was quite frequent:

> 'I think when I started teaching I felt science was fact and that every-
> thing I read was the truth. I was quite happy to go along with that
> philosophy and teach it to pupils.'

'The fact that it's probably a "best guess" at explaining phenomena around us as opposed to "this is what somebody has said so I'm going to go along with that because it makes sense to me" . . . it's something that is mutable and can change and it does quite often.'

This teacher presented a view especially related to the new GCSE courses:

'I think if you look at the How Science Works section in the new GCSE specifications, as well as the substantive knowledge, there's a whole section which is how science works, definitions if you like, and the last paragraph of that is basically [to] say we don't know all the answers. We have ideas based on evidence, but that's all they are. They're not proven facts about many things and with a lot of things we haven't even got that. It's important that kids know that.'

Moving on to objective 2, this is more about the systematic approach and rational argument. There were several examples here but then this is a message that has permeated practical science in the UK for the last 15 years:

'These sorts of arguments you have with kids who aren't used in the science classroom to not getting something right or wrong. It's either right or wrong and I think we need to encourage kids that it's not about right or wrong. It's about backing up your opinions with evidence and reasons.'

'It's not about just following instructions or getting them to think up experiments, but more about planning and getting precise and reliable results and about what to do with those results once they've got them.'

'. . . relating that to the science theory you're trying to get across, but then evaluating what it was about that experiment that possibly could have gone wrong.'

There was some recognition that the way things are done in school perhaps cannot mirror 'real world' science because of assessment pressures:

'What we've been teaching in school is "These are hoops you have to jump through in a specific way in order to get the marks" which obviously is not the way in universities and other establishments as how it would be done.'

The theory-laden nature of observation in objective 9 and the problems it can cause was recognized by one teacher:

'If they don't have some idea of what it is they're actually looking for then they struggle to find it. I would have done a similar thing this year with stomata with the fifth form and having put up the slide that showed a number of stomata and guard cells and so on they immediately found it.'

Seeing science as part of social or cultural traditions in objective 12 was mentioned by two teachers:

'I think when we did microscopes last week, the one that I think that really amazes them is the electron microscope and to think that it's only been about for 55, 60 years and the changes in biology over the last 60 years as a result of someone just developing this very sophisticated microscope.'

'But I think in the case of Pasteur and the discovery of penicillin you certainly see a human side to that and the Jenner one, they see a human side to that in their decision-making and the dilemma and ethics and I think there's a lot more mileage in that one.'

Another teacher recognized the religious and spiritual dimension of teaching science in a denominational school:

'. . . as a Catholic school we spend a great deal of time on RE [religious education], which is compulsory, and there are ethical and philosophical concepts. The idea that some things you develop your belief on and you learn a fact about it. It's very much developing your own opinions and that's part of being a scientist and a human being.'

Following on from this, objective 13 emphasizes the relationship between science and technology:

'. . . but with ammonia and the Haber process, for example, I point out that Haber was trying to do it for the good of mankind in artificial fertilizers and everything. And then he also kept on wanting to extend his knowledge and found that it could be used for explosives. So what was good science became what you might call bad science. Who was to blame? Haber? The German government? So I start bringing things in like that.'

Finally, objective 14 is about how scientific ideas are affected by the social and cultural context which this teacher saw in terms of the history of science:

'I read a lot about the history of science, in which I'm very interested, about how science ideas have developed over centuries, and I try and bring those ideas into my lessons as much as I can.'

Another teacher recognized the potential opportunity to make links between science and other subjects in the curriculum:

'I was there thinking, "Am I doing a history lesson?" This is the "How Science Works" bit, which is making a very big impact. I'm pleased with that. In the past, if you tried and do anything cross-curricular you'd have been put off but I do think they're going to understand better why it was an issue if they know the steps that happened. Halfway through doing this I was thinking, "Gosh, how much science have I done yet?" So should I be moving on to do a bit more? But I think this is important. It is how science works and it's the key bit.'

This leaves quite a few gaps. There was little evidence, for example, of scientists being creative (objective 10) or the communication of science (objectives 7 and 8).

There were some aspects which, while not included in Bill McComas' list, reflect teachers' beliefs and understandings about the nature of science. This teacher believes that science produces knowledge, but that science cannot necessarily give uncontested answers on social controversies. He is more tentative about using science to generate definitive statements:

'I think whenever you're dealing with a controversial issue or something that needs discussion and debate I think we have to get the kids to understand that it's not about right and wrong, but about opinion and based on evidence. And I had a heated discussion with a fellow teacher not a million miles away in the school on a CPD day I was delivering about controversial issues, who was of the opinion that unless the children knew as much science as he does their opinion wasn't as worthy as his and he believed that 100 per cent. How can you formulate an opinion about something if you don't know all the facts?'

In another instance, there was an allusion to scientists being human and that the way they work is not the systematic process it is sometimes thought to be – sometimes science can be 'messy'.

At several points in this book, we have discussed the use of different sorts of models and of the process of modelling. Despite the lack of formal exposure to ideas about the nature of science, teachers have been exposed to the use of models in their own learning and are keen to develop their own models to enhance their power in helping their students learning. They need, however, to cope with the potential problems when their students find out that models used in earlier years of schooling are modified or replaced later.

Concrete, formulaic and mathematical models all need to be introduced and used sensitively. They are important devices in science to express and test relationships and describe phenomena. We suggest that their importance perhaps justifies the understanding of them (not just their use) to be included in any list of objectives in learning about the nature of science for both students and teachers.

The nature of science and the curriculum

We have already mentioned, in the teacher accounts, how a new way of describing scientific inquiry which attempts to incorporate something about the nature of science that has come into being in GCSE courses for 14–16-year-old students and is likely to feature in the curriculum for younger students in due course. The criteria for these GCSE courses, issued by the Qualifications and Curriculum Authority (QCA), provide a framework that those bodies responsible for developing examinations must conform to in designing their syllabuses (now called specifications). The section of the criteria called 'How Science Works' includes, as well as something about practical and inquiry skills for planning and carrying out investigations, a consideration of data, evidence and theories, and something about how scientific knowledge is developed and validated. At the centre of these criteria is the procedural understanding that we have referred to elsewhere in this book (see pp. 44–53), focused towards the use of evidence and making judgements. This is supported by recent research (Gott and Duggan 2003) and, although the term itself has not been used, by work on 'argumentation' which we mentioned in an earlier chapter (see p. 68).

Although many elements from the McComas list are present in these criteria, there are some that are missing. For example, although there is a recognition of the role of the scientific community in validating scientific knowledge, there is nothing explicit about the cultural context in which that community operates or the contribution of other cultures to the development of scientific ideas in the past or in the present. What sort of image of science is being presented to students and how adequate is it? Perhaps the greatest weakness is the treatment of methodological issues. While those writing about the philosophy of science might see a variety of different ways in which scientific knowledge is generated, the QCA criteria (or more specifically the examination specifications produced to conform to them) present a rather prescriptive view of how science works – one which, through its treatment of experimental design and variables is still perhaps more suited to the physical sciences than the biological and environmental sciences. However, the QCA list itself is a significant improvement on what it replaced and does present a more comprehensive picture of both science itself and its relationship to its socio-economic and technological context.

Developing teachers' and students' understanding of the nature of science

Our standpoint would be that in order for students to develop even a basic understanding of the sort of aspects we have described above and which are now part of the curriculum, teachers need to develop their understanding to a deeper level. Curriculum and examination changes are important but without teachers having a more sophisticated perspective their impact will be limited and there is even the danger of a false or partial picture being presented. Even our highly accomplished science teachers recognized this as an area for their own professional learning. Other studies confirm that even experienced teachers can have fairly naïve views on the nature of science (Abd-El-Khalick and BouJaoude 1997). There have been some interesting studies which give some hope that more explicit attention to developing science teachers' knowledge and understanding of issues to do with the nature of science through both initial training or CPD programmes can have an influence on the images of science and scientists developed by students (Lederman 1992, 1999; Hashweh 1996; Schwartz and Lederman 2002). Citing other research, van Driel *et al.* (2001: 146) suggest that:

> explicitness and reflectiveness with respect to the nature of science are the most important features of programs that appeared successful in facilitating teachers to develop conceptions of the nature of science that are consistent with those advocated by current reforms, and to translate these conceptions into an appropriate classroom approach.

Monk and Dillon (2000) provide a short introduction to some of the issues as does Duschl (2000). The book *Young people's images of science* (Driver *et al.* 1996) is a really good read to see things from the students' perspective. Ros Driver's earlier book *The pupil as scientist* (1991) was one of the first studies to try to link the nature of the subject of science itself to students' ideas. An article by Dhingra (2003) considers the picture of science that students get from television, which is becoming an increasingly important source of information for young people.

If you want to delve more deeply into the nature of science itself, *Science in schools* (Brown *et al.* 1986) contains an excellent series of chapters by different authors (including Einstein!) to present science as a human and cultural activity – 'real science' – before plunging into 'school science'. Lewis Wolpert's *The unnatural nature of science* (1992) presents the way science and common sense often seem to be in opposition – which is a problem for many students in understanding science concepts. Of course, all bookshops today have a 'popular science' section and there are many books which tell stories *about* science and scientists, and along the way tell the story *of* science. *The Faber book of science* (Carey 2005) and *Galileo's commandment* (Blair Bolles 1997) are good anthologies. A few hours spent with these books may give you a refreshing view of your own subject and cause you to ask yourself questions about how the curriculum represents or misrepresents it.

If you only want to explore one topic within the nature of science, then it might be the whole area of models, modelling and analogies. The use of models and analogies was identified by Shulman as being characteristic of PCK and has been a focus for consideration of PCK in science particularly (Justi and van Driel 2005). It was also a recurring theme in the lessons and discussions with our group of highly accomplished teachers and features in several of the teacher accounts and commentaries. The use of models in science education has been a fertile area for research (Justi and Gilbert 2002; van Driel and Verloop 2002; Halloun 2006) and it seems clear that teachers' ideas are often confused and, therefore, there is a risk of this confusion being passed on to their students.

If you are feeling brave, then you could try Nott and Wellington's article 'Your nature of science profile' (1993) which enables you to review your own position in relation to a number of key dimensions – are you a positivist or a relativist? – a realist or an instrumentalist? In a follow-up article (1995), these authors consider the way in which your own personal position can influence your practice and through the examination of 'critical incidents' consider how sometimes even experienced teachers use strategies that they call 'rigging' and 'conjuring' to achieve experimental outcomes that fit with particular perspectives on 'right' answers.

This chapter has only give a brief insight into issues concerning the nature of science in science education, let alone the complexities of philosophical stances on science outside education. We hope it might have given you a taste for more. We have to admit passing through much of our own teaching careers with little idea about these issues and only coming to understand their significance in more recent times. Having started to find out more, we have been fascinated and have seen ways in which professional learning in this area could really enrich science teaching and impact on the images of science which our students develop. We hope you will become enthusiastic too.

7   The student voice

How do we engage our students in their science education? This is a key question that troubles all science teachers, and not just those at the beginning of their careers. The answer to it is complex and depends on many factors. This chapter is devoted to capturing the voices of the students taught by the highly accomplished science teachers we observed, in the belief that a better understanding of what students think can only be helpful to teachers as they research, plan and prepare their lessons.

What do we mean by the 'student voice'? There is a lot of recent research that can be used to find out more about the concept but for the purposes of this book the 'student voice' is the combination of views that students hold about what makes their science lessons interesting, what helps them see the connections with the 'real world' of science outside the classroom and what are the approaches that allow them to learn best.

Why is listening to the 'student voice' important?

First of all you have to believe that what students think and say could affect your practice as a science teacher and could make your science teaching more engaging for the students. If you do not believe this, then there is little point in reading further. However, if you are not sure, a good starting point to convince you would be Michael Reiss' longitudinal study of a small group of students in the UK progressing through their five years of secondary science education from 11 to 16 (Reiss 2000). The story provides ample evidence of what can be learned by listening to students.

Our view is that it would seem odd to make no attempt to find out, or even be aware of, what the students you teach think of their science education or what they expect from it. Outcomes from a recent large UK government-funded project maintain that student involvement is fundamental to school improvement. But this research warns that there are both 'comfortable and uncomfortable learnings for teachers' (McIntyre *et al.* 2005). What emerged is that students can offer a surprisingly perceptive and constructive focus on learning. For students, the process of consultation is significant as it makes them feel that they are being treated as adults and that they should, therefore, take more responsibility for their own learning. For teachers, the choice is whether or not to listen and whether or not to respond. However, the evidence suggests that the student voice offers exciting possibilities for innovative and creative science teaching and enhanced student engagement.

From our own research, and from research in the public domain, we advocate that listening to students is an essential part of any science teacher's professional learning. The intention in this chapter is to provide insights into students' perspectives by analysing the ways they respond to the science 'brought' to them by the teachers we observed. We then try to show how the subject and pedagogical knowledge components of a teacher's professional knowledge impacts on students' interest and motivation in science. We anticipate these analyses will offer readers an intuitively accessible approach to what accomplished science teachers know and can do.

Students' attitudes towards science: what the research shows

If you carry out any of your own research with students, make sure you distinguish between attitudes towards 'school science' and attitudes towards 'science'. School science and science in the world outside are very different things in the minds of students. School science may shape students' impressions of science and whether they might want to pursue careers in science, but it does not necessarily affect their interest or enthusiasm for wanting to know about science-based issues. What the research shows is that most students would really like to make these connections because they think science is important. However, they cannot do it alone. They need science teachers who can point the way. For a deeper discussion on what is meant by *attitudes* towards science, Osborne *et al.*'s (2003) article provides a very thorough analysis of some of the recent research and the chapter by Shirley Simon on students' attitudes towards science in *Good practice in science teaching* (Monk and Osborne, 2000) offers a very helpful theoretical discussion of what is implied and included in the term 'attitudes'.

One of the largest international comparative surveys of students' attitudes towards science that has been carried out in recent times is the Relevance of Science Education project (the ROSE project: www.ils.uio.no/english/rose). Covering some 35 developed and developing countries, this project aims to shed light on students' (mostly 15–16-year-olds) perceptions of the importance of science and technology. Fascinating for the beginning- and early-career science teacher, though, is what can be learned by studying the questionnaire. Among other things, students are asked about their science lessons, what they want to learn about, what they think about science and technology, what their future jobs might be and their views regarding the environment. Although it is huge, the questions have been very carefully piloted and could form the basis of some investigative work with your own students (for full details of the questionnaire see Schreiner and Sjøberg 2004).

Research from the ROSE project and from other studies (e.g., Osborne and Collins 2000; Osborne *et al.* 2003) confirms the view that school science is becoming increasingly off-putting to many students, leading them into thinking 'it's not for me'. This decline in students' attitudes has been the trend for some years, but the reasons for it are complex. Science teachers themselves will tell you that increases in subject choice, a preference to mix arts and science subjects, the apparent difficulty of science as a subject and the constraints of the science curriculum, are all reasons why students are not choosing to continue post-16 study in science.

However, research suggests that science teaching itself is also part of the problem. A survey carried out by one of the examining bodies in the UK found that over 50 per cent of the 1000 or so Year 9, 10 and 11 students (13–16 age group) surveyed, said that science lessons were 'boring, confusing or difficult' (OCR 2006: 1), while another survey of over 800 Year 9 students (13–14 age group) across 36 schools carried out by the University of York and funded by the AstraZeneca Science Teaching Trust found that only 27 per cent of the students thought it would be 'good' to become a scientist (Bennett 2007).

Findings from these kinds of studies do not make pleasant reading for politicians and industrialists looking at the prospects for the economic health and future of the country (see House of Lords 2006). However, they are not all bad news. In the York study over 50 per cent of students agreed that science is important for wealth creation and that people were disadvantaged if they knew little of science in today's society. Haste (2004) in her research with students aged 11–21, found an appreciation of the benefits science can bring. And contrary to expectations, girls are just as interested in science as boys, although their interests lie in different areas. Nevertheless, the challenge remains for the scientific community to find ways to enthuse and inspire students and reverse the trend so that careers in science are perceived as an attractive option.

So what can the students themselves tell us about their experiences of learning science in the secondary school? Our conversations with students left us with the feeling that, with sensitivity and effort, there is much that can be done.

What did we ask the students involved in our research?

Our argument in this chapter is that having a good understanding of what your students think about science and school science is both important and beneficial. We talked mostly to students right across the 12–15 age bracket, although the majority were from Year 10 (14–15 age group). Interestingly, we found them to be much more perceptive about science teachers and their teaching than might have been expected given the outcomes of the surveys reported previously. In fact, like McIntyre *et al.* (2005) we found them to be mature and insightful, and ready to acknowledge the relevance of science in their lives and its place in their futures.

We asked them questions along these lines:

- Do you think knowing about science is important?
- What do you like about science? What gets you interested? What makes science come alive for you?
- Do you like school science? How does it compare in difficulty with other subjects?
- How do you think science in school connects with everyday science in the world outside the classroom? Can you think of some connections?
- What sort of things help you remember what you are taught, i.e., capture your interest, get you involved? Can you think of some examples?
- How do you like to be taught science? What sort of teaching in science helps you learn best? What activities do you like? What is good about them?
- Do you like to understand the science, or are you happy just to learn what is needed for tests and exams?
- What sort of teaching approaches help you with understanding the science?
- Do all of you in this group like the same things in science? Do you think your science teachers recognize how you are different and perhaps use different teaching/learning approaches?
- Are any of you likely to continue with science at A level?

Rather than treat the process as a kind of group interview, the students were encouraged to use the questions as the basis of a dialogue, so they could comment on one another's views. This led to some interesting conversations. We analysed all the data using a qualitative software package called NVivo to draw out common themes. Although this resulted in a complex picture, it was evident that when given an opportunity to talk freely, all students (not just the articulate) could express quite insightful views about the place of science and its value to them as individuals and to society as a whole. What emerged very strongly was that they could recognize when their science teachers were trying really hard to find imaginative ways to enthuse and inspire them. It is these findings we will report here.

What do students think about the science teaching they receive?

Students' views about the kind of science teaching they receive are instructive. A number of points emerged which are worth illustrating. Science teachers who 'make an effort', as they put it, to capture the students' interest are well regarded. This is seen as a mark of 'caring' about what they teach. Students could also tell if their teachers were just going through the motions, or whether they were really interested in what they were teaching – 'Were they passionate?' was the question they asked. Such teachers were also good at explaining the science. If they could not help you see it one way, they always had other ways of explaining it. They also did not make you write everything down. Science teachers who were determined to engage students used writing for good reasons to do with learning, not just for management purposes.

Making an effort

Students were forthright in their opinion that they respected the teacher if the teacher 'made the effort'. To them this was a clear indication that the content mattered because the teacher was trying hard to make it interesting and relevant:

> 'They make an effort. They won't just like read out of a textbook. They'll go and research something and give you examples and try to make the lessons as interesting as they can and you can hear it in their voice but when we're having discussions they'll get really into it and get really excited about their subject.'

Thorough preparation was clearly noticed by the students. If it was not apparent then, for some students, there was an element of reciprocity in their thinking:

> 'A lot of the time I think if there's not a lot of effort in it the lesson isn't going to succeed, because if the teacher hasn't put effort into what they're trying to teach, then the children won't put effort into trying to learn it.'

Caring

The issue of making an effort blends into students' beliefs about their teachers' attitudes towards them. If their science teachers can be seen to be making an effort then it is because they care, and because they also think your learning is important:

> '. . . that he prepares and he thinks about it and obviously cares about it'.

> 'And if you can see that he's interested in it, and he's trying for us . . .'

And if they also take the trouble to get to know you as individuals then that is another sign of respect:

> 'He knows every pupil individually and we're giving him respect back because he gives us respect.'

Being 'passionate'

Another component of caring about the science you teach is showing outwardly that you are interested in the subject matter. In fact, the students looked for more than that – they wanted to see enthusiasm, even passion. And they can easily tell whether their science teacher is or is not interested in what they are teaching, just as Donnelly and Jenkins (1999) discovered – students could easily detect their teachers' attitudes towards what they were teaching, 'Biology with you is OK. Chemistry is fun. But you like physics don't you?'. (p. 16).

In short, the students' view was that they wanted to see their science teachers 'being passionate' about what they teach, almost on the basis that if *they* are not interested in the subject, why should we be? Some of the comments we heard in relation to the highly accomplished science teachers we observed made this point quite firmly:

> 'He's so passionate about what he does and you really want to learn.'

> 'But it's interesting if they're passionate about their subject. And they can tell you extra bits of information that you find quite interesting . . . like the stories.'

It is clearly no good if a science teacher begins a lesson or topic by apologizing for some aspect of what they are about to teach: then the students know it is going to be boring! According to the students in our conversation groups, science teachers were heading for trouble if they publicly admitted at the outset that they had little interest in the topic, and even more so if they were evidently not going to try to make it interesting:

> 'If you see your teacher cares about their subject and likes it and is really into it . . . if they're not really interested in their subject it makes you not interested in it.'

In contrast, the students had respect and admiration for those science teachers that did their best to find ways to make the science capture their interest.

Explaining the science

It will come as no surprise that students like science teachers who are good at explaining (see Ogborn *et al.*'s 1996 book *Explaining science in the classroom*). Not only that, the students were adamant that teachers who got frustrated with them when they did not 'get it' the first time were not good science teachers. When asked about what good science teaching is about, the responses were along the lines of:

> 'Someone who explains it. If someone in the class doesn't understand they come over to us and say, "Right this is basically what I mean, but in a simpler version." '

> '. . . because I always remember what the teacher said and if the teacher explains it then I remember'.

> 'Some teachers just think you should have understood it and will get angry if you don't and they'll think you weren't listening. It's not that you don't listen, but you just don't understand, so they need to break it down into a simpler version. Just a way we'll keep in our brain.'

> 'They don't just tell you straight facts but explain behind the facts – why it works.'

> 'And then you understand and you can relate back to why it happens, and you can work out how it happens.'

For the students, it is the science teacher's responsibility to make it simpler. Of course, with good PCK, a highly accomplished science teacher will know what the alternative explanations might be that the student will find easier to follow. Sometimes these are the anecdotes or the stories drawn from personal experience that can be so vital in helping students get another perspective.

Writing for a purpose

Following a monitoring exercise, one of the highly accomplished science teachers, also a head of science, was concerned that staff in her department were getting the students to write unnecessarily:

> 'I had books in and was getting very worried about the amount of notes in books, because the department has spent a lot of money on a textbook for every child, and it seemed to me we were having little mini-textbooks in these notebooks and that's not what I wanted at all.'

More fundamentally she was concerned about the quality of learning if the main activity was student writing.

The students were quite indignant when they were told to copy out of books or undertake what they saw as activities designed just to keep them occupied. Astutely, they commented, 'as if we don't know why they are getting us to write!' They were not fooled. They knew when they were being managed as opposed to being taught. Unfortunately, being asked to write without a clear purpose is one of the quickest ways to evoke the cry 'science is boring!'. Students also suggested that writing for the sake of writing was not good for learning:

> 'You'd almost think they hadn't been in school themselves sometimes because they can be really strict or think that they have to be really mean. They don't seem to realize that we want even just a little bit of fun. We just take notes the whole time.'

> 'Sometimes I like school science, but it can get boring when it's just written work and you're not quite understanding what's going on.'

> 'She actually does say if we start talking a lot, "Do you want to do this? Do you want to work out of a book?" And she knows that we'll behave then because we like to interact with one another and do that rather than just sit down writing questions out of a book.'

And of course students can soon detect when writing is being used as a threat. The highly accomplished science teacher, referred to above, was clear about her purposes for students writing in notebooks:

> 'They're just simply a reflection of what's been covered. The textbooks

are for revision. The books are for practising original writing and thought.'

What these students said about writing resonated strongly with findings from the ESRC-funded Teaching and Learning Research Programme that was running between 2000 and 2003, and reported in *Consulting pupils*, a fascinating book written by Flutter and Rudduck (2004). They too explored students' views about writing:

> It was clear, however, that classroom activities that did not involve writing were more likely to engage pupils' interests and pupils said that they liked tasks that were 'different' or involved some degree of physical movement . . .
>
> (p. 114)

The need to find ways to involve students in physical activity, or movement of some kind, was a fundamental belief underlying the practice of virtually all the highly accomplished science teachers we observed.

What engages the students in learning science?

Engagement is the word on the lips of so many commentators and politicians who seek to increase the number of students taking science further. Robin Millar (2006: 70), in the Wellcome Trust publication *Engaging science*, makes the important point that, 'The key to greater student engagement is making stronger and clearer links between the science that young people hear about outside school and the science they learn in school.'

The students' idea of engagement is when the teacher uses devices to capture their interest, or grabs their attention with a dramatic experiment or activity. What most highly accomplished science teachers mean by engagement is the hook, stimulus or trigger they use initially to capture the students' imagination, but as a precursor to *involvement*, where they engross students in a learning journey that is both motivating and intrinsically of value from an intellectual perspective. At this level, highly accomplished science teachers aim to enable students to see the *relevance* of science knowledge in their lives and futures. They contrive activities to enable students to begin to see the legitimate connections between school science and what they refer to as 'real world' science.

'Engagement', as a concept, appears to be somewhat elusive. The suggestion from many observers is that once we engage the students in science all else will follow, i.e., more students will opt for science at A level, thus more students will go on to study sciences at university and as a consequence more trained scientists will be available to the workforce both at technical and research levels. Well, let us hope so!

Fun and enjoyment

Students clearly associate learning with science that is enjoyable or made 'fun'. The idea that science means fun and enjoyment clearly influences attitudes towards the subject. As one student put it:

> 'I really think that if you have a teacher who is fun and puts fun into science then you will learn more from it because if you go into a lesson thinking, "Oh I've got so and so . . ." and instead you go in thinking, "Oh yes, I've got a really cool teacher, even though I don't like science . . ." they'll make it more interesting for you. And if they can link humour to science, it's great.'

Is it the teacher who is fun, is it the lesson, or is it both? And what is the relationship with learning? We believe some care is needed here. The questions we should ask perhaps, are; 'Are fun and enjoyment the same thing?', 'What are the roles of fun and/or enjoyment in learning science?', 'Are they essential, or just desirable preconditions for the promotion of learning?' and 'How are these conditions created?' Common sense, of course, would suggest that if students believe science is neither fun nor enjoyable, and associate it with boredom, then positive attitudes towards science will be harder to foster.

If we are not careful, one obvious danger is that students come to view science (or even the science teacher as the quote above suggests) as entertainment. Pyrotechnic experiments, bangs and surprises are then seen as the norm and anything less is a disappointment or even a turn-off. The pressure on the science teacher then to 'perform' every lesson becomes unreasonable, if not intolerable. For beginning- and early-career teachers who try to entertain the students there is the additional danger that they may confuse positive or enthusiastic responses with meaningful learning.

From our research with the students, there is good evidence that highly accomplished science teachers really do raise students' expectations of what they can expect from science. Indeed, these teachers see it absolutely as their responsibility to foster positive attitudes towards science. However, although they are naturally inclined to find ways to capture the students' interest, they never put themselves in a position where students come to expect to be passive observers of teacher-led spectacles. Their belief in engaging the students through intellectual engagement means that the activities they design result in active participation. A good example of this is Eric. He described for us in some detail how he was prepared to use himself to engender an atmosphere of fun and enjoyment in his lessons. Clearly, Eric was aiming to establish a positive emotional state in his classes in the belief that making the lesson fun promoted involvement. Indeed, the students were never left in any doubt as to what his expectations were of them.

Getting students' interested

The students' idea of engagement was what they call 'getting us interested'. They made reference to their science teachers' little stories or anecdotes. As one student acknowledged:

> 'It's weird because there's a fine line between teachers who completely make you switch off and then teachers who really interest you because the work they do is exactly the same but it's just the way they teach it.'

This is an interesting comment as it is tantamount to student recognition of teachers' PCK. It is not what science teachers know, it is the way they transform what they know that has the effect of engaging the students or not.

All our highly accomplished science teachers made reference to the stories of science, their personal anecdotes, the references they could make to what they knew of the history of science or links to contemporary science because of what they had read in recent times.

Clearly such asides are important to students because they bring the subject to life. When science teachers offer different explanations and utilize 'attention grabbers', such as the exploding jelly baby experiment (carefully placing a jelly baby into heated potassium chlorate to demonstrate the oxidation of sugar), they have an impact:

> 'She said, "Have you seen the jelly baby blow up?" and we were all like, "What was that?" and she made us stand around and blew up a jelly baby and it was like, "Let's see that again" and she acts like one of us but she's still fun because she teaches us at the same time.'

Other highly accomplished science teachers had their own 'tricks of the trade', as they called it, which they used in various circumstances to encourage students to engage with the science. These were their hooks, stimuli or triggers. Examples would be particular starter activities or material that shows the development of science from an historical perspective. This is where books, such as *The Faber book of science*, can be effectively exploited for their quirky and surprising stories (see Carey 2005), or you might also consider consulting ideas texts, such as Keith Gibbs' (1999) publication from the Institute of Physics.

Involvement

We would argue that engagement is just one stage in drawing the students into an appreciation of the value of a good science education. It is, of course, a vital precursor, but it is not sufficient to bring about learning. For that to happen, students need to be *involved* in their learning of science. This is where science teachers need to be imaginative – for example, in transforming their subject knowledge, their knowledge of the curriculum, their knowledge of the students and their knowledge of learning in order to conceive activities and materials that will generate in students an intrinsic interest and involvement in the content.

How is involvement brought about in learning science? For our highly accomplished science teachers it is about providing the framework in which students are actively engaged in thinking about both the content and the procedures of science. They talked of 'active processing', meaning that students needed to be set intellectual challenges involving translating information from one form to another (see earlier chapters for examples of practice). The highly accomplished science teachers saw this approach as a key strategy to promote involvement by giving the students responsibility, treating them as adults and encouraging them to become independent learners.

By the same token, students wanted to be active learners. They appreciated the opportunity to have discussions, and share and test their ideas in a non-threatening environment. They argued that not only did this help them think, but it clarified their ideas at the same time. Such social constructivist approaches to learning are as important in science as in any other discipline. The students appeared to have an intuitive appreciation of the potential of learning through social discourse:

> 'You're actually hearing what's going on and you're not reading it out of books, but actually thinking yourself.'

> 'But if you know something, say with IVF, we knew a bit of information so we could actually go into our groups and discuss what we knew and what we thought.'

Involvement was a recurrent theme in our students' responses to our questions. They appreciate the opportunity to be involved in discussion. This does not mean they do not want the science. Far from it – they want to have informed discussion. It is in this way they can make sense of the science. But they like hearing others students' opinions and are prepared to debate them seriously.

In Vygotskian terms the students' social interaction within a group allows them to develop and structure their thinking from the social plane where they first engage with the ideas and language, to the personal plane where they can begin to internalize and make sense of what they are learning (Vygotsky 1978; Edwards 1995). In this way they have the opportunity to restructure their own understandings and become more confident within the inter-personal discourse operating in the group. As a consequence they become more prepared to hear what others have to say and willing to share their ideas publicly:

> 'Because we got put in groups and didn't have to work on our own, group work is often easier.'

> 'You get varied opinion don't you?'

> 'You get everyone's opinion and you can figure it out in the end. But if we'd all been put on our own then that would have been near impossible to do that lesson.'

Making the science relevant

Really important to students was the idea that their school science should be 'relevant' to their lives. They wanted to be able to see how what they were being taught could be useful to them. This came through strongly time and time again. Interestingly, they were not entirely utilitarian in their view. Some were honest about the kinds of intellectual benefits a science education brings and saw that science as an intellectual pursuit could develop the mind:

> '. . . because it gives you an analytical approach to it and makes you see the different steps you can take to solve a problem. There's a very logical way through it.'

Unsurprisingly, this view was relatively rare, but most students saw science as a subject with a utility value:

> 'In school it prepares you for what there is in the real world because if you wanted to go into a job to do with science you'd have a basic knowledge that would help you and you would know what jobs were out there and what to expect.'

> 'It might not be affecting us now but it could when we're grown up and in our lifetime.'

'It teaches you not so much life skills, but general knowledge as well.'

'Relation to everyday life is really important. Like in chemistry when we were learning about lime, mortar, cement, concrete, now I walk down the street and it's really sad but I think "I know what that's made of, I know how to make it." Really simple things but that makes you feel really clever and you have an understanding of it.'

'But the main thing is relating it to you.'

The emphasis on relevance apparent in the last couple of comments, however, was typical. We found the students' ideas in our study bore a remarkable resemblance to many of the findings of the ROSE project (see also Jenkins and Nelson 2005 for a really good overview of the findings from the ROSE project). There is much for science teachers to learn from the ROSE project as the insights it offers should alert us all to students' orientations towards school science. Above all, we should acknowledge that it is possible for students to find science interesting and relevant but, sadly, we probably have to accept that it is often not taught in ways interesting enough to raise it above other subjects when students have to make choices.

Each group of students we interviewed were adamant about the different ways that science was important, but they struggled to say exactly what it was that they thought they needed to learn. Both boys and girls often gave utilitarian answers, such as it was important to learn about the human body and the effects that various drugs have on it, but they were less likely to identify concepts in science which we as science educators might think essential to developing scientific understanding.

What can science teachers learn from students' views?

Many of the points made to us during our conversations with the students are probably quite unsurprising. They like to 'learn by doing', to do activities that act as memorable events in helping them associate the learning that accompanied those events. They said they responded to those science teachers who got to know them as individuals and who treated them as adults by giving them responsibility for their learning. Those teachers were approachable, did not get angry if you did not understand, had time for you and recognized that you liked to learn in different ways. The language of learning styles, the visual, auditory and kinaesthetic approaches now common in the language of so many schools, is not only appreciated, but used by the students themselves.

Learning by doing

The expression 'learning by doing' is most often attributed to Dewey (1983). It is a phrase that both the highly accomplished science teachers and the students used frequently to describe how they think students learn best. Perhaps it should be noted that the act of 'doing' does not necessarily result in 'learning'. Once again we should remember Driver's aphorism, 'I do and I am even more confused!' (1991: 9), or the expression 'hands on, minds off'. Numerous comments from the students were along the lines of:

> 'By making it memorable and fun, with a hands-on approach, you can get stuck into how you're doing it, and you remember it.'

> 'Practicals keep you busy and you're actually doing something and you can remember better rather than just learning out of the book.'

The highly accomplished science teachers, however, although themselves often expressing beliefs that students should be active, were more circumspect in relation to what that actually meant. Generally, they used the term 'active' to describe what the students should be doing, but by that they meant 'intellectually engaged'. Emma, for example, was absolutely clear that students should be 'processing' ideas or information. Naturally this would include practical activity, but she was not suggesting that practical activity alone would in any way secure the learning she was seeking.

Responsibility

We were impressed by the way that students from all the ability groups were able to recognize how being given responsibility impacted on their attitudes. In some cases this manifested itself in quite basic terms:

> 'I think he treats us like adults actually. I don't know. He makes jokes sometimes and actually makes you feel like adults.'

> 'As long as they don't talk to you like you're an idiot.'

> 'As long as they don't go, "Ooh! Let's get up and play." As long as they talk to you not like a student really, but more like an equal.'

Other students were aware that they were being given the opportunity for ownership over what they were doing and that their science teacher wanted them to take responsibility for their learning:

'That's what's good about the lessons where we have to think for ourselves. She gives a point of focus and then we go off and do it. I think that's really good.'

Underlying the practice of all the highly accomplished science teachers was a complex set of beliefs that brought together concepts, such as ownership, responsibility, developing thinking skills, promoting independent learning, developing relationships at an adult level, the need for mutual respect, and so on. Unravelling all of this is not easy, but such belief systems are driven ultimately by the educational aims of these teachers and the values they hold dear. As a beginning- or early-career teacher it is important for you to begin to articulate the beliefs and values you think should drive your practice.

Learning styles

In science education there are always opportunities for devising resources, materials and activities which could match students' visual, auditory and/or kinaesthetic learning preferences. If, indeed, you believe that students should be seen as individuals who like to learn in different ways, then it is your ability to transform the subject matter, in conjunction with your knowledge of learners and learning, that may allow you to meet, as far as possible, the diverse needs of the students in your classes. Clearly the language of learning preferences has reached the students, and they are aware of what their science teachers are trying to do in order to acknowledge that they are different and like to learn in different ways. Put somewhat crudely, one student expressed it thus:

'. . . because some people can't learn as much if their teacher knows what they know in their way, but if they teach it in the way we like it we understand it a lot more and get things quicker'.

In recent times teachers too have become more thoughtful about the way they conceive and construct activities. Many, including these highly accomplished science teachers, have been strongly influenced by professional development programmes that introduced them to the concept of multiple intelligences (Gardner 2006):

'Learning about how the brain works and the different ways of learning, visual and kinaesthetic. Things that nobody had ever talked to me about before when I was training, certainly not in my first school. So that was all very new to me and I found teaching a lot easier after that, a lot more interesting. The students got a lot more out of it. It just made much more sense.'

Apart from presenting ideas or concepts in multiple ways, some highly accomplished science teachers liked to use the students themselves as alternative interpreters of information. This was seen by the students as 'student-friendly' and a refreshing alternative to the teacher as always being the final arbiter of knowledge. Those highly accomplished science teachers who used this approach were, of course, very careful about how and when this was done in order to avoid sowing the seeds of further misconceptions.

Implications of the student voice for learning science teaching

Throughout this chapter we have highlighted a number of issues that students identified in our conversations with them. What seemed to be uppermost in their thinking was what they regarded as the effort made by their science teachers to find interesting and relevant ways to engage them. In their opinion, these teachers were prepared to work hard for them, they were sometimes unpredictable, or quirky, but they cared. How did the students know this? Because they took an interest in them, they saw them as individuals with different learning needs and they established relationships with them built on trust and mutual respect. These were people who did not get angry, but had a sense of humour, who would join in and not be afraid of making fools of themselves if it helped engage the students in their learning. Above all, the students respected these science teachers for what they knew and how they were able to transform what they knew into materials and activities that enabled the students to link the science outside school with the science they learn inside it.

Can the beginning- and early-career teacher learn from listening to the student voice? Evidence from our research and from the research reported in many other studies both nationally across the UK and internationally through projects, such as the ROSE, would suggest the answer is a resounding 'Yes!'.

What should the learning science teacher do? Well! First, be prepared to listen. As we said at the beginning of this chapter McIntyre *et al.*'s (2005), research indicated there are both 'comfortable and uncomfortable learnings' for teachers. The process of consultation is a delicate one. Be wary of hearing only the most articulate voices. We aimed to avoid this by asking our highly accomplished science teachers to provide us with students who represented a cross-section of ability and aptitude and by drawing on a range of classes across the different schools with students who posed different levels of challenge.

The 'comfortable learnings' from our research are that students are able to focus on what helps them to learn. The 'uncomfortable learnings' are that sometimes students can pinpoint what is not working for them and teachers might find the responses a little threatening.

8 Professional learning

How teachers learn is emerging as an important field of research (Loughran 2006a; Beijaard *et al.* 2007). In many countries across the western world, governments make the point that the most important factor in determining the achievement of students is the quality of the teaching they receive (see Darling-Hammond 2000; DEST 2003). As a consequence, attention is now turning strongly to examining the nature of professional development available to teachers and what they do or do not learn from it. In the UK, for example, the advent of the Teacher Learning Academy in 2004 (see www.gtce.org.uk/tla) has intensified the pressure on schools to take professional learning seriously and to consider how they might go about establishing their own professional learning communities. For science teachers in the UK, the new network of Science Learning Centres (see www.science learningcentres.org.uk) provides a new set of opportunities for professional learning.

But how can we be sure that the opportunities created for science teachers, first, are appropriate, and second, likely to lead to changes in teacher practice that could result in improvements in student achievement? Unfortunately, we cannot! All the evidence from research into professional development suggests that we cannot be sure that the mere provision of numerous professional development opportunities alone will achieve either of these. So what do we need? In our view, what is actually required are science teachers who are clear about their professional learning priorities and, therefore, in a better position to be pivotal in determining what the professional development provision should be.

One thing of which we can be certain is the commitment to professional learning shown by the highly accomplished science teachers we worked with as the basis of this book. It is that commitment to professional learning that characterizes these teachers and which has resulted in them gaining the respect and recognition of their colleagues and peers and becoming the teachers they are. Most of the highly accomplished science teachers would probably argue that they are on a long-term journey and that their learning will only stop when they do. In fact, it is the possibility that their work is forever open to revision and change that keeps and maintains their love of teaching science.

Our view is that right from the point of entry to the profession, science teachers should be inducted into the process of learning science teaching by learning how to learn from experience. There can only be a few programmes of initial teacher education/training (ITE/T) across the world that do not involve at least one, if not two or three, periods of school experience. Furthermore, it is imperative that such programmes should involve experienced science teachers who, themselves, are also committed to continuous professional learning in order that they can provide the support and mentoring to beginning- and early-career teachers necessary to set these new entrants to the profession on their own individual learning journeys. In our research, there is clear evidence from the highly accomplished science teachers we worked with that they are the very kinds of science teachers who have the skills necessary to do this. The challenge, though, is how do we increase their numbers to a critical mass that a commitment to professional learning in science education becomes the norm rather than the exception?

What is professional learning?

So what do we mean by professional learning? Rather than try to offer a formal definition, we would direct you to sources, such as Michael Eraut (1994), whose research has focused on a deep analysis of what professionalism and professional learning are. However, we also anticipate that you will be able to make meaning for yourself regarding what constitutes professional learning through the contents of this chapter. Most importantly, we are quite deliberately rooting this discussion about professional learning firmly in the practices of the highly accomplished science teachers. Where appropriate we have used the teachers' own words to try to expose their thinking. Significantly, all the highly accomplished science teachers are engaged in supporting beginning- and early-career teachers in a variety of roles – for example, perhaps as mentor, or head of department, or induction tutor. What they said to us we believe is likely to be entirely typical of the kind of language and advice that beginning- and early-career teachers might receive from them. Indeed, it is this very kind of advice that beginning- and early-career teachers have to interpret, and make sense of, for themselves.

Throughout this book, we have tried hard to help the reader get some insight into the professional knowledge of the science teacher. To achieve this we used the technique of VSR as a way of getting the highly accomplished science teachers to talk and guide us through their decision-making, and then, through the detailed analyses of their practice in Chapters 3–5, we tried to reveal something of the knowledge bases they have developed and how they draw on them. Although we have relied extensively on Shulman's (1987) categorization of the knowledge bases for teaching as a useful way of describing what the highly accomplished science teachers know and can do, we recognize that this is not the whole story.

Reviewing your professional knowledge

Becoming reflective

It is one thing to be exhorted to reflect and become a reflective practitioner, it is another to do it. Learning to reason from a pedagogical perspective does not necessarily come naturally. Such skills have to be learned through apprenticeship, learning from others through professional dialogue and by learning the discourse of pedagogy. Fortunately there are many good sources that can help you to develop your skills. Schön's *Educating the reflective practitioner* (1987) is as good a place to start.

Our highly accomplished science teachers were all dedicated to the concept of being reflective, learning from the process of reflection and building new learning into practice. No one expects this skill to be instantly acquired; it develops over time. In fact, many argue that for most teachers a learning period of five years or more is common. For Iain it was longer:

> 'I think the fundamental shift I've made is that I've become much more reflective and much more self-critical and I've got the confidence to become critical and say, "That wasn't particularly good" or "I don't think that worked particularly well. What could I do next time round?" That sort of constant reflection and modification has gradually evolved into an improvement I think in teaching. That's about a seven-year process, and I'm now ten years into my teaching.'

Other highly accomplished science teachers recognized that developing the capacity to reflect involves a learning curve. And they see it as their duty to encourage, support and challenge beginning- and early-career teachers in their efforts to learn how to be reflective:

> '. . . what they're doing is going through a very steep part of their learning curve and if they're prepared to make adjustments they'll improve. So it's how you actually instil that mindset of reflection. I think that's the key.'

As an advanced skills teacher, however, Derek was keen to acknowledge his position as a role model and saw it as vital that he both demonstrated and promoted such reflective practice with newly-qualified teachers. He was generally critical of the superficial approach beginning- and early-career teachers often take to reflection and analysis because, as he put it, 'They don't ask themselves the basic question – why?':

> 'What newly-qualified teachers always want to do is say what worked and what didn't, and "what worked I'll try and do that again and what didn't I'll never try again". What's difficult is to get them to think about why something worked and why something didn't, and whether that was anything to do with the fact that it would never work again, or that it didn't work because there are things that work one lesson and not the next.'

Derek actually had a novel expression to describe how he conceived the process of thinking more deeply about what can be learned both from what works and what does not work in the classroom. In getting newly-qualified teachers to reflect on their practice, Derek introduced the interesting concepts of a *toolkit* and a *recycling bin*. But he found that newly-qualified teachers were too quick to say that the things that do work should go into the toolkit, and the things that do not work should go into the recycling bin. As a consequence he said of the newly-qualified teachers:

> 'The things in the recycling never come out again and the things in the toolkit come out every time. In a way, that's wrong, because, if you're like me, some things work one lesson and won't work ever again. Or it may in the next lesson things that don't work may not then, but will work really brilliantly in another lesson or another context.'

What he meant by this was that initially newly-qualified teachers were indiscriminate in their use of the things they had put in their toolkit. By the same token, ideas, activities and resources that did not work went into the recycling bin for a rethink, even though they might have worked well for different reasons with a different class. Derek's view was that without regard for the situation or context, this was all too superficial.

Essentially, Derek is stressing the *situated* nature of learning as a teacher (Lave and Wenger 1991) where 'situatedness' is determined by the factors that define the context. Through experience, Derek is now highly sensitive to the context and the situated nature of professional knowledge. As a consequence, his pre-active decision-making (and interactive decision-making) are shaped by reflection and analysis. The difference compared with the newly-qualified teacher is that context will influence strongly what he will take from the toolkit and how he will use it. Furthermore, his recycling bin will contain ideas and resources which he believes can be reshaped to better fit new situations.

We would maintain further that the way Derek uses his contextual knowledge has an important bearing on his PCK. In other words, he analyses every situation very carefully and as a result makes different decisions about how to transform his subject knowledge according to the situation. This, in part, may explain why the expert teachers in Berliner's (2004) study, we referred to in Chapter 1, were so reluctant to have their expertise examined in unfamiliar contexts.

Other highly accomplished science teachers took a more pragmatic line that in effect said that if beginning- and early-career teachers do not make the effort to learn how to reflect on practice, job satisfaction will be hard to come by. Above all else, a capacity to be self-critical was fundamental to professional learning:

> '. . . giving them the assurance that what they're doing is very good at that initial level . . . but if they are prepared to invest time on their knowledge base and pedagogical knowledge they will get better. And if they continue to reflect they will continue to get better. I honestly think the bottom line is preparedness to be self-critical and reassess what you do, and after that you'll celebrate your successes because if you don't do that you'll have a fairly miserable existence.'

Professional learning needs

Having the capacity to reflect on your own practice paves the way to making decisions about the nature of the professional learning that will improve your practice. We remind you here that any reflection and analysis should help you identify your needs both in improving what you already know and can do and in recognizing what you do not know. The former is relatively easy in that improving your current capabilities relies on an analysis of what is already quite familiar to you. Perhaps, for example, you feel that your questioning techniques are closing down opportunities for students to develop their inquiry skills. Having realized this you can seek professional development activities that meet your needs and provide the support and challenge that will result in both change and improvement in practice. The latter, however, is not so easy. In effect we are referring here to being in the state of 'unconscious competence'. We will say more about this in Chapter 9. What is significant about identifying your needs in this situation is that you need to enlist the help of more experienced others to hold a mirror to your practice. Alternatively we hope the content of this book has already alerted you to areas of practice that you recognize either you know very little, or nothing at all, about.

So what can you learn from the highly accomplished teachers described in this book? First, they are all travelling on very different personal learning journeys – there is no one path. Second, a strong sense of intrinsic self-motivation drives them to continue their learning journeys. Interestingly, at the outset their journeys began largely without experienced others pointing the way. They were beginning- and early-career teachers just as many readers of this book will be now. For many of them, their expertise is now recognized among colleagues and peers, but still they continue to seek guidance from others who have professional learning experiences that they have not. Their minds are always open to new possibilities. Practice simply does not stand still.

Chapter 9 will take further the idea of auditing professional learning needs. It will attempt to say more about how you might go about this, how you might identify opportunities for learning and how you might create them to ensure that the professional development you undertake actually aligns with your learning needs. In the meantime, we will take forward the idea that much professional learning should come through learning from colleagues and peers and that the science department is almost uniquely placed among subject departments for having the potential to foster multi-disciplinary learning through a community of practitioners (see Wenger 1998).

Collaborative learning in a professional learning community

The science department in a secondary school can comprise a considerable number of people. In our experience the number can sometimes exceed 20, including full-time and part-time science teachers and technicians, pre-service teachers, science consultants from local education boards and authorities, science educators from higher education institutions, sometimes local scientists from industry, and so on. Everyone in the community has the potential (if not always the will) to learn and all have experiences to share.

So where does the beginning- and early-career teacher fit into this? First, it is vital for everyone to recognize that beginning- and early-career teachers can often be entering the profession with a wealth of experience behind them. For any science department, not to acknowledge this would be unwise. However, in terms of the practice of the community they are essentially 'newcomers' (Lave and Wenger 1991). They are there as apprentices to engage in 'legitimate peripheral participation'. According to Lave and Wenger, this is a way of trying to understand how learning may occur within a community. We maintain that some of the most valuable experiences beginning- and early-career teachers will have is while they are in the science department learning from the practice of more seasoned and experienced others. Of course, no one person is the repository of all the knowledge in a science department; knowledge is distributed unevenly and disparately across all its members. For instance, there were clear examples in our conversations with highly accomplished teachers of the fact that technical staff hold a special but unique form of professional knowledge. This is not necessarily knowledge of classroom experience that many beginning- and early-career teachers believe they are there to acquire but specialized knowledge, that is essential for the efficient working of the department. Sadly, school administrators are all too likely to see science technicians as expendable in times of financial constraint, but their loss can deny newcomers key knowledge that sometimes the 'old-timers' do not realize they have.

An effective leader within a science department will recognize the distributed nature of knowledge across it and know how the various knowledge bases relate to one another. A department that works well as a collaborative community of learners will also devise ways to ensure that such professional knowledge can be shared and accessed by all staff, and by newcomers in particular. We would anticipate learning taking place through a clearly defined professional discourse within the department. But such a discourse does not come about by accident. A discourse of collaboration also needs a vocabulary and a language.

The nature of collaborative learning

The early stages of a teacher's career are marked by the first encounters in professional discourse with colleagues. Essentially this is an introduction to the language of the pedagogy of teaching and learning. David Hopkins made this point clearly in a speech to the UK Teacher Training Agency in 2005 when he remarked:

> Language defines us. If teachers had a more extensive vocabulary of professional practice, they could exercise more control over the learning environments of their students and their own professional development. A key task for those committed to enhancing the learning of pupils, therefore, is to expand the vocabulary of teaching.

This issue of language and the nature of professional discourse emerged clearly through our research with highly accomplished science teachers. Acquiring and using the language of professional discourse is a characteristic of apprenticeship in joining the community. Our highly accomplished teachers were comfortable in using the language of pedagogy to express their thinking and to articulate practice, thus allowing the apparently implicit, or tacit, knowledge of teaching science to become explicit. If beginning- and early career-teachers are to engage in legitimate peripheral participation then within any community of science practitioners there must be members proficient in the discourse of collaboration.

In Chapter 1 we introduced Lave and Wenger's concept of 'communities of practice'. We think the concept is particularly useful in providing a framework within which language (a vocabulary for the pedagogy of science teaching), knowledge and experience can all be shared and developed. As indicated previously, the science department in most secondary schools forms a natural community, but whether it is a learning community or not depends very much on the nature of the leadership the department enjoys. We talked at length to the highly accomplished science teachers about how they learned from other science educators and what kinds of early learning opportunities they experienced when joining the profession. What emerged is that there was absolutely no pattern of experience! Learning was serendipitous. If you were lucky enough to find yourself in a department where teachers actively engaged in learning from one another, then you were indeed fortunate.

Productive disequilibrium

For professional learning to occur, what matters most, it would seem, is the nature of the interactions the highly accomplished science teachers received – not only when they started out, but as they have continued on their learning journeys. It appears that the often serendipitous nature of many interactions, and the almost certain lack of any theoretical structure for them, renders those interactions somewhat unproductive. However, to address this issue, we believe Wilson and Berne (1999) offer a way of structuring interaction which may be helpful to any collaborative activity and lead to what Lave and Wenger (1991) call a 'learning curriculum'. They define a learning curriculum for legitimate peripheral participation as 'a field of learning resources (or situated opportunities) in everyday practice viewed from the perspective of the learner' (1991: 97). Wilson and Berne (1999: 203) suggest that the purpose of any interaction between collaborating colleagues should be, in their words, 'to create and sustain productive disequilibrium, through self-reflection, collegial dialogue and on-going critique'.

The concept of productive disequilibrium is interesting. It would suggest that although it may be uncomfortable, those involved in the interaction must accept that dearly-held assumptions or preconceptions need to be open to testing and evaluation. For beginning- and early-career teachers this may be less difficult as they are in the process of developing their values about the purposes of education in general and their theories and beliefs about science teaching and learning in particular. Perhaps the effectiveness of professional learning may be indicated by the extent to which collegial dialogue promotes self-reflection and critical analysis. Ultimately, the test of the quality of professional learning, through collaborative activity and interaction, is the impact of teacher learning and how closely it is linked to (change in) teacher practice and to student achievement.

Learning science departments

Learning science departments have to be created! Some departments that the highly accomplished science teachers described to us were self-evidently proactive in creating a pool of shared resources and in their approach to sharing knowledge and learning from one another. Simple sharing of resources is one dimension:

> 'The school always gets a *New Scientist* and ASE membership, so we get their publications, which have lots of ideas. And just trying to build up the background sources because textbooks date in a flash. We've also subscribed recently to online things.'

> 'We have a section on the Science Network [i.e. school intranet] where we just put all our resources to share so that whenever you're teaching them you can just pull up what everyone else has done and see if there's something they've done which is good.'

In other departments it was less clear how they worked but they seemed to have an unwritten code of collaboration and mutual support which helped sustain a learning community. This would seem to be closer to the idea of developing a discourse of collaboration which beginning- and early-career teachers might see as evidence of a learning curriculum for them:

> 'So that support exists, that informal climate. I couldn't put my finger on how that climate was started but the very fact that people are willing to give their time to each other is really key.'

> '. . . so we've made it very positive, and it's now such a positive atmosphere and it's happened over the last ten years so that people now have conversations not only about what people have read and ideas people have, but also about learning and the students and talking about the students as individuals rather than bodies.'

Science departments may find it helpful to be clear about the purposes and the nature of the kinds of collaborative learning they wish to promote. Wilson and Berne (1999), once more, suggest collaborative learning can be viewed in terms of three knowledge categories: opportunities to talk about students and learning; opportunities to talk about and do subject matter; and opportunities to talk about teaching (p. 177). Arguably these categories are not discrete. Subject matter cannot be isolated and divorced from those for whom it is intended. Nevertheless, it is better to be transparent about how the learners, and the content being prepared for them, are related. If this can be achieved, beginning- and early career-teachers will find it much easier to see into the 'situatedness' (see previously) of teaching and should be clearer about the focus of the discourse.

Research and practice

What is the role of research in influencing practice? You can find numerous articles in academic journals and elsewhere that suggest educational research has little to offer teachers. As researchers ourselves we would obviously disagree, but we would say that wouldn't we! In fact, Hemsley-Brown and Sharp (2003: 461) confirm that 'empirical research shows that there is no direct positive relationship between systematic dissemination of research findings and impact on policy and practice'. This is probably not surprising, but there is better evidence to suggest that where research is conducted through networks that involve researchers in conjunction with classroom practitioners the impact of practice has the potential to be much greater (DETYA 2000). The Children's Learning in Science project (CLIS 1987) is one example of a participative research project that has had huge influence on science teaching; another is the Cognitive Acceleration through Science Education (CASE) project (Adey *et al.* 2001). Recent projects funded by the ESRC such as the Evidence-based Practice in Science Education (EPSE) project have already yielded really interesting results (Millar *et al.* 2006).

The question as we see it for beginning- and early-career teachers is twofold: how do you access and use the outcomes of research in science education; and how do you engage in meaningful research into your own practice? Both, we believe, can result in the development of new professional knowledge. From our research there was good evidence to show that all the highly accomplished science teachers had used published outcomes of major research projects in one way or another and that some, to varying degrees, had engaged in research themselves.

Using the outcomes of research

Currently there is a lot of interest in using 'evidence-based practice' in teaching (see Elliott 2001 for a comprehensive account of the issues). For science, the EPSE programme (2001–3) offers an excellent introduction to the issues surrounding the process (see www.tlrp.org/proj/phase1/phase1bsept.html). As an outcome of the programme, Millar *et al.*'s recent book *Improving subject teaching* (2006) focuses specifically on science teaching and reports the effects of science teacher-/educator-designed interventions on teacher practice. If any text can give an insight into the role research can play in helping to understand and improve practice, this one leads the way. This is because it explains very clearly how the interventions were created through a participative process, what they were intended to achieve and how evidence of their efficacy was collected and evaluated.

We alluded earlier to influential research projects such as CASE which resulted in carefully designed programmes of intervention. With such projects there is always the danger that if the user is not fully aware of the theoretical basis of the research, the intervention based on that research may be misinterpreted or misused. As a consequence, when the intervention fails to yield the anticipated outcomes, the blame falls squarely on the intervention rather than on the way the intervention was introduced. Having said that, CASE, through its *Thinking science* (Adey *et al.* 2001) publication (now in its third edition) has had a huge take-up across the UK and influenced the practice of many science teachers. Where at one time few science teachers knew what 'metacognition' or 'social constructivism' were, now they know and can utilize the ideas more broadly in their practice.

Currently there are a number of other research-based interventions for science education that you might investigate. Among these is the IDEAS project, which emanated from King's College London. IDEAS is an acronym for ideas, evidence and argument in science. It is based on research conducted with schools in the London area and incorporates Stephen Toulmin's philosophy of argument as a theoretical framework for helping teachers explore the basis of scientific argument with students. It provides science teachers with a number of alternative ways to introduce argumentation into their science lessons. This in itself would offer an ideal focus for a science teacher wishing to improve the scientific quality of the kind of classroom talk they would like to promote with students. Understanding argumentation's theoretical background, however, is absolutely essential if the intervention is to have any chance of success. Simon *et al.* (2006), in their article in the *International Journal of Science Education*, give a well documented overview of the current thinking about the place of argumentation in science teaching. For a really good set of accounts about argumentation directed specifically at classroom practitioners see Erduran (2007).

Engaging in research

We strongly recommend that all science teachers, newcomers and old-timers, should participate in the process of research as an effective way of developing reflective and analytical capacities. For example, in one of our own projects at the University of Bath (Bullock *et al.* 2002), teachers from ITE/T partnership schools reviewed their own practice to provide key insights into what enhances student learning through coursework. Moreover, if the capacity to engage in pedagogical discourse is important, then participation in research offers another effective route to accomplishment.

You might consider the approach we took to gather data for this book, i.e., VSR. Stimulated recall has a long history. Over 25 years ago, Calderhead (1981) reviewed the benefits of the technique, although he noted the crucial and possibly distorting role the interviewer could play in the subsequent discussion. A few years later Meade and McMeniman (1992) confirmed the efficacy of VSR for gaining a profound insight into the implicit theories and beliefs of teachers. Since then it has been used as the basis of some significant pieces of research. More recently in the UK, the National College for School Leadership (NCSL) published a short document by McMeniman *et al.* (2003) reporting how researchers in Australia used VSR to explore teachers' decision-making as a measure of the extent to which published research impacted on their practice (for the full report see DETYA 2000).

Without doubt, videoing your teaching can offer you a powerful way of analysing your practice, particularly if you can enlist the support of other science teachers to explore the reasoning behind your approaches to teaching and learning. In fact, not only should it help you to develop your capacity to engage in pedagogical discourse, but such collaborative analysis can also help more experienced colleagues articulate their tacit knowledge, i.e., they should be able to articulate the reasoning behind their decision-making both in preparation for teaching (pre-active decision-making) and while teaching (interactive decision-making). Gaining insights into the tacit knowledge of the highly accomplished science teacher is a very effective way of learning the discourse of collaboration, and thus to become a legitimate peripheral participant.

We advocate classroom research as an essential tool for professional learning. In science there is no shortage of dimensions of practice that could be tackled through this process. From explorations into scientific inquiry as a basis for learning science to the use of different types of discussion to promote the social construction of knowledge, there is more than enough to keep even the most dynamic of advanced skills teachers busy. For beginning- and early-career teachers, however, it offers the opportunity to develop the range of capacities that highly accomplished science teachers demonstrate. We have called these 'professional learning capacities' which, when taken together, provide a basis for the development of professional knowledge and its deployment for the enhancement of student learning.

Professional learning capacities

Throughout this book we have argued that professional learning is not simply a process devoted to acquiring knowledge: it is a more complex interrelated set of capacities, all of which can be discerned in the practice of the highly accomplished science teachers involved in this research (see Figure 8.1). We have attempted to identify the key capacities that provide the stepping stones to accomplishment. We have exemplified each professional learning capacity with an extract from one of the participating teachers. We offer them here as a precursor to further discussion in Chapter 9.

Professional learning capacity	Evidence
1 Ability to be reflective and analytical with regard to own practice.	'. . . the reason I want to spend more time on this is because last year's Year 8 who I taught, when they had their end of unit test for this, enzymes was the bit they didn't get. So I wanted to spend much longer on it with this class than my other class.'
2 Ability to determine personal learning needs and priorities.	'So for me, I think pedagogical change was probably that creativity, having to change to engage kids. Having to change. That's what comes from working in schools with challenging kids.'
3a Ability to identify opportunities for learning.	'I guess as you teach more and more you learn what works and what doesn't and if you're like me you're trying new things all the time.'
3b Ability to create opportunities to learn.	'I take risks and I'm probably better equipped to deal with the failures, but I still will fail sometimes and have to put it down to experience that I'll lock away in my mind as "I'm not doing that again" or "if I do it again I'll do it in a slightly different way".'
3c Ability to learn from or in collaboration with (more experienced) colleagues.	'And I think I've done it through trial and error to a certain extent and also through watching other people and seeing the way they've presented things. Going and watching other people teach, especially if you're not a specialist. I went to a biologist and a physicist and asked how they taught that. "I struggled with teaching that. How did you present that?" And they would come to watch me doing something and say, "I didn't think of using that way to do that. That's really good. I'd like to use that." The more you can get links with other people and going into each other's rooms, the better.'
4 Ability to manipulate and transform subject knowledge.	'I tried to think of ways of learning it myself and then think of the way of getting that information over to students. I think that probably is true of what's happened over the years and obviously that's changed with experience.'

5 Ability to engage in pedagogical reasoning.	'I think it's important to allow pupils to discuss concepts in small groups early on – this gives them confidence in their ideas as others validate them and reminds them of other people's opinions. The discussion will allow me to find out what their current knowledge is and what misconceptions exist.'
6 Ability to store knowledge for future use.	'The way I approach it with them [another but less able group] will be very different because they won't come up with the same responses. Certainly I'll take out all the isotopes bit. That will go because I think that more than anything will confuse them. But probably the same start with that slide and pictures to get them thinking about that. But cut down a lot of the substantive knowledge aspect.'

Figure 8.1 Capacities for professional learning.

Concluding remarks

To conclude this chapter we leave you with two thoughts from David Hopkins in a speech he gave to the General Council for Teaching (England) at the inaugural conference of the Teacher Learning Academy on 7 July 2005. First, Professor Hopkins reaffirms the value of research as an authentic mechanism for professional learning:

> If you want to improve teaching, the most effective place to do so is in the context of a classroom lesson. If you start with lessons, the problem of how to apply research findings in the classroom disappears.

Second, he reinforces the need for a cultural shift in teachers' attitudes towards their own development:

> Put simply, unless teachers see their continuing development as an essential part of their professionalism, the system will be unable to make the next big step forward in standards of learning and achievement.

The commitment towards their own learning development displayed by the highly accomplished science teachers is a commitment, we believe, that can only be encouraged more widely when schools themselves promote a culture that values and resources adequately teacher professional learning.

9 Professional knowledge in context

This book started with a consideration of the knowledge base for teaching as a starting point for examining the professional knowledge of the highly accomplished science teachers whose practice and thinking is at the core of the central chapters. In this chapter we wish to return to the issue of how helpful it is to characterize knowledge for teaching in this way and return to that particular sort of knowledge called pedagogical content knowledge. We are then going to conclude by examining some of the links between two concepts that have been a strong thread throughout this book – professional *knowledge* and professional *learning* – and then, to consider a third – professional *development*.

Standards

In Chapter 1 we presented some different approaches to 'codifying' the knowledge base for teaching, starting with the seven categories proposed by Lee Shulman and going on to other attempts to produce frameworks for the purpose of assessing teaching competence. Often the word 'standards' is introduced – sets of teaching standards have been developed in most countries both to mark entry points into the profession or to regulate progress within it. In the UK, the Training and Development Agency (TDA) has produced a framework for progression from initial qualification through four stages to Advanced Skills Teacher. Other countries have similar systems, either compulsory for all teachers or on an incentive basis – success in meeting the standards is a requirement for crossing a salary bar for gaining promotion. Although it can be argued that these standards provide some kind of statement that sets out a baseline regarding what teachers are expected to know and be able to do, they are generic and do not capture the specialized knowledge of the subject teacher. Our focus in this book has been on science teaching but the standards movement has generally opted for a generic approach. There are a few examples of standards which are subject-specific. In Chapter 1 we referred to the professional standards for accomplished science teachers set out by the NBPTS (see www.nbpts.org) in the USA. Meeting these standards leads to certification and that may lead to job security and salary enhancements. The approach in Australia, also mentioned in Chapter 1, is interesting in that a subject teaching association took the initiative and worked with government agencies to generate, by science teachers and science educators working together, not so much a set of standards but a set of descriptions of highly accomplished science teachers (ASTA 2007). By adopting a slightly more holistic approach, these descriptions provide much more helpful statements about what science teachers might aspire to in their careers. The project leader, Lawrence Ingvarson, has stressed the value of having such a framework to encourage teachers to reflect on and improve their teaching. He goes further in showing how they can gain recognition for their achievements through a portfolio-based certification process (see Ingvarson and Semple 2006).

If you wish to review your own professional knowledge, these kinds of professional standards offer a detailed picture of what accomplished science teaching is about and might be as good a place to start as any. You could also look at the National Science Learning Centre's website (www.sciencelearningcentres.org.uk) in the UK where an audit/planning tool is available which can be used to review your science professional knowledge. This tool is based on one produced by science teachers for the Science Education Forum (www.scienceeducationforum.org.uk), using a framework based on the ASTA standards but which also provides opportunities to self-assess at different levels, thus allowing for progression. We believe this tool to be unique in providing a career-long framework for professional knowledge development for science teachers. It is not intended to be a stick to beat teachers with but rather a way of science teachers being able to take some control of their professional learning.

The idea behind a diagnostic or auditing tool is to encourage a process of self-evaluation whereby you can pinpoint your professional development priorities for improving your science teaching. Self-evaluation, however, requires a high degree of self-awareness and that in turn depends on your capacity to be honest with yourself about your learning needs. In Chapter 2 (p. 19) we made reference to Dubin's dichotomy (Dennison and Kirk 1990: 22) which relates the two interrelated dimensions of consciousness and competence. Before developing this further we should recognize the associations with this idea of competence. Nobody likes to think of themselves as 'incompetent' and there are undoubtedly negative connotations to that word, particularly in education. Dubin did not mean it that way – he placed no such lay value judgements on the term. He was talking about a spectrum from a relatively low level of performance to a relatively high level. So, in those terms, we all need to be aware that there are for all of us areas of 'incompetence'. Dubin's concern was to look at the relationship between competence and consciousness, and to suggest a progression through a sequence of learning states. But before learning can begin there is the pre-learning stage of 'unconscious incompetence' – not knowing what you do not know! In carrying out any kind of audit of your knowledge, you must be sensitive to areas of knowledge which as yet you do not know about – areas of 'unconscious incompetence'. At the end of the sequence, the things we know best, almost intuitively or automatically, are in the domain that Dubin calls 'unconscious competence'. This is part of the problem in clearly articulating the practice of our highly accomplished teachers. It is one thing to know how to ride a bicycle, it is another to explain to someone how to do it. Dubin suggests that 'conscious incompetence' is the state of readiness to learn and that through learning we reach, initially, conscious competence, and then, with practice and experience, the end state of unconscious competence. Some sort of audit can help to identify those areas of conscious incompetence. The audit will also identify the things you *do* know, so should not be seen as only focusing on the negative, but should provide some positive reinforcement as well.

Knowledge, knowing and PCK

Having introduced some of the issues relating to the identification and classification of professional knowledge in Chapter 1, we came down to using six of Shulman's categories in analysing the practice of our highly accomplished teachers. In reviewing Shulman's categories, we resisted trying to treat PCK in the same way as the other six. We suggested that it was perhaps hard to isolate this sort of knowledge as a 'type' or 'category' without diminishing it. To some, PCK may simply be the metaphors, stories or models which Shulman alluded to, but we feel that there is more to it that that. Just knowing *that* it is possible to use a particular analogy – Eric's students throwing bits of paper to represent radioactive decay, for example – is different from knowing *when* and *how* to deploy such knowledge. We called this a 'meta-knowledge' – a 'knowledge about knowledge' – and it is that sort of knowledge that we believe to be important in accomplished science teaching. We hope that the accounts in Chapters 3–5 have given some insight into the PCK of our highly accomplished teachers. It comes through in the way that they talk about and think about their teaching, and in their decision-making before, during and after their teaching. We believe that these teachers are drawing on a range of knowledge bases in their professional practice and that this is our interpretation of Shulman's use of the metaphor of an 'amalgam' – a mixture of different metals which together can have distinctive properties different from its constituents. Our metaphor was more dynamic – the spinning top. Our contention which we hope we have demonstrated through these teachers' accounts is that, rather than seeing PCK as a different 'type' of knowledge, it is more about the sophisticated process of combining knowledge bases together for particular contexts in relation to classes, topics or other factors. Thus, we might see an amalgam in terms of the constituent knowledge bases which these teachers draw on, but the key knowledge that these teachers have is how and when to combine them together and in what proportions.

In reviewing PCK, others have presented alternative perspectives. John Barnett and Derek Hodson (2001: 426) present their concept of 'pedagogical context knowledge' in an attempt to synthesize 'a number of models, metaphors, and notions already described in the literature about teachers' knowledge'. Their views are very much in sympathy with those expressed in this book regarding the limitations of an approach which is restricted to trying to codify and tightly define through 'standards' the knowledge of, in particular, more experienced and accomplished science teachers. They refer to those such as Connelly *et al.* (1997) who stress the value of thinking about 'personal practical knowledge' in guiding teaching:

> The significant aspect of this 'teacher's knowing of a classroom' is that it is not objectivist, not a body of pre-existing knowledge to be acquired by teachers and subsequently applied to practice. Rather, it is transient, subject to change, and situated in personal experience both inside and outside the classroom.
>
> (Barnett and Hodson 2001: 431)

They also stress the situated nature of teachers' knowledge and its generation within communities of practice in schools and science departments. We found examples with our highly accomplished teachers where change of 'situation' led to the need for re-learning – for example, moving to a new school. Berliner (2004) in his study with expert teachers found that when they were placed in new surroundings they became much more frustrated about their performance than novice teachers. Perhaps what is being revealed is a greater awareness of what they believe to be necessary in terms of developing relationships with their students in order to enable them to perform at the standard they know they are capable of.

Barnett and Hodson's 'pedagogical *context* knowledge' links together conceptual and experiential knowledge. Their 'PContextK' is not so much a form of knowledge itself but the integration of four other knowledge bases: 'classroom knowledge'; 'professional knowledge'; 'academic and research knowledge'; and 'pedagogical content knowledge'. Together these form 'knowledge landscapes' (Connelly *et al.* 1997):

> Having an overview of the nature of pedagogical context knowledge enables teachers to look around the knowledge landscape, to look inward for reflection, and to look outward for other sources of

knowledge and criticism. It enables unexplored or inadequately explored areas of the landscape to become 'friendly places' and fruitful avenues for the acquisition of professional expertise, rather than places to be feared and avoided.

(Barnett and Hodson 2001: 440)

We feel this view is very much in accord with the sort of approach to professional learning through the professional learning capacities we proposed in Chapter 8.

Taking a slightly different angle, Cochran *et al.* (1993) suggest 'pedagogical content *knowing*' (PCKg) as being a desirable attribute of accomplishment in teaching. At least this is a more active conception than a static 'type' of knowledge and one which is closer to our spinning top metaphor. The additional strength that we believe there to be in our spinning top is the way that it links the underlying knowledge bases with the active processing that we discussed in Chapter 2 – what we referred to there as 'pedagogical reasoning'. We believe that this is a key feature of the highly accomplished teacher – this, often tacit, 'knowing' which these teachers were able to bring to bear in transforming their subject knowledge, matching their teaching to the needs of their learners. The importance of pedagogical reasoning is stressed by its inclusion as one of our professional learning capacities in Chapter 8. The issue is perhaps not just stressing its importance but suggesting ways in which it might be developed. It may be one of those things which needs to be learned but which is hard to 'teach'. We hope that this book has at least uncovered and illustrated instances of pedagogical reasoning and perhaps given some shape to a quality of thinking about science teaching of which readers might not have previously been aware – a shift from 'unconscious incompetence' to 'conscious incompetence'.

So we started with one PCK and ended up with three! There are other attempts to make sense of this in the literature. Certainly the book edited by Julie Gess-Newsome and Norman Lederman, *Examining pedagogical content knowledge* (1999), provides some fascinating ideas about what it might be and discusses other issues such as how it might be assessed. We would strongly recommend Loughran *et al.*'s book *Understanding and developing science teachers' pedagogical content knowledge* (2006) which through its CoRe (content representation) and PaP-eRs (pedagogical and professional-experience repertoires) approach give some fascinating accounts of teacher thinking about a wide range of science topics. Although it does not explicitly use the notion of PCK, another very useful book which presents teachers' knowledge and exposes their thinking in a detailed way is *Analysing exemplary science teaching*, edited by Alsop *et al.* (2006). Half of the book contains accounts of exemplary practice, the other half contains analyses built around these accounts but exploring a wide range of issues.

Shulman certainly started a ball rolling when he initially (and quite loosely) formulated the concept of PCK. It may continue to be one those unfolding stories where the journey is more important than the destination. Even if the 'elusive butterfly' is never pinned, much has been learned about what characterizes high quality science teaching and PCK has exposed some important issues which stress that perhaps it is not so important what you *know* as what you can *do* with it – *quantity of knowledge vs. quality of thinking*.

Professional development

We started this book with professional knowledge and pedagogical reasoning and then shifted the focus, particularly through the teachers' accounts of their practice, to one of professional learning. There is another related field which we would now like to move to – that of professional development. We have tried to show the importance both of the knowledge the highly accomplished teachers have and of the ways in which they bring it to bear on their teaching. Professional development is perhaps best considered as a 'facilitating mechanism' for the learning which teachers undertake to improve their practice. There are two tensions, however. The first is that professional development is often driven by the needs of the system or the institution and less often by the personal needs of the individual teacher. The second tension is that it is more often concerned with generic rather than subject-specific needs. We suggested in Chapter 8 some ways in which professional learning towards highly accomplished science teaching might take place, but what opportunities can professional development (as a 'facilitating mechanism') offer?

Opportunities for professional development vary considerably from country to country, from public to private sectors and from phase to phase. In some European countries professional development is compulsory and expressed in terms of entitlements. Within the UK, the situation in Scotland is much more positive that in England. In Scotland, there is the expectation that teachers will be involved in a minimum of 35 hours of professional development per year. This is linked with a Chartered Teacher scheme which provides salary incentives linked with professional development goals. In England, there is no such entitlement at the time of writing and the picture of provision is much more variable. For science teachers, particularly, there are many opportunities. Figure 9.1 attempts to show something of the range.

Notwithstanding the opportunities, the issues are to do with access, resources and prioritization. Our highly accomplished science teachers do not seem to have waited for professional development to be done to them. They have taken a much more autonomous perspective – taking responsibility themselves for their development. Although they have taken advantage of courses, they have also done a lot in their own schools, working with

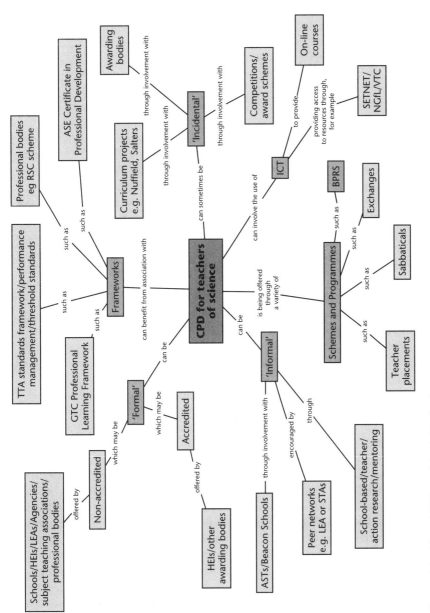

Figure 9.1 Map of CPD provision in England

colleagues in the science department, other departments in the school, and even beyond school. They have also done a lot of work on their own – reading, Internet research and activities with professional associations like the ASE. Theirs seems to be an eclectic approach to professional development – selecting from here and there, from a wide variety of sources to meet their needs – but they have been in control.

It may be helpful to look at what is known about effective professional development for science teachers in order to develop fresh ideas which might be helpful in planning your own route through the maze of opportunities.

Our story here again goes back to the 1980s and to the seminal work of Bruce Joyce and Beverley Showers (see Joyce and Showers, 2002 for the latest version of their original book) who, through a study of a large number of 'in-service training' courses for teachers, suggested the relationship between levels of impact and the components of the training. Levels of impact ranged from raising awareness through to change of practice in the classroom, that is, according to Hopkins (2007):

- presentation of theory or description of skill or strategy;
- modelling or demonstration of skills or models of teaching;
- practice in simulated and classroom settings;
- structured and open-ended feedback (provision of information about performance);
- coaching for application (hands-on, in-classroom assistance with the transfer of skills and strategies to the classroom).

Although these are not strictly speaking in a rigid hierarchical sequence, there is a sense in which 'presentation of theory' (e.g., through a one-off workshop) is only the first stage in a developmental series to support the introduction of new teaching ideas in the classroom, ultimately through something like coaching. In their research, Joyce and Showers found (perhaps unsurprisingly) that training courses often expected high levels of impact (i.e., real changes in what happens in classrooms) from just the first stage. This would accord with many teachers' experiences of attending a one-day course and being expected to apply new ideas to their practice without further support. It is one reason why many teachers are at best sceptical and at worst cynical about this sort of professional development, which has been criticized for being neither 'professional' nor 'development'. We would wish to distance ourselves from any conception of professional development which is seen to be exclusively externally determined or provided. Professional development for the sort of professional learning we are advocating in this book will involve a variety of different approaches, but will be individually driven, holding the needs of the teacher and his or her institution in balance.

How much better if professional development programmes allowed a teacher to go from the initial presentation of ideas to modelling, practice, and then feedback and coaching? Current interest in coaching can be traced back to the work by Joyce and Showers and their more recent work has been in this field. But this sort of view of how professional development (or staff development, as David Hopkins refers to it) might be conceptualized has implications for teachers and schools. According to Hopkins (2007: 4):

> This implies changes to the way in which staff development is organised in schools . . . In particular, this means providing the opportunity for immediate and sustained practice, collaboration and peer coaching, and studying development and implementation. Instructional leaders realise that one cannot 'ad hoc' staff development – time has to be found for it.

Studies on professional development for science teachers (Dillon *et al.* 2000; Denley *et al.* 2004; Wellcome Trust 2006) have suggested that schools have not made the changes that Hopkins is suggesting. They show a messy picture of teachers not always being aware of what CPD opportunities are available to them, a lack of transparency in policy at departmental and school levels and still quite a heavy reliance on short courses with little if any follow-up; certainly not the comprehensive approach advocated by Joyce and Showers.

There are very few examples of professional development programmes which are designed around a more sustained approach, but we would like to mention two. We have referred elsewhere the CASE project (see p. 193). CASE has not only developed an innovative approach to science teaching with clear benefits in student attainment but has also produced in parallel an innovative professional development programme which combines elements of Joyce and Showers' components, particularly the use of in-class support, feedback and coaching (see Adey 2004). Another project-based professional development programme is explored by Bell and Gilbert (1996), again with key elements of support, feedback and reflection in their account of the Learning in Science Project.

Secondary schools in England have been involved in a national government-funded initiative through what started as the 'Key Stage 3 Strategy' but is now the 'Secondary National Strategy', of which science is a part. A multi-million pound programme of CPD for teachers has been running which has involved some 'off-site' courses but also a lot of work in schools and departments through strategy consultants. Although there is an overall evaluation of this initiative through Ofsted (2005), this contains little detail about the professional development model used or how effective it has been.

The other major science initiative in England currently is the establishment of the network of Science Learning Centres. We have written about this elsewhere (Bishop and Denley 2006) in terms of how such a network might have an important role in leading practice in professional development. Leach *et al.* (2005) present a vision of how they see these centres providing high quality and effective professional development opportunities for science teachers and other science educators.

All these examples of CPD for science teachers are to varying extents part of a 'top-down' and external conception of professional development. They provide structures and resources which teachers may or may not wish to take up – how does this fit with our vision of professional learning which suggests trying to make the system work for you rather than you working for the system? The highly accomplished teachers with whom we worked took advantage of the professional development opportunities which were available to them but also created their own within and beyond their schools. They are reflective and analytical and proactive in their learning – going back to some ideas from Chapter 1, they are (within limits) autonomous professionals. In the next section, we would like to explore two of the professional learning communities from the last chapter to show ways in which you might try to become more active in controlling your professional development and look for and make your own opportunities, rather than waiting for them to be offered, or worse, having them forced on you.

Identifying and creating opportunities for professional learning

To make the most of learning opportunities we believe it is essential to be strategic and purposeful. Like the highly accomplished science teachers in this book, you need to be clear about your educational values (Corrigan *et al.* 2007) and your theories and beliefs (philosophy) about teaching and learning. We will draw again on some of our teachers' accounts to illustrate possible approaches.

Identifying opportunities

Enthusiasm for learning is a characteristic trait of the highly accomplished science teachers involved in this research. Wherever they find opportunities to extend their knowledge, they take them and find ways to build new knowledge into their existing professional knowledge. For instance, Derek knew something already about Bloom's taxonomy (Bloom 1956) with respect to assessment in the cognitive domain but had not appreciated how the taxonomy might be utilized to improve his questioning technique. Not only that, he also saw it as a way of encouraging the students to think more deeply. It therefore coincided with his philosophy that his teaching should help the students develop their thinking skills. Some further research allowed him to exploit this new knowledge further.

Some highly accomplished science teachers identified specific gaps in their knowledge. Eric was concerned that his view of science lacked an historical perspective:

> 'When I first started teaching I didn't have time to read around it because I was so engrossed in the actual subject matter, but I read a lot of popular science. I read a lot about the history of science, in which I'm very interested, about how science ideas have developed over centuries, and I try and bring those ideas into my lessons as much as I can.'

It was quite evident from Eric's lesson how he used historical asides to provide a human dimension to the science he was asking the students to engage with. Evidence from the students supported his view that anecdotes and other 'bits of information' captured their interest and gave them the feeling that they were always going to learn something in his lessons.

Almost every day publicity material of one kind or another comes into schools advertising external courses or other activities. Judging the value of such training as opportunities for professional learning can be difficult. Our highly accomplished science teachers appeared to make limited use of such courses as very little of what was offered had a subject focus. Orla was quite scathing about the fact that much of what was on offer related only to generic aspects of teaching and learning:

> 'I don't want to know about behaviour for learning in science, I want to know about science! Every Saturday and Sunday I get the paper and sniff out as many articles as I can, even adverts, cut them out and I've got a big box of laminated articles for them to rummage through so you can say, "We're going to learn about this in science. Have you seen this?" MMR, things like that. There are so many opportunities to slot in where they've heard it outside and make that link.'

Consequently Orla identified many opportunities for herself to develop her own subject matter knowledge, but acknowledged it was hard work.

A theme emerging from our research for this book is that deep subject matter knowledge is fundamental to good science teaching. Of course, this is not a new theme (see McDiarmid *et al.*'s excellent article 'Why staying one chapter ahead doesn't really work: subject-specific pedagogy' from 1989). Consistently, the highly accomplished science teachers created genuinely interesting science lessons for their students because they either knew the subject matter extremely well already or they had made a considerable effort to research it. Either way, the strength of the lesson lay in how they subsequently transformed that content into activities and materials which both involved the students and enabled them to learn.

Creating opportunities

Sometimes it is necessary to manufacture opportunities for professional learning. There were numerous examples where risks were taken in order to test the effects of a new idea, or the modification of an existing one. Failing was part of the process but, if other things were in place, such as having established effective relationships with the students, the risks would be calculated rather than complete unknowns. In the lessons we happened to observe, Eric, Isabel, Emma and Alison all took risks of one kind or another in order to learn how the students would respond and to assess how the quality of the learning compared with other approaches they had tried in the past.

Eric in particular, appeared to see risk-taking as an essential component within his overall strategy for professional learning. As head of a science department there were occasions where he found himself teaching the same module in parallel with another colleague. Knowing that there would be clashes in relation to the supply of equipment and other resources, he allowed his colleague to follow the path determined by the scheme of work while he deliberately sought to find an alternative route. He did this on the basis that having to experiment with an alternative route through the content would provide him with the opportunity to test the sequencing of the concepts:

> 'Sometimes I'll take a scheme of work and actually teach it in a different order just for my own experimentation really. This has arisen because occasionally we have clashes of equipment, so it's necessary for someone to go out of sync with someone else. So I'll quite often say, "OK, you teach in that order and I'll teach in a different order" and sometimes that's quite useful in terms of viewing a whole topic from a different stance because you know where you want to end up by the end of the topic, but there's actually quite a few different ways of getting there. It's not just the way that's been written into a scheme of work. There are probably five or ten different ways of getting through some material and by making yourself do it in a different order it's actually quite interesting ... I've quite often taught about electric motors, showing kids motors that are working, getting them to build their own motor and then talking about magnetism and current and the interaction between them. There's no need to go through it in what you might consider to be the accepted order simply because that's the way it's written into the scheme of work. It's by looking at those different

ways that actually you come across, sometimes better ways of doing things.'

In some instances opportunities for professional learning can be created by engagement with the scientific community itself. Personal connections or links with local higher education institutions or industry all offer possibilities for updating science knowledge. For example, Emma said:

'Probably my best source of up-to-date knowledge are discussions with other scientists. My husband is a scientist and a lot of friends from my degree and teaching are scientists and obviously everybody in the department here.'

All our highly accomplished science teachers contrived opportunities of one kind or another which they thought would help them reflect on and be exposed to alternative teaching techniques and approaches. In some instances this was pursued by working with colleagues to create in-school opportunities for professional learning:

'I've done it through trial and error to a certain extent and also through watching other people and seeing the way they've presented things. Going and watching other people teach, especially if you're not a specialist. I went to a biologist and a physicist and asked how they taught that. "I struggled with teaching that. How did you present that?" And they would come to watch me doing something and say, "I didn't think of using that way to do that. That's really good. I'd like to use that." The more you can get links with other people, and going into each other's rooms, the better.'

Being involved in team teaching, peer observations or supporting pre-service or novice science teachers were all activities the highly accomplished science teachers undertook in order to learn from colleagues and peers while at the same time broadening and deepening their knowledge and understanding of teaching science. Whatever they did, they understood in principle that they would learn more through collegial and collaborative activities than from individual classroom experience alone. Hence the concept of a professional learning community comes quite naturally to teachers committed to continuous learning.

Being a teacher researcher

Another way of looking at professional learning is as research on your own practice. Numerous variants of 'action research', 'collaborative research' or just 'teacher research' have been around for over 20 years but more recently they have gained some status through their leading to higher degree qualifications or other forms of recognition (such as the Best Practice Research Scholarships until recently available through the DfES in England). Most of our highly accomplished science teachers had either undertaken or were in the process of completing a master's degree which usually required some form of school-based inquiry. One teacher was successful on two occasions in her applications to carry out BPRS (Best Practice Research Scholarship) supported research in her teaching of chemical equations.

There is good evidence to suggest that one of the most powerful ways to develop classroom practice is to engage in some form of classroom research. The highly accomplished science teacher who carried out research funded by the BPRS scheme was certain that it made a marked impact on her practice:

> 'It was about chemical equations and why students find them so hard, when to me they're quite logical and straightforward. What is it that they find so difficult exactly? So I did research into that just by trying different methods of teaching it and comparing them. And now I don't actually teach that section the same as I did, so it's had an influence on my teaching. I now make sure that when I teach that section I don't just do what I always used to.'

Research can take other forms too. Iain had been a researcher in plant physiology himself in the past. He was keen to show his students that research was still important to him and that the outcomes of his research could enliven his teaching. He saw this as increasing his credibility with the students as well as demonstrating the relevance of science to their lives by trying to show them how it happens right on their doorstep:

> 'I'm doing a project at the moment on the competition between native and non-native species of red and grey squirrels and we have a forest just up the road here where they're using conservation techniques to try and preserve the red squirrel. We have an agricultural research centre just up at the top of the road so we talk about things like tissue culture, micro-propagation. If you can refer them to somewhere close to base then they'll think, "Oh so that goes on there".'

A welcome move at government level would be to encourage CPD funding to be made available to schools to be used in support of science teachers trying to raise the level of engagement and involvement of students in science through classroom research. The TDA in England provides funding through university education departments. Organizations, such as the Association for Science Education in the UK (www.ase.org.uk), the National Science Teachers Association in the USA (www.nsta.org) and the Australian Science Teachers Association (www.asta.edu.au), all promote in one way or another the value of collaborative research in recognition of the potential for learning that accompanies such activity. These organizations should be able to advise on potential sources of funding and provide some support for science teachers wishing to undertake both research into their teaching or science research in their schools. Local university education and science departments are worth contacting to see what opportunities are available to get involved in their research projects. Also, STEMNET (www.stemnet.org.uk) should have a local office which will provide support.

Even if you cannot get funding, it is still possible to work on your own or with colleagues in the department. Good starting points for developing your understanding of classroom research are either David Hopkins' book *A teacher's guide to classroom research* (2002) or *Practitioner research for teachers* by Steve Bartlett and Diana Burton (2004). And to understand more about the research process itself, Jerry Wellington's (1996) short reader on *Methods and issues in educational research* summarizes neatly most of the issues you need to consider.

Recognition for your professional learning

We have already mentioned the possibility of classroom-based research leading to units or modules in a master's degree programme but that is not the only route to some sort of recognition for your learning. The ASE offers a way of submitting a portfolio of evidence to be considered for the award of Chartered Science Teacher status (www.ase.org.uk/htm/thease/siteguide.php). On the other hand, you might just be interested in putting together a portfolio record of your past learning and plans for the future. The National Science Learning Centre (www.sciencelearningcentres.org.uk) allows you to create an online portfolio in which you can store information about your achievements but also resources and materials and link in with discussion groups.

A model for professional learning

If we need some sort of formalization of the professional learning process then we could develop a tentative model (see Figure 9.2) showing the relationship

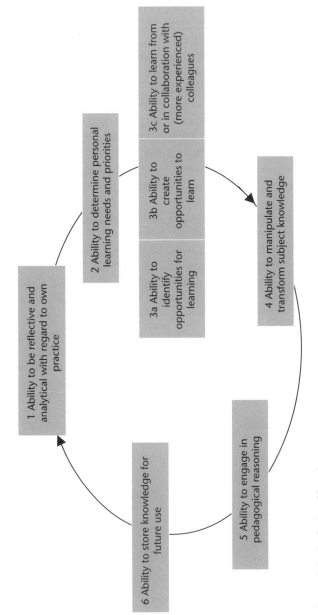

Figure 9.2 Professional learning.

between the professional learning capacities we suggested in the previous chapter (see Figure 8.1 on pp. 196–7). The model links to the examples we have given throughout the book from our group of highly accomplished science teachers where these capacities are seen in their classroom practice. It suggests a way in which a teacher working within a professional learning community might review his or her on-going development. It also emphasises the cyclical nature of professional learning and may suggest a sequence for planning ways forward.

Conclusion

The major theme running through this book, is the idea that learning to be a science teacher is an intellectual pursuit and that in order to be at the forefront of developments in science education, it is necessary to be a continuously learning science teacher.

From the interviews documented here it is evident that highly accomplished science teachers are actively seeking to find ways to build and extend their knowledge bases to embrace new knowledge, new ideas, skills and techniques. This is particularly important in a subject like science which is not only constantly changing in itself but where the underlying concepts are often difficult for young people to learn. We have tried to illustrate the ways that highly accomplished science teachers integrate their subject knowledge with their knowledge of teaching and learning, to present their learners with difficult ideas in an accessible form. At several points we have asserted that the amount you know is not itself sufficient for accomplished teaching – it is whether you are able to manipulate that knowledge, sensitively and creatively, to make it accessible to your students that matters.

We have emphasized the importance of considering the professional learning of teachers in the context of the subject being taught and in relation to the professional communities in which they work. We have tried to show how they work within their communities and make meaning from their experiences. As they grow their sense of identity develops, helping them to establish their role both as learners and teachers.

This then brings us to the end of our exploration of science teaching. We hope you have found this book useful and that it will inspire you to work towards becoming a highly accomplished teacher of science – we wish you well!

Appendix: commentaries from Chapters 3, 4 and 5

Derek (biology)	Isabel (chemistry)	Emma (biology)	Ursula (chemistry)	Orla (chemistry)	Eric (physics)	Aaron (physics)	Alison (physics)	Iain (biology)
Raising student self-esteem.	Learning styles and preferences.	Training the students.	Language in science – words as labels (Sutton).	Assessment for learning.	Modelling.	Monitoring learning.	Ownership.	Using analogies.
Science education for citizenship.	Security vs. unpredictability.	Misconceptions in science.	Learning by doing.	Active processing.	Developing relationships – risk-taking.	Misconceptions.	Developing relationships.	Making science relevant.
Promoting student discussion.	Models and modelling.	Using ICT.	Integrative theme.	Engagement and involvement.	Teaching for understanding.	Language in science – everyday and scientific usage.	Students' images of the nature of science.	Theory-dependent observation.
	Reinforcing learning.	Social construction of knowledge.	Science and special educational needs.		Student engagement.	Constructivist approaches to science teaching.		Questioning.

References

Abd-El-Khalick, F. and BouJaoude, S. (1997) An exploratory study of the know-ledge base for science teaching, *Journal of Research in Science Teaching*, 34: 673–99.

Adey, M., Shayer, P. and Yates, C. (2001) *Thinking science* (3rd edn). Cheltenham: Nelson Thornes.

Adey, P. (2004) *The professional development of teachers: practice and theory*. Dordrecht: Kluwer.

Alsop, S., Bencze, L. and Pedretti, E. (2006) *Analysing exemplary science teaching*. Maidenhead: Open University Press.

Argyris, C. and Schön, D. (1974) *Theory in practice: increasing professional effectiveness*. San Francisco, CA: Jossey Bass.

ASTA (Australian Science Teachers Association) (2007) *National professional standards for highly accomplished teachers of science*. Available at: http://www.asta.edu.au/membership/benefits/recognition/profstds/ accessed 4 April 2007.

Ausubel, D. (1968) *Educational psychology: a cognitive view*. New York: Holt, Rinehart and Winston.

Barnett, J. and Hodson, D. (2001) Pedagogical context knowledge: toward a fuller understanding of what good science teachers know, *Science Education*, 85(4): 426–53.

Bartlett, S. and Burton, D. (2004) *Practitioner research for teachers*. London: Paul Chapman.

Beijaard, D., Korthagen, F. and Verloop, N. (2007). Understanding how teachers learn as a prerequisite for promoting teacher learning, *Teachers and Teaching: Theory and Practice*, 13(2): 105–8.

Bell, B. and Gilbert, J. (1996) *Teacher development: a model from science education*. London: Falmer Press.

Bell, D. (2002) Making science inclusive: providing effective learning opportunities for children with learning difficulties, *British Journal of Support for Learning*, 17(4): 156–61.

Bennett, J. (2007) *Annual national survey of Year 9 students' attitudes to science* (funded by the AstraZeneca Science Teaching Trust). York: Science Education Group, University of York.

Berliner, D.C. (2004) Describing the behavior and documenting the accomplishments of expert teachers, *Bulletin of Science, Technology Society*, 24, available at: http://bst.sagepub.com/cgi/content/abstract/24/23/200

Bishop, K.N. and Denley, P. (1997) The fundamental role of subject matter knowledge in the teaching of science, *School Science Review*, 79(286): 65–72.

Bishop, K.N. and Denley, P. (2006) Science Learning Centres and governmental policy for continuing professional development (CPD) in England, *Journal of Inservice Education*, 32(1): 85–102.

Bishop, K.N., Reid, A., Stables, A., Lencastre, M., Stoer, S. and Soetart, R. (2000) Developing environmental awareness through literature and media education: curriculum development in the context of teachers' practice, *Canadian Journal of Environmental Education*, 5: 268–86.

Black, P. and Harrison, C. (2000) Formative assessment, in M. Blair Bolles (ed.) (1997) *Gallileo's commandment: an anthology of great science writing*. London: Abacus.

Blair Bolles, M. (ed.) (1997) *Gallileo's commandment: an anthology of great science writing*. London: Abacus.

Bloom, B.S. (1956) *Taxonomy of educational objectives*. London: Longman.

Brickhouse, N.W. (1990) Teachers' beliefs about the nature of science and their relationship to classroom practice, *Journal of Teacher Education*, 41(3): 53–62.

Brown, J., Cooper, A., Horton, T., Toates, F. and Zeldin, D. (1986) *Science in schools*. Milton Keynes: Open University Press.

Bullock, K. and Wikeley, F. (2006) *Whose learning? The role of the personal tutor*. Maidenhead: Open University Press.

Bullock, K., Bishop, K.N., Martin, S. and Reid, A.D. (2002) Learning from coursework in English and Geography, *Cambridge Journal of Education*, 32(3): 325–40.

Calderhead, J. (1981) Stimulated recall: a method for research on teaching, *British Journal of Educational Psychology*, 51(2): 211–17.

Calderhead, J. and Miller, E. (1997) Teachers: beliefs and knowledge, in D.C. Berliner and R.C. Calfee (eds) *Handbook of educational psychology*. New York: Macmillan.

Carey, J. (2005) *The Faber book of science*. London: Faber and Faber.

Chalmers, A.F. (1999) *What is this thing called science?* Buckingham: Open University Press.

Clark, C.M. and Peterson, P.L. (1986) Teachers' thought processes, in M.C. Wittrock (ed.) *Handbook of research on teaching*, 3rd edn. New York: Macmillan.

Claxton, G. (1997) Science of the times: a 2020 vision of education, in R. Levinson and J. Thomas (eds) *Science today: problem or crisis?* London: Routledge.

CLIS (Children's Learning in Science) (1987) *Children's Learning in Science project – CLIS in the classroom*. Leeds: Centre for Science and Mathematics Study, University of Leeds.

Cochran, K.F., De Ruiter, J.A. and King, R.A. (1993) Pedagogical content knowing: an integrative model for teacher preparation, *Journal of Teacher Education*, 44: 263–72.

Connelly, F., Clandinin, D.J. and Ming Fang He (1997) Teachers' personal practical knowledge on the professional knowledge landscape, *Teaching and Teacher Education*, 13(7): 665–74.

Corrigan, D., Dillon, J. and Gunstone, R. (2007) *The re-emergence of values in the science curriculum*. Rotterdam: Sense Publishers.

Darling-Hammond, L. (2000) *Teacher quality and student achievement: a review of state policy evidence*. Education policy analysis archives, available online at: http://epaa.asu.edu/epaa/v8n1/ accessed 4 April 2007.

Denley, P., Bishop, K., Oakes, M. and Ingram, M. (2004) *An audit of CPD opportunities for science educators*. London: The Wellcome Trust.

Dennison, W. and Kirk, R. (1990) *Do, review, learn, apply: a simple guide to experiential learning*. Oxford: Blackwell.

DEST (Department of Education, Science and Training) (Australia) (2003) *The National Statement from the profession on teacher standards, quality and professionalism*. Canberra: DEST.

DETYA (Department of Education Training and Youth Affairs) (Australia) (2000) *The impact of educational research: research evaluation programme*, available at: http://www.detya.gov.au/highered/respubs/impact/splitpdf default.htm

Dewey, J. (1983) The child and the curriculum, in J.A. Boydston (ed.) *John Dewey: the middle works, 1899–1924, Volume 2: 1902–1903*. Carbondale, IL: Southern Illinois University Press.

Dhingra, K. (2003) Thinking about television science: how students understand the nature of science from different program genres. *Journal of Research in Science Teaching*, 40(2): 234–56.

Dillon, J., Osborne, J., Fairbrother, R. and Kurina, L. (2000) *A study into the professional views and needs of science teachers in primary and secondary schools in England*. London: King's College.

Donnelly, J. and Jenkins, E. W. (1999) *The expertise and deployment of science teachers at Key Stage 4*. Leeds: Centre for Studies in Maths and Science Education, University of Leeds.

Doyle, W. (1990) Themes in teacher education research, in W.R. Houston (ed.) *Handbook of research on teacher education*. New York: Macmillan.

Driver, R. (1991) *The pupil as scientist*. Buckingham: Open University Press.

Driver, R. and Oldham, V. (1986) A constructivist approach to curriculum development, *Studies in Science Education*, 13, 105–22.

Driver, R., Guesne, E. and Tiberghien, A. (1985) *Children's ideas in science*. Buckingham: Open University Press.

Driver, R., Asoko, H., Leach, J., Scott, P. and Mortimer, E. (1994a) Constructing scientific knowledge in the classroom, *Educational Researcher*, 23(7): 5–12.

Driver, R., Squires, A., Rushworth, P. and Wood-Robinson, V. (1994b) *Making sense of secondary science: research into children's ideas*. London: Routledge.

Driver, R., Leach, J., Millar, R. and Scott, P. (1996) *Young people's images of science*. Buckingham: Open University Press.

Duggan, S. and Gott, R. (2000) Understanding evidence in investigations: the way to a more relevant curriculum, in J. Sears and P. Sorensen (eds) *Issues in science teaching*. London: RoutledgeFalmer

Duggan, S. and Gott, R. (2002) What sort of science education do we really need? *International Journal of Science Education*, 24(7): 661–79.

Duit, R. and Treagust, D.F. (2003) Learning in science: from behaviourism to social constructivism and beyond, in B. Fraser and K. Tobin (eds) *International handbook of science education*. Dordrecht: Kluwer.

Duschl, R.A. (2000) Making the nature of science explicit. In R. Millar, J. Leach and J. Osborne (eds) *Improving science education: the contribution of research*. Buckingham: Open University Press.

Edwards, A. (1995) Teacher education: partnerships in pedagogy, *Teaching and Teacher Education*, 11(6): 595–610.

Elliott, J. (2001) Making evidence-based practice educational, *British Educational Research Journal*, 21(5): 555–74.

Entwistle, N.J. (1988) *Styles of learning and teaching: an integrated outline of educational psychology for students, teachers, and lecturers*. London: David Fulton.

Eraut, M. (1994) *Developing professional knowledge and competence*. London: Falmer.

Erduran, S. (2007) Special editorial: argument, discourse and interactivity, *School Science Review*, 88(324): 29–30.

Erduran, S. and Osborne, J. (2005) Developing arguments, in S. Alsop, L. Bencze and E. Pedretti (eds) *Analysing exemplary science teaching*. Maidenhead: Open University Press.

Etzioni, A. (ed.) (1969) *The semi-professions and their organisation*. New York: The Free Press.

Fenstermacher, G.D. (1994) The knower and the known: the nature of knowledge in research on teaching, in L. Darling-Hammond (ed.) *Review of research in education*. Washington, DC: American Educational Research Association.

Flutter, J. and Rudduck, J. (2004) *Consulting pupils: what's in it for schools*. London: RoutledgeFalmer.

Gardner, H. (2006) *The development and education of the mind: the selected works of Howard Gardner*. Abingdon: Routledge.

Gess-Newsome, J. and Lederman, N.G. (eds) (1999) *Examining pedagogical content knowledge: the construct and its implications for science education*. New York: Kluwer.

Gibbs, K. (1999) *The resourceful physics teacher: 600 ideas for creative teaching*. Bristol: Institute of Physics Teaching.

Gilbert, J. (2006) *Science education in schools: issues, evidence and proposals. A commentary by the Teaching and Learning Research Programme*. London: TLRP, available online at: http://www.tlrp.org/dspace/handle/123456789/633

Gilbert, J. and Boulter, C. (2003) Learning science through models and modelling, in B. Fraser and K. Tobin (eds) *International handbook of science education*. Dordrecht: Kluwer.

Goldsworthy, A., Watson, J.R. and Wood-Robinson, V. (1999) *Investigations: getting to grips with graphs*. Hatfield: Association for Science Education.

Gott, R. and Duggan, S. (1996) Practical work: its role in the understanding of evidence in science, *International Journal of Science Education*, 18(7): 791–806.

Gott, R. and Duggan, S. (2003) *Understanding and using scientific evidence*. London: Sage.

Halloun, I.A. (2006) *Modeling theory in science education*. Dordrecht: Springer.

Hashweh, M. (1996) Effects of science teachers' epistemological beliefs in teaching, *Journal of Research in Science Teaching*, 33(1): 47–63.

Haste, H. (2004) *Science in my future: a study of values and beliefs in relation to science and technology among 11–12-year-olds*. London: Nestlé Social Research Programme.

Hay McBer (2000) *A model of teacher effectiveness*, available at: www.teachernet. gov.uk/haymcber/

Hemsley-Brown, J. and Sharp, C. (2003) The use of research to improve professional practice: a systematic review of the literature, *Oxford Review of Education*, 29(4): 449–70.

Hennessy, S., Deaney, R. and Ruthven, K. (2003) *Pedagogic strategies for using ICT to support subject teaching and learning: an analysis across 15 case studies*. Cambridge: Faculty of Education Research Report 03/1, University of Cambridge.

HM Treasury (2004) *The ten year Science and Innovation Investment Framework 2004–2014*. London: HMSO.

Hodson, D. (1990) A critical look at practical work in school science, *School Science Review*, 71(256): 33–40.

Hodson, D. (1991) The role of philosophy in science teaching, in M.R. Matthews (ed.) *History, philosophy and science teaching: selected readings*. New York: Teachers College Press.

Hodson, D. (1998) *Teaching and learning science: towards a personalized approach*. Buckingham: Open University Press.

Hopkins, D. (2002) *A teacher's guide to classroom research*, 3rd edn. Buckingham: Open University Press.

Hopkins, D. (2005) *Creating powerful learning experiences: the contribution of the GTC Teacher Learning Academy*. Speech given by Professor David Hopkins at the first conference of the Teacher Learning Academy, 7 July. Available at: http:// www.gtce.org.uk/newsfeatures/features/tlaspeech1 accessed 4 April 2007.

Hopkins, D. (2007) *Instructional leadership and school improvement*. Nottingham: National College for School Leadership, available at: www.ncsl.org.uk/media/ 1D3/BF/instructional-leadership-and-school-improvement.pdf

House of Lords (2006) *Science teaching in schools*. Tenth report of Session 2005–6, Science and Technology Committee. London: HMSO.

Ingram, J. (2004) *The velocity of honey, and more science of everyday life*. London: Aurum Press.

Ingvarson, L. and Semple, A. (2006) *How can professional standards improve the quality of teaching and learning science?* Available online at: http://www.acer. edu.au/documents/RC2006_IngvarsonandSemple.pdf, accessed 17 September 2007.

Jenkins, E.W. and Nelson, N.W. (2005) Important but not for me: students' attitudes towards secondary school science in England, *Research in Science & Technological Education*, 32(1): 41–57.

Jensen, E. (1998) *Teaching with the brain in mind*. Alexandria, VA: Association for Supervision and Curriculum Development.

Joyce, B. and Showers, B. (2002) *Student achievement through staff development*, 3rd edn. Alexandria, VA: Association for Supervision and Curriculum Development.

Justi, R.S. and Gilbert, J.K. (2002) Science teachers' knowledge about and attitudes towards the use of models and modelling in learning science, *International Journal of Science Education*, 24(12): 1273–92.

Justi, R.S. and van Driel, J.H. (2005) The development of science teachers' knowledge on models and modelling: promoting, characterising, and understanding the process, *International Journal of Science Education*, 27(5): 549–73.

Korthagen, F. (2004) In search of the essence of a good teacher: towards a more holistic approach in teacher education, *Teaching and Teacher Education*, 20: 77–97.

Lave, J. and Wenger, E. (1991) *Situated learning: legitimate peripheral participation*. Cambridge: Cambridge University Press.

Leach, J. and Scott, P. (2000) Children's thinking, learning, teaching and constructivism, in M. Monk and J. Osborne (eds) *Good practice in science teaching: what research has to say*. Buckingham: Open University Press.

Leach, J., Holman, J. and Millar, R. (2005) The continuing professional development of science teachers: a discussion paper, *School Science Review*, 87(318): 105–11.

Lederman, N.G. (1992) Students and teachers' conceptions of the nature of science: a review of the research, *Journal of Research in Science Teaching*, 29: 331–60.

Lederman, N.G. (1999) Teachers' understanding of the nature of science and classroom practice: factors that facilitate or impede the relationship, *Journal of Research in Science Teaching*, 36(8): 916–29.

Lenton, G. and Stevens, B. (2000) Numeracy in science: understanding the misunderstandings, in J. Sears and P. Sorensen (eds) *Issues in science teaching*. London: RoutledgeFalmer.

Loughran, J. (2006a) *Developing a pedagogy of teacher education*. Abingdon: Routledge.

Loughran, J. (2006b) Towards a better understanding of science teaching, *Teaching Education*, 17(2): 109–19.

Loughran, J., Berry, A. and Mulhall, P. (2006) *Understanding and developing science teachers' pedagogical content knowledge*. Rotterdam: Sense Publishers.

Luft, J. and Ingham, H. (1955) *The Johari Window: a graphic model of interpersonal awareness*, in Proceedings of the Western Training Laboratory in Group Development. Los Angeles, CA: UCLA Extension Office.

Marshall, B., Hodgen, J. and Harrison, C. (2005) *Science inside the black box*. Slough: National Foundation for Educational Research.

McComas, W. (ed.) (1998) *The nature of science in science education: rationales and strategies*. Dordrecht: Kluwer.

McComas, W., Clough, M. and Almazroa, H. (1998) The role and character of the nature of science, in W. McComas (ed.) *The nature of science education: rationales and strategies*. Dordrecht: Kluwer.

McDiarmid, G.W., Ball, D.L. and Anderson, C.W. (1989) Why staying one chapter ahead doesn't really work: subject-specific pedagogy, in M.C. Reynolds (ed.) *Knowledge base for the beginning teacher*. Oxford: Pergamon Press.

McIntyre, D., Pedder, D. and Rudduck, J. (2005) Pupil voice: comfortable and uncomfortable learnings for teachers, *Research Papers in Education*, 20(2): 149–68.

McMeniman, J., Cumming, J., Wilson, J., Stevenson, J. and Sim, C. (2003) *Teacher knowledge in action: the impact of educational research*. Nottingham: National College for School Leadership.

Meade, P. and McMeniman, M. (1992) Stimulated recall – an effective methodology for examining successful teaching in science, *Australian Educational Researcher*, 19(3): 1–17.

Millar, R. (1996) Towards a science curriculum for public understanding, *School Science Review*, 77(280): 7–18.

Millar, R. (2006) *Engaging science*. London: Wellcome Trust.

Millar, R. and Osborne, J. (eds) (1998) *Beyond 2000: science education for the future*. London: King's College.

Millar, R., Leach, J., Osborne, J. and Ratcliffe, M. (2006) *Improving subject teaching: lessons from research in science education*. Abingdon: Routledge.

Monk, M. and Dillon, J. (2000) The nature of scientific knowledge, in M. Monk and J. Osborne (eds) *Good practice in science teaching: what research has to say*. Buckingham: Open University Press.

Monk, M. and Osborne, J. (eds) (2000) *Good Practice in science teaching: what research has to say*. Buckingham: Open University Press.

Mortimer, E. and Scott, P. (2003) *Meaning making in secondary science classrooms*. Maidenhead: Open University Press.

NBPTS (National Board for Professional Teaching Standards) (2005) *National Board for Professional Teaching Standards: guide to national board certification*, available at: http://www.nbpts.org/candidates/guide/whichcert/19AdolYoungScience 2004.html accessed 4 April 2007.

Newton, D. (1988) *Making science education relevant*. London: Kogan Page.

Newton, D. (2000) *Teaching for understanding*. London: Falmer.

Nott, M. and Wellington, J. (1993) Your nature of science profile: an activity for science teachers, *School Science Review*, 75(270): 109–12.

Nott, M. and Wellington, J. (1995) Critical incidents in the science classroom and the nature of science, *School Science Review*, 76: 41–6.

Novak, J.D. and Gowin, D.B. (1984) *Learning how to learn*. New York: Cambridge University Press.

OCR (2006). *Students and science report*. Cambridge: OCR.

Ofsted (Office for Standards in Education) (2005) *The secondary national strategy: an evaluation of the fifth year*. London: Ofsted.

Ogborn, J., Kress, G., Martins, I. and McGillicuddy, K. (1996) *Explaining science in the classroom*. Buckingham: Open University Press.

Osborne, J. and Collins, S. (2000) *Pupils' and parents' views of the school science curriculum*. London: King's College.

Osborne, J., Simon, S. and Collins, S. (2003) Attitudes towards science: a review of the literature and its implications, *International Journal of Science Education*, 25(9): 1049–79.

Paatz, R., Ryder, J., Schwedes, H. and Scott, P. (2004) A case study analysing the process of analogy-based learning in a teaching unit about simple electric circuits, *International Journal of Science Education* 26(9): 1065–81.

Press, H.J. (1998) *The little giant book of science experiments*. New York: Sterling.

Ratcliffe, M. and Grace, M. (2003) *Science education for citizenship*. Maidenhead: Open University Press.

Reiss, M. (2000) *Understanding science lessons: five years of science teaching*. Buckingham: Open University Press.

Roberts, G. (2002) *SET for success: the supply of people with science, technology, engineering and mathematics skills*. London: HM Treasury.

Schön, D. (1983) *The reflective practitioner: how professionals think in action*. New York: Basic Books.

Schön, D. (1987) *Educating the reflective practitioner: toward a new design for teaching and learning*. San Francisco, CA: Jossey-Bass.

Schreiner, C. and Sjøberg, S. (2004) *Sowing the seeds of ROSE (Relevance of Science Education)*. Oslo: Department of Teacher Education and School Development, University of Oslo.

Schwartz, R. and Lederman, N.G. (2002) 'It's the nature of the beast': the influence of knowledge and intentions on learning and teaching nature of science, *Journal of Research in Science Teaching*, 39(3): 205–36.

Scott, P. and Mortimer, E. (2006) The tension between authoritative and dialogic discourse: a fundamental characteristic of meaning-making interactions in high school science lessons, *Science Education*, 90(4): 605–31.

Shulman, L.S. (1987) Knowledge and teaching: foundations of the new reform, *Harvard Educational Review*, 57(1): 1–22.

Simon, S., Erduran, S. and Osborne, J. (2006) Learning to teach argumentation: research and development in the science classroom, *International Journal of Science Education*, 27(14): 137–62.

Smith, A. (1996) *Accelerated learning in the classroom*. Stafford: Network Educational Press.

Stenhouse, L. (1975) *An introduction to curriculum research and development*. London: Heinemann.

Sternberg, R.J. and Horvath, J.A. (1995) A prototype view of expert teaching, *Educational Researcher*, 24(6): 9–17.

Sutton, C. (1992) *Words, science and learning*. Buckingham: Open University Press.

Sutton, C. (2003) New perspectives on language in science, in B. Fraser and K. Tobin (eds) *International handbook of science education*. Dordrecht: Kluwer.

Taber, K. (2001) When the analogy breaks down: modelling the atom on the solar system, *Physics Education*, 36: 222–6.

Treagust, D.F. (1988) Development and use of diagnostic tests to evaluate students' misconceptions in science, *International Journal of Science Education*, 10(2): 159–69.

Turner-Bisset, R. (1999) The knowledge bases of the expert teacher. *British Educational Research Journal*, 25(1): 39–55.

van Driel, J.H. and Verloop, N. (2002) Experienced teachers' knowledge of teaching and learning of models and modelling in science education, *International Journal of Science Education*, 24(12): 1255–72.

van Driel, J.H., Beijaard, D. and Verloop, N. (2001) Professional development and reform in science education: the role of teachers' practical knowledge, *Journal of Research in Science Teaching*, 38(2): 137–58.

Vygotsky, L.S. (1978) *Mind in society: the development of higher psychological processes*. Cambridge, MA: Harvard University Press.

Wellcome Trust (2006) *Believers, seekers and sceptics*, available at: http://www.wellcome.ac.uk/assets/wtx028430.pdf

Wellington, J. (1996) *Methods and issues in educational research*. Sheffield: Department of Education, University of Sheffield.

Wellington, J. (ed.) (1998) *Practical work in school science: which way now?* London: Routledge.

Wellington, J. (2000) *Teaching and learning secondary science*. London: Routledge.

Wellington, J. and Osborne, J. (2001) *Language and literacy in science education*. Buckingham: Open University Press.

Wenger, E. (1998) *Communities of practice: learning, meaning, and identity*. Cambridge: Cambridge University Press.

White, R.T. (1993) *Learning science*. Oxford: Blackwell.

Wilson, S.M. (ed) (2004) *The wisdom of practice: Lee S. Shulman*. San Francisco, CA: Jossey-Bass.

Wilson, S.M. and Berne, J. (1999) Teacher learning and the acquisition of professional knowledge: an examination of research on contemporary professional development, *Review of Research in Education*, 24: 173–209.

Wolpert, L. (1992) *The unnatural nature of science*. London: Faber and Faber.

Wood-Robinson, V. (2006) *ASE guide to secondary science*. Hatfield: Association for Science Education.

Woolnough, B.E. and Allsop, T. (1985) *Practical work in science*. Cambridge: Cambridge University Press.

Wynn, C.M. and Wiggins, A.W. (1997) *The five biggest ideas in science*. New York: John Wiley.

Index

Related books from Open University Press

Purchase from www.openup.co.uk or order through your local bookseller

LANGUAGE AND LITERACY IN SCIENCE EDUCATION

Jerry Wellington and Jonathan Osborne

All teachers look and hope for more scientific forms of expression and reasoning from their pupils, but few have been taught specific techniques for supporting students' use of scientific language. This book is full of them . . . In this very practical book, Jerry Wellington and Jonathan Osborne do much more than summarize research which shows how very much language, in all its forms, matters to science education. They also show teachers what can be done to make learning science through language both more effective and more enjoyable.

> Jay L. Lemke, Professor of Education, City University of New York

Science in secondary schools has tended to be viewed mainly as a 'practical subject', and language and literacy in science education have been neglected. But learning the language of science is a major part of science education: every science lesson is a language lesson, and language is a major barrier to most school students in learning science. This accessible book explores the main difficulties in the language of science and examines practical ways to aid students in retaining, understanding, reading, speaking and writing scientific language.

Jerry Wellington and Jonathan Osborne draw together and synthesize current good practice, thinking and research in this field. They use many practical examples, illustrations and tried-and-tested materials to exemplify principles and to provide guidelines in developing language and literacy in the learning of science. They also consider the impact that the growing use of information and communications technology has had, and will have, on writing, reading and information handling in science lessons.

The authors argue that paying more attention to language in science classrooms is one of the most important acts in improving the quality of science education. This is a significant and very readable book for all student and practising secondary school science teachers, for science advisers and school mentors.

Contents
Acknowledgements – Introduction: the importance of language in science education – Looking at the language of science – Talk of the classroom: language interactions between teachers and pupils – Learning from reading – Writing for learning in science – Discussion in school science: learning science through talking – Writing text for learning science – Practical ploys for the classroom – Last thoughts . . . – References – Appendix – Index.

160pp   0 335 20598 4 (Paperback)   0 335 20599 2 (Hardback)